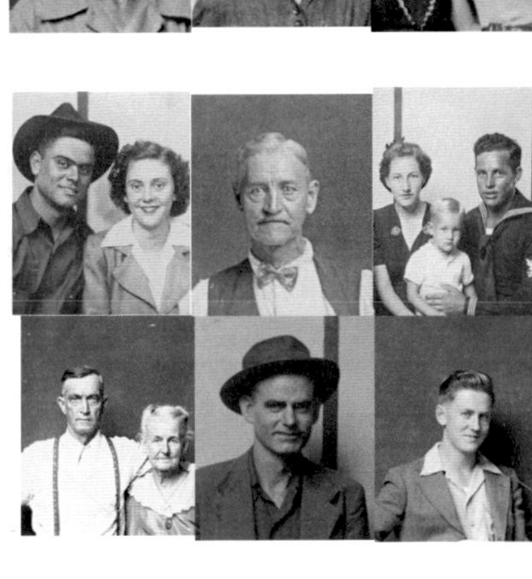

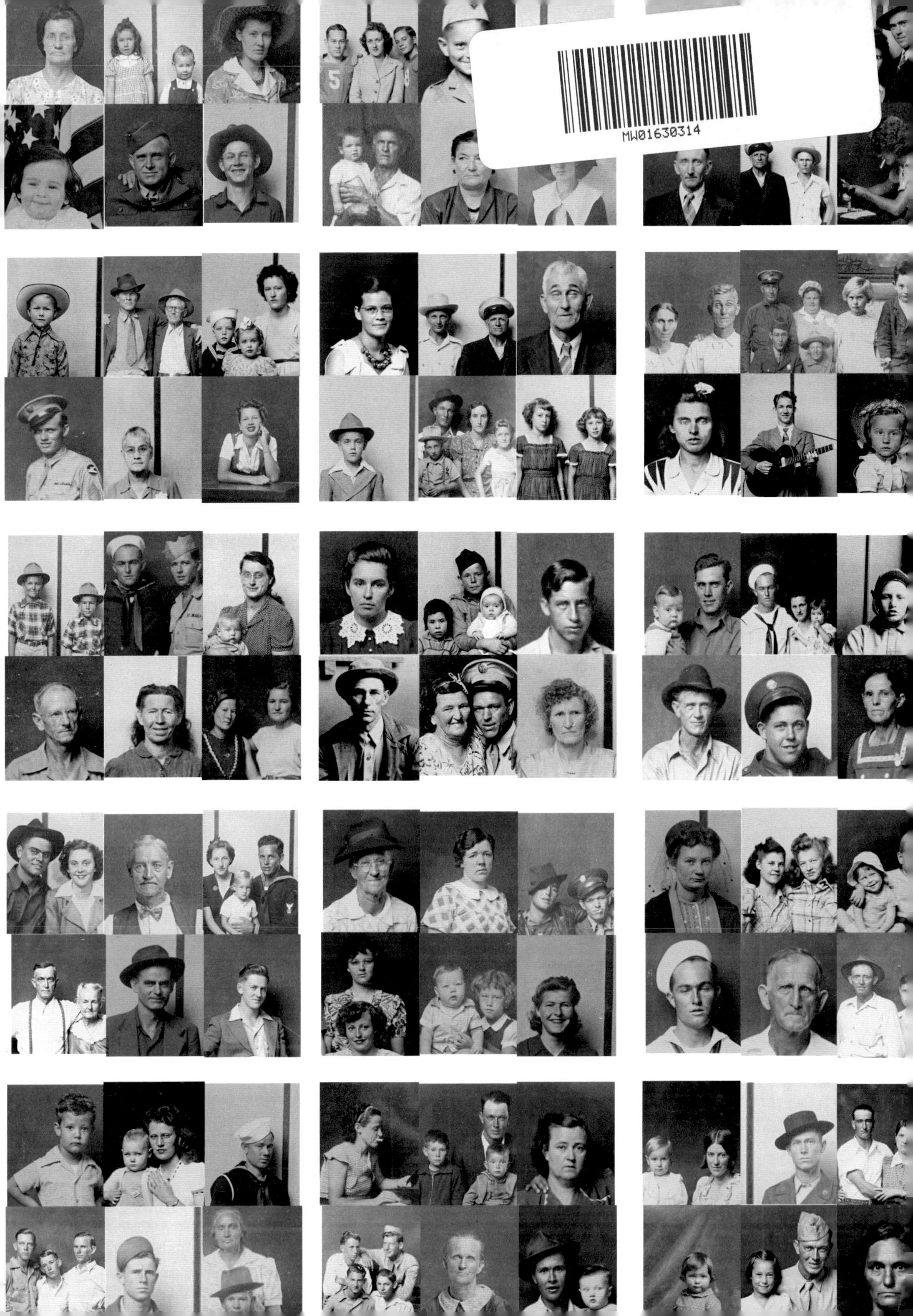

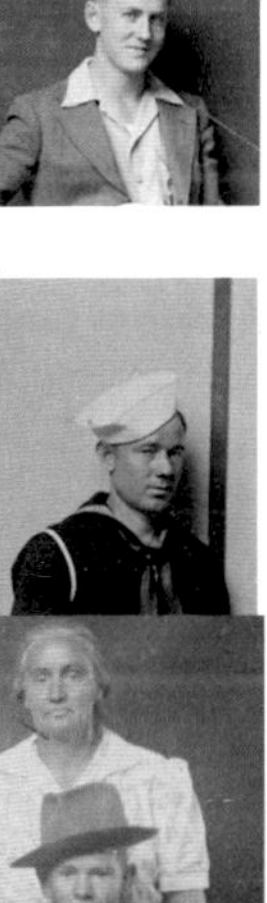

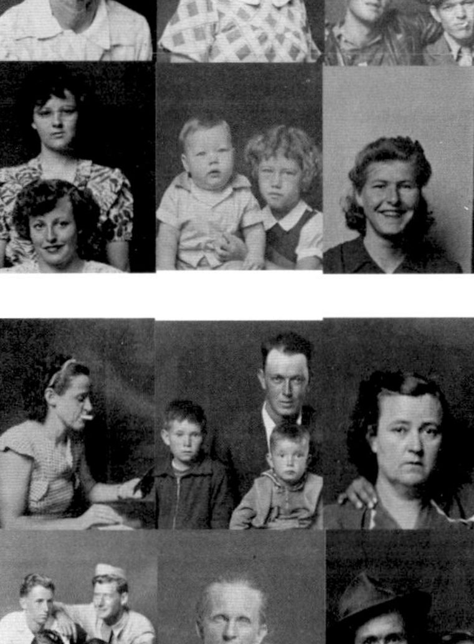

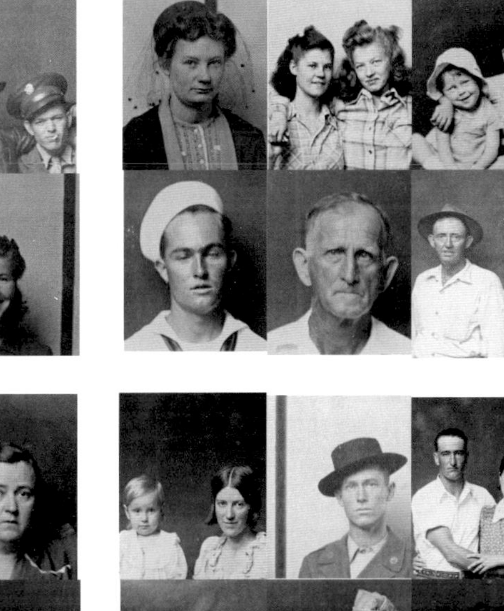

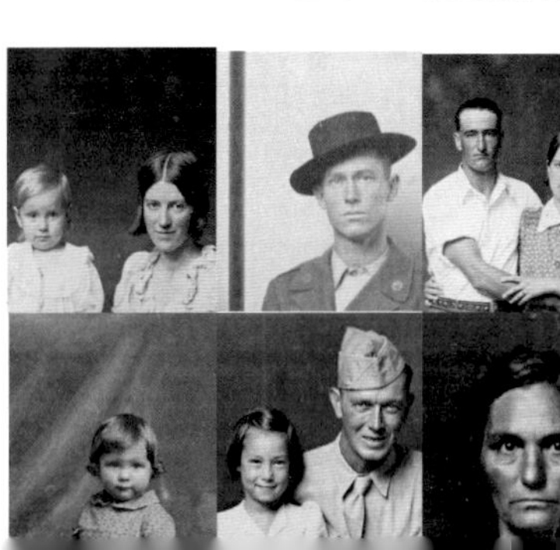

DISFARMER

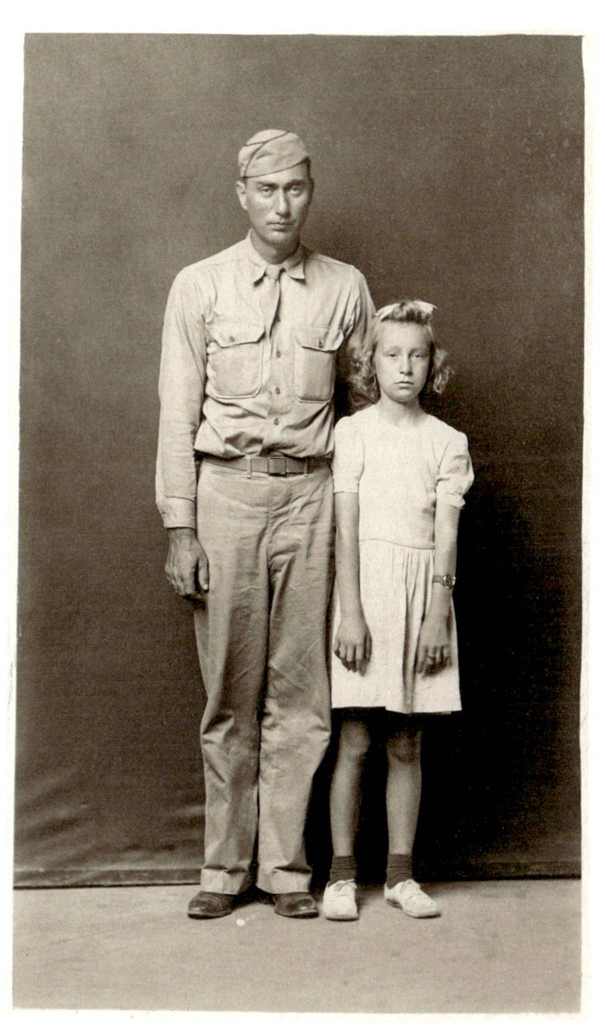

DISFARMER

The Vintage Prints

Edwynn Houk
Gerd Sander
Richard B. Woodward
Michael P. Mattis

Winnie Rose Reyes-Maye
March 2013

Edwynn Houk Gallery NY
pH powerHouse Books New York, NY

Foreword

by Edwynn Houk

This publication accompanies the exhibition *Disfarmer: The Vintage Prints* at the Edwynn Houk Gallery from 8 September–15 October 2005. For almost thirty years the Edwynn Houk Gallery has mounted exhibitions, published catalogues, and acquired photographs for museums and collectors. We have introduced the work of unknown and young artists who have gone on to receive significant acclaim. We have also represented artists already well established for whom we have tried to add to their known body of work with exhibitions and publications.

A few of these artists, like Brassaï and André Kertész, on several occasions led us to sources that turned out to own photographs highly important to their careers, long thought to have been lost. In addition, the Gallery has represented estates such as those of Dorothea Lange and Bill Brandt where in the course of our research we tracked down significant works which were not part of the estate collection and occasionally not even part of the artist's known oeuvre. We have also made a number of always-surprising discoveries of great individual works in the course of our various activities.

It is quite fair to say, however, that in almost thirty years in the field of photography, I have never had an experience comparable to the discoveries which make up *Disfarmer: The Vintage Prints*. The scale, the thoroughness of the undertaking, and the exciting success of the search are without precedent in the history of the Edwynn Houk Gallery. We have, I believe, rediscovered and redefined a body of work by one of the medium's great artists. On a personal level, this project owes much to the inspiration and experience gained while working with the estate of the great German photographer August Sander in 1976, an opportunity for which I shall always be indebted to gallerist Tom Halsted and to the family of August Sander.

Above all, I would like to thank collector Michael Mattis who conceived of this historical reclamation project nearly two years ago, and had the vision, passion, and tenacity to carry it to completion. The reconstitution of the life's work of a great artist that resulted from this vision is an invaluable contribution to both the cultural and art history of America.

Introduction

by Gerd Sander

> Photography is a re-creation of nature, with all visible forms appearing in it exactly reproduced.
> —August Sander

August Sander, born 1876 in Herdorf, Germany and Mike Disfarmer, born eight years later in the American Midwest, have one thing in common. Both grew up in rural communities. Sander described his childhood as a happy one. His mother taught him to observe nature, to learn about the herbs, both the healthy and dangerous ones, to respect the changing seasons and to live accordingly. With no electricity, television or radio, the long evenings of the winter were spent huddled around the one big stove in the main room of the house. His father, as he recalled, would draw in his free time, with August watching him. The meaning of the three words, *Seeing*, *Observing*, and *Thinking*, which would become the mainstays of his life and the foundation for his photographic vision, were planted in him during this time. I can only assume that Disfarmer's childhood was quite similar. Little is known about Disfarmer, but his photographs reveal a passion for his fellow man, much like Sander's work.

Sander, who never lost the desire to learn, read every day. In his library we found a book by Franz Grillparzer, titled *About the Spiritual in the Arts*. Sander had marked several pages. The one I found most characteristic reads as follows: "The artist whose 'originality' is emphasized as his distinctive quality belongs for that reason in the second rank; for those in the first rank are characterized by their sense of the natural. They do it like everybody else, only infinitely better." Sander's sense for the 'natural' came out of a deep love and empathy for humanity, coupled with a curiosity for the past and a searching for the future. He never forgot that we are all here just for a short time, and that, as artists, we have the possibility to leave something behind when we are gone, something the world might gain knowledge from and perhaps a bit of pleasure in as well.

A former assistant of Sander's during the difficult times of the thirties wrote to him in June 1961 the following: "I believe that you have answered the question of the meaning of life in your own way. You had something essential to say to your contemporaries and to posterity, and manifested this with the means appropriate to you. Can one do more than that as a human being?"

If you dislike what you photograph and approach every subject with a negative attitude, a negative image will appear; too much is omnipresent today.... Sander and Disfarmer are gone physically, but not in spirit. When we ask ourselves what is so extraordinary about the images these two very different men left us, inevitably the answer is the simplicity and the respect for life that the two shared.

When we look at the work of both men, we see ourselves, and we have the choice to admire or recoil from what we see. This decision is always ours.

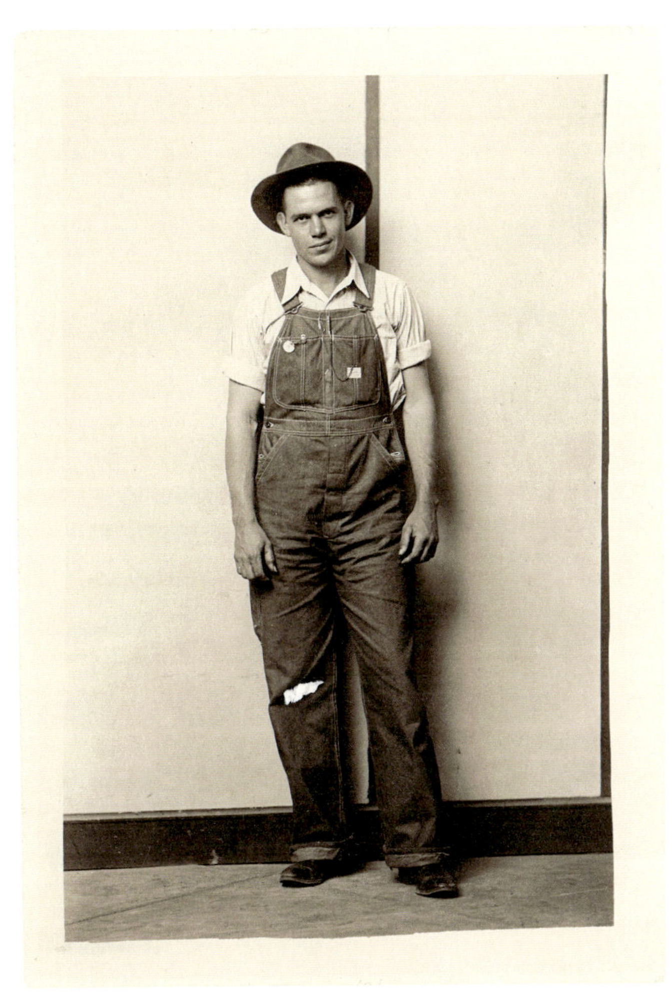

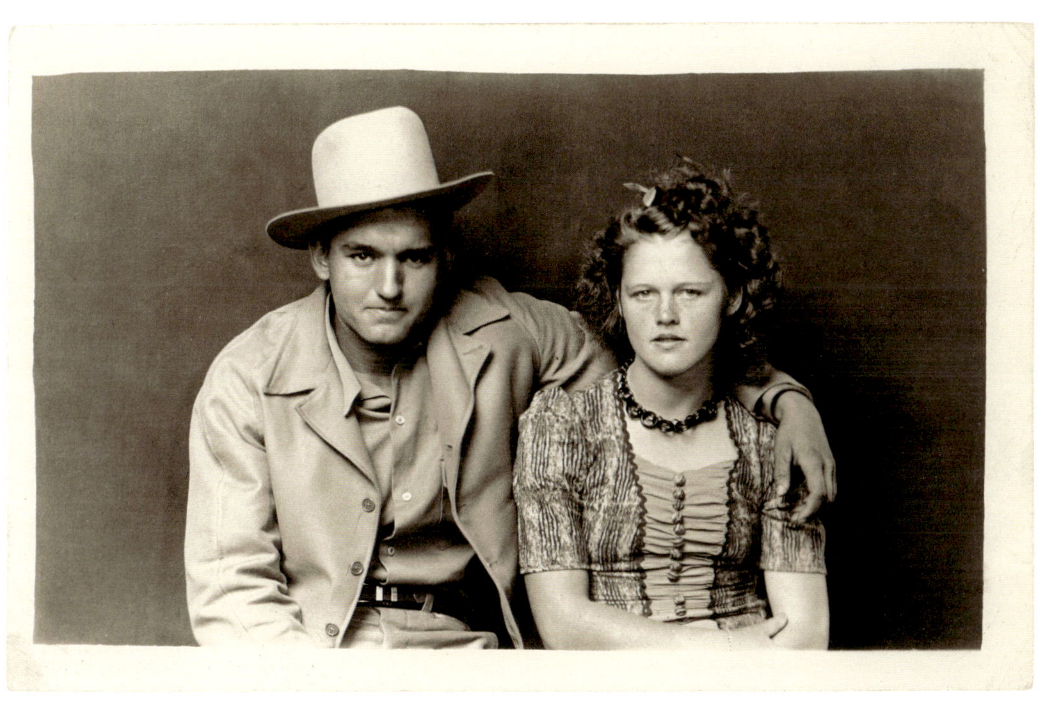

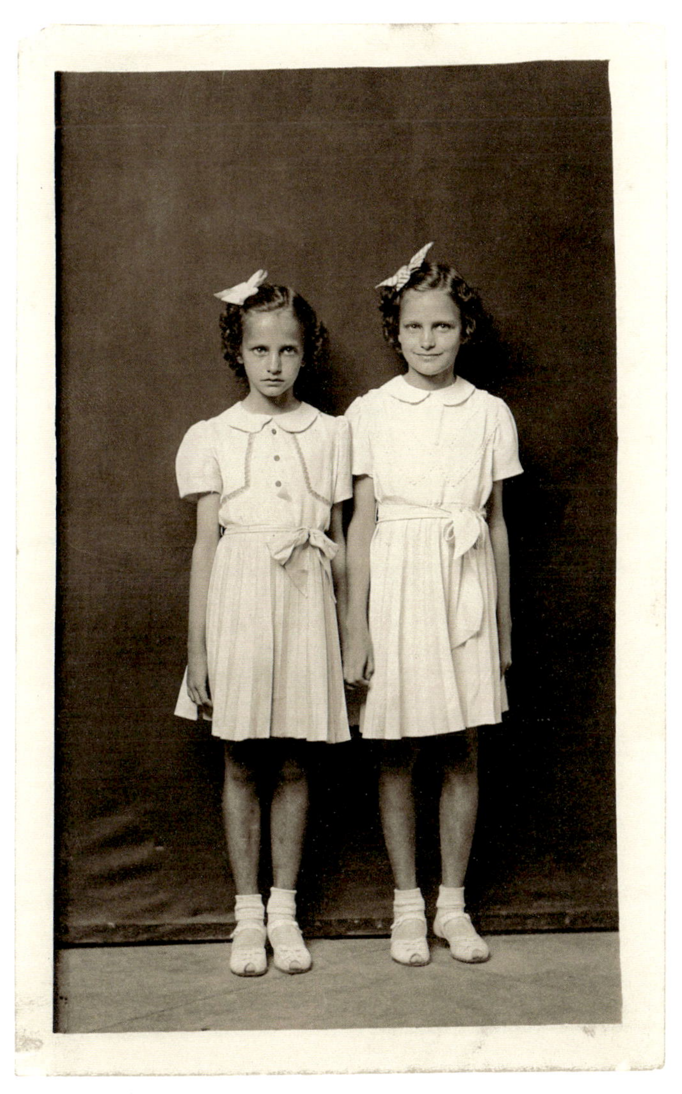

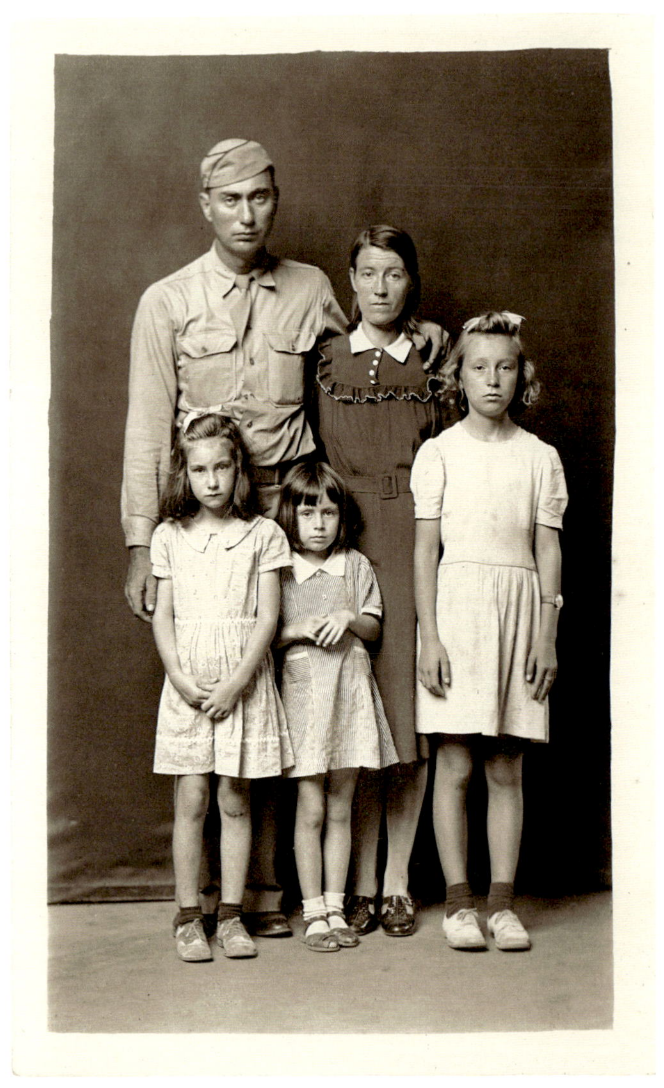

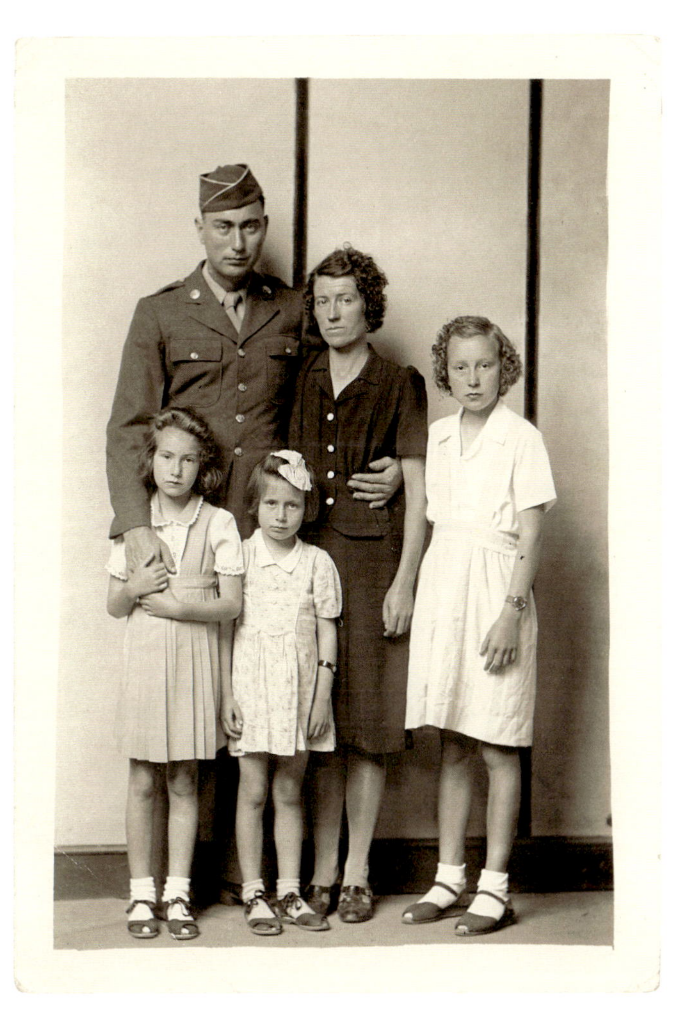

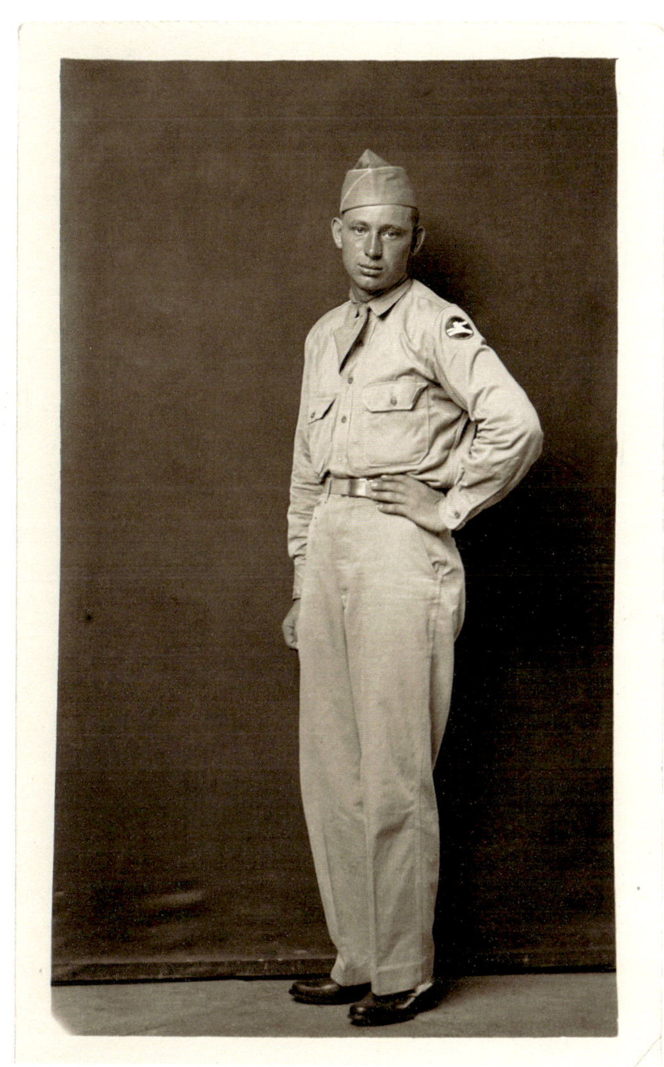

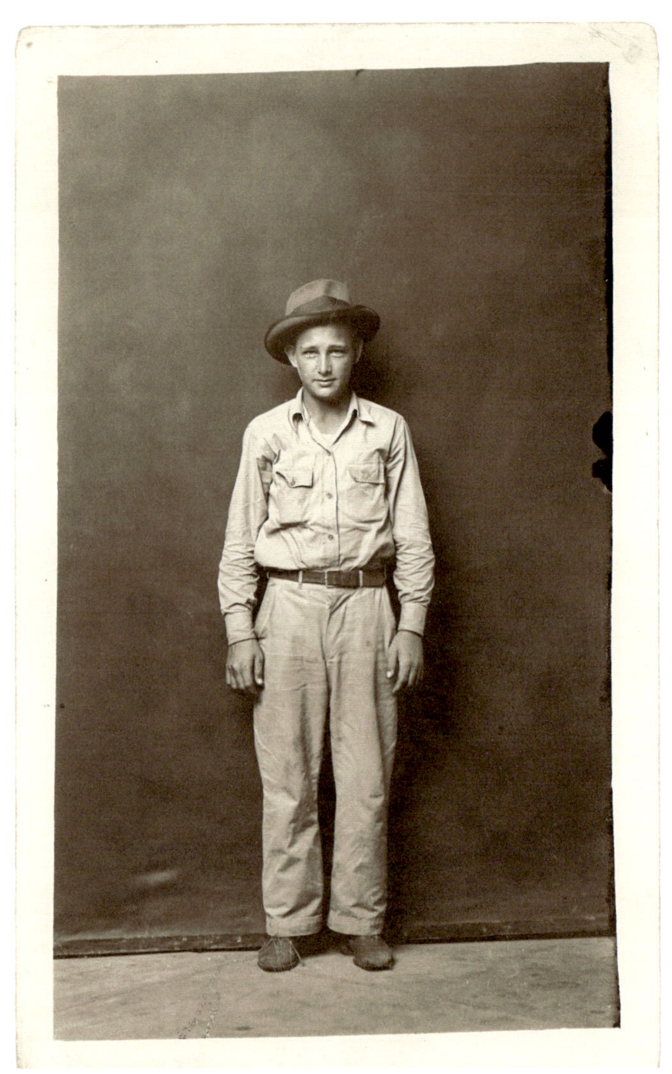

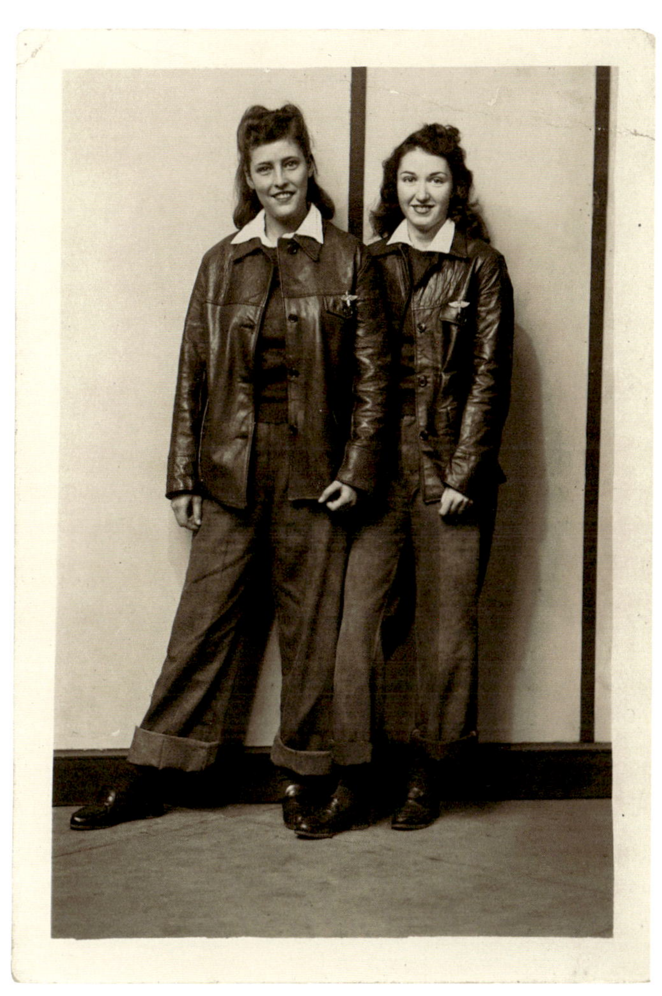

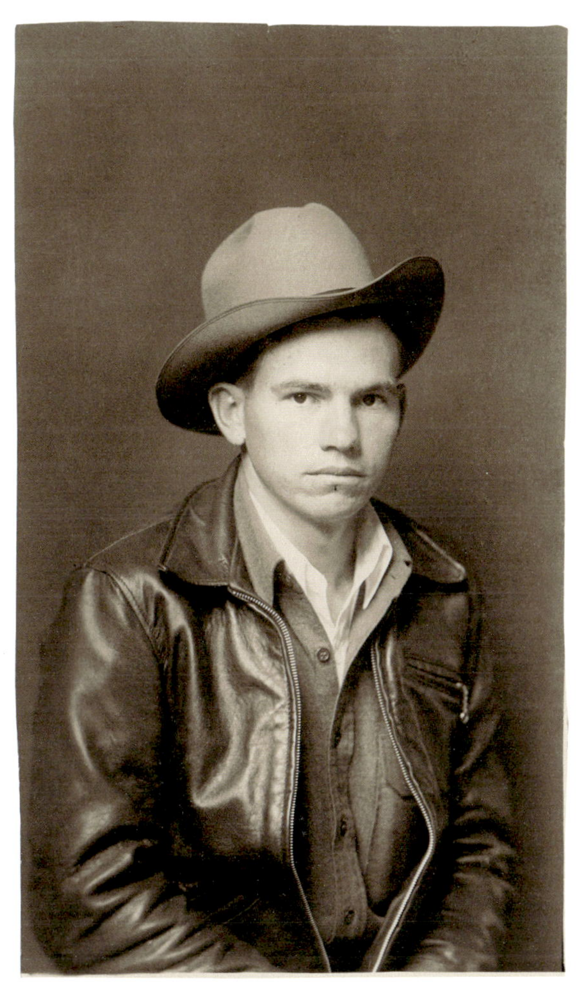

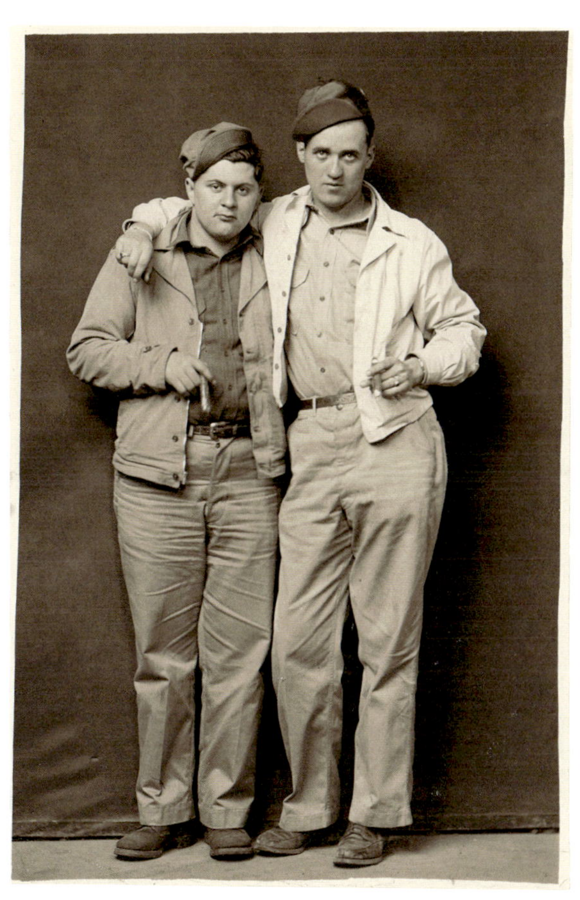

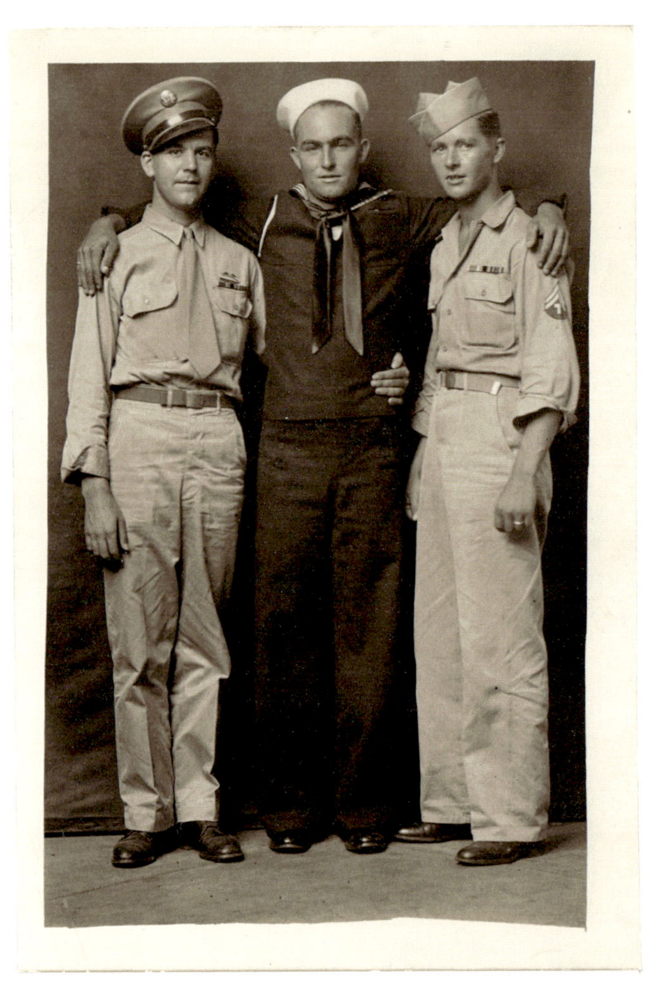

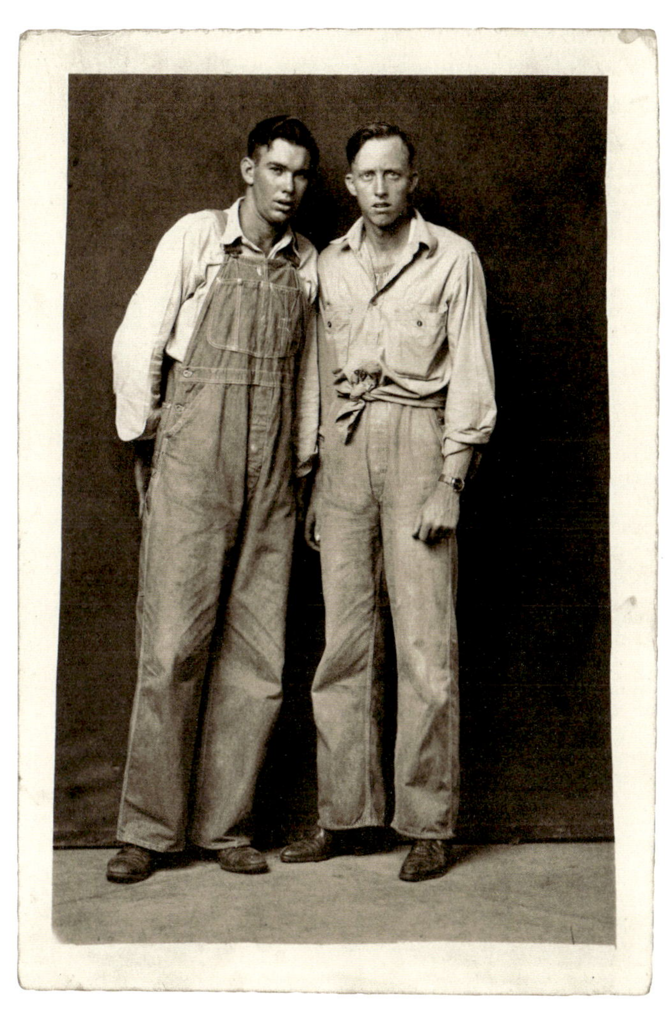

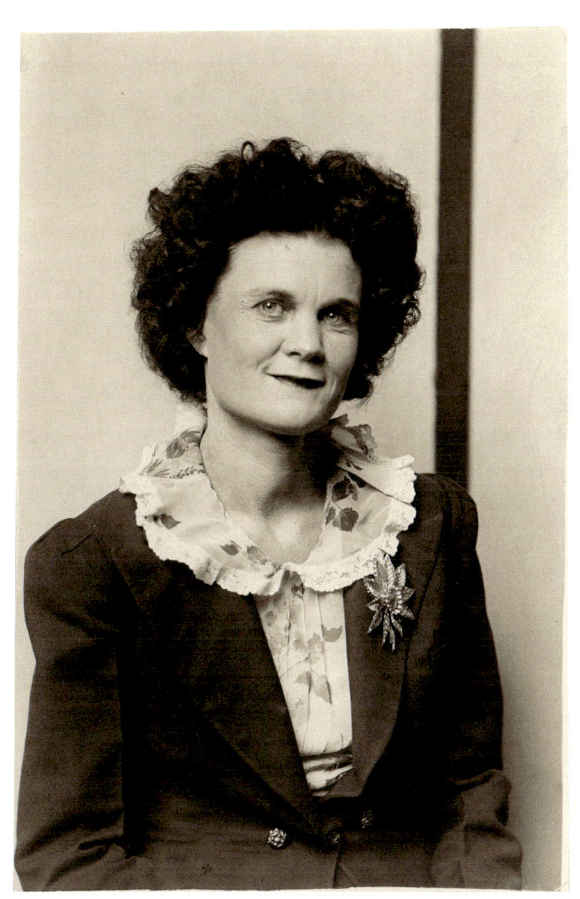

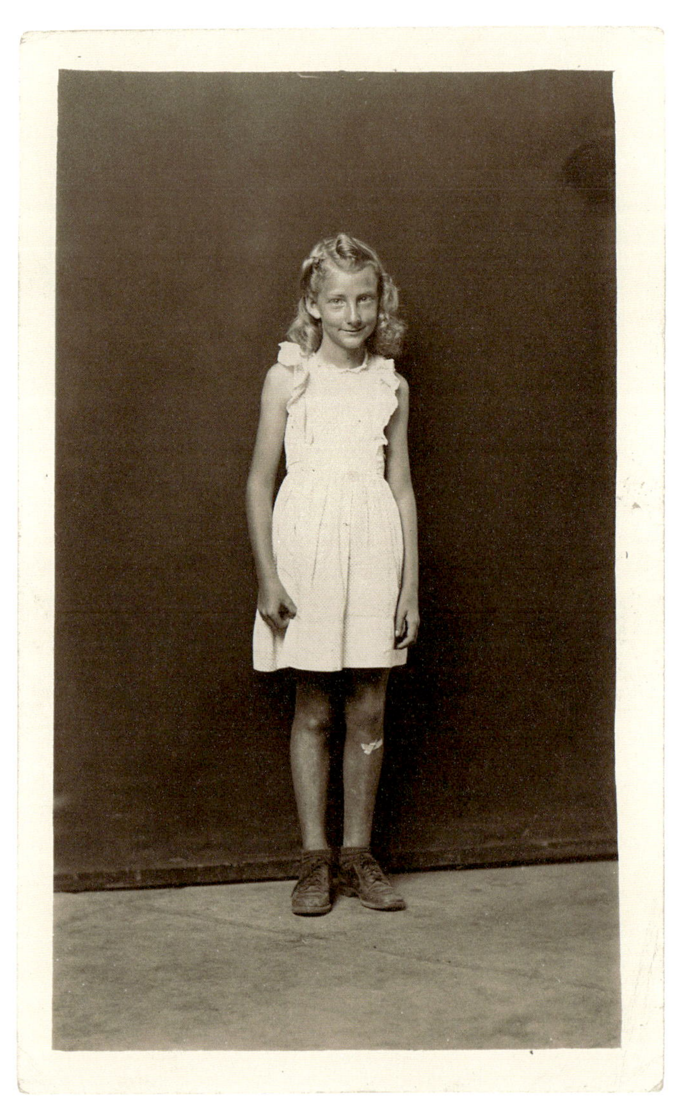

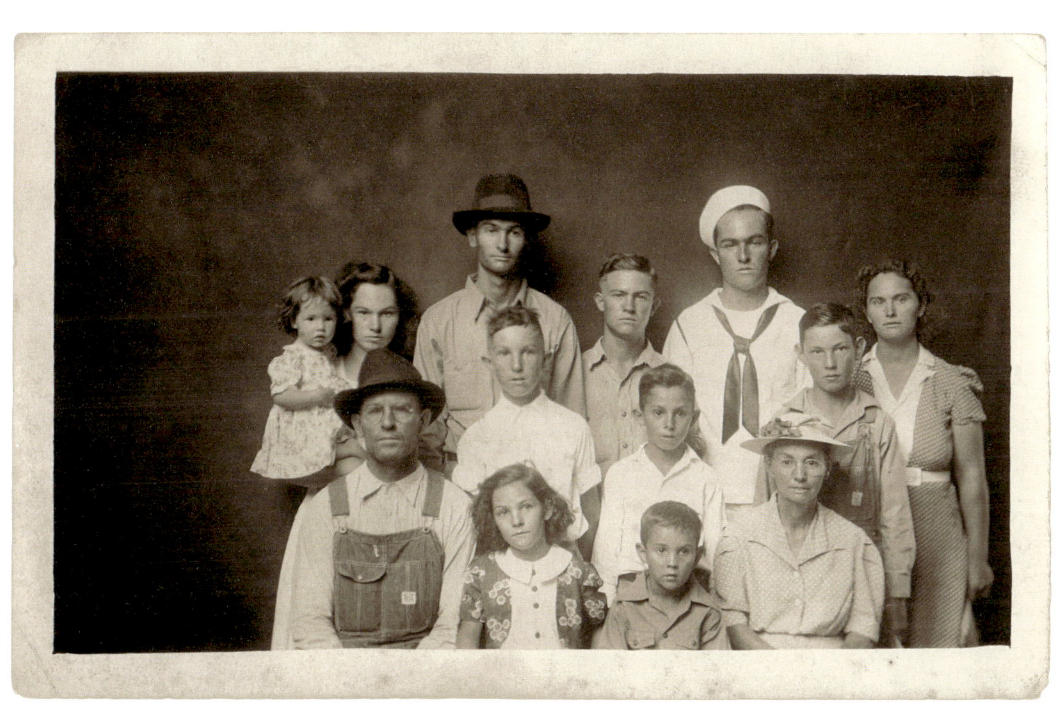

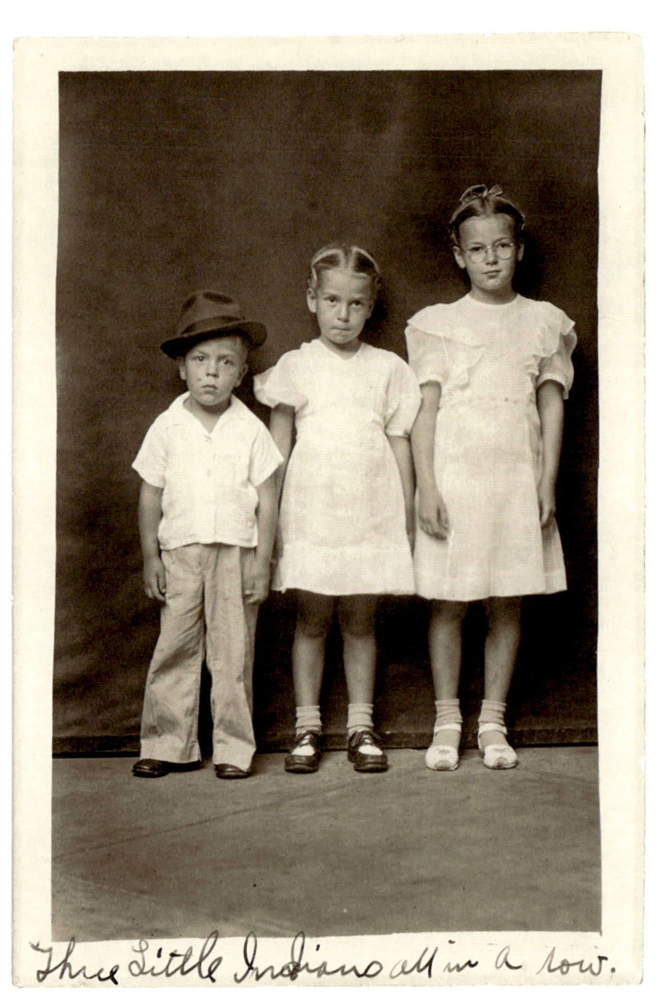
Three Little Indians all in a row.

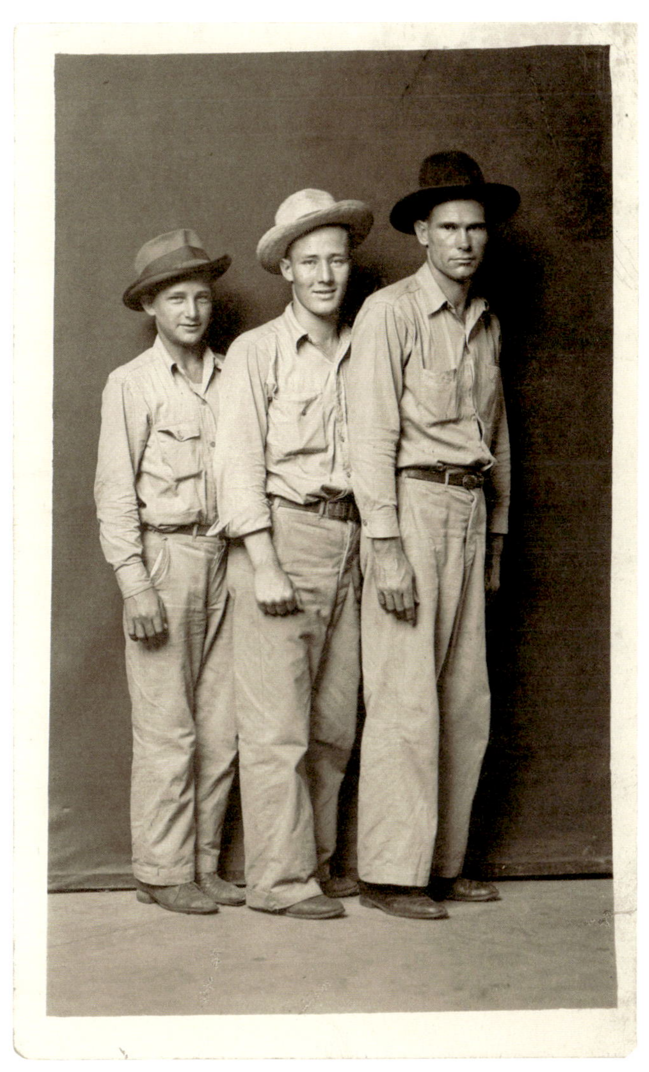

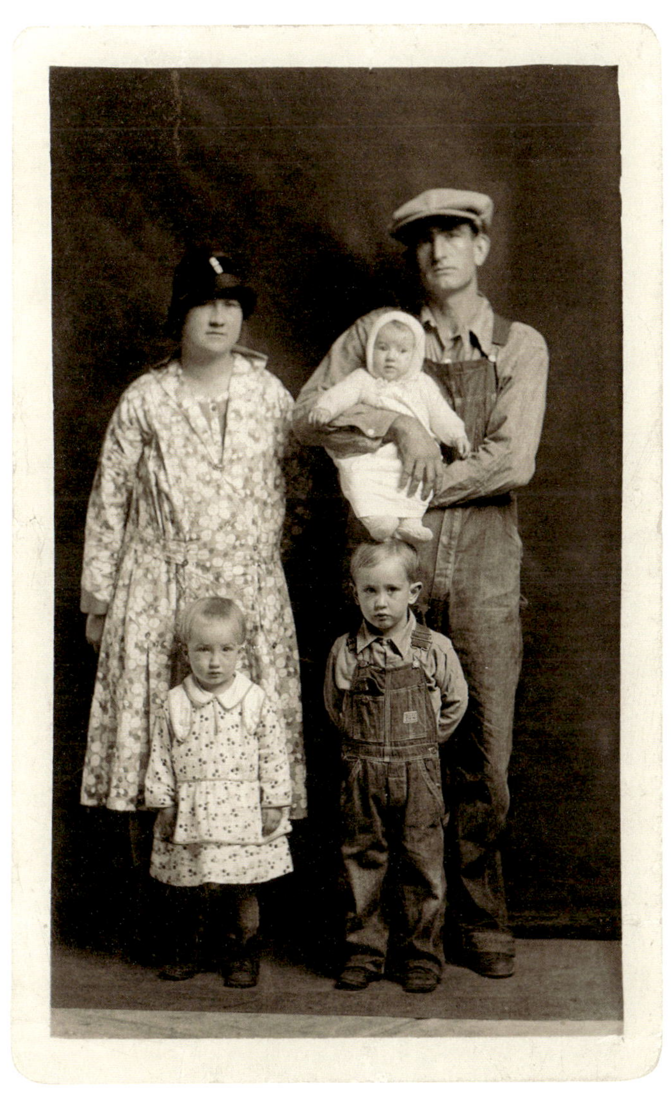

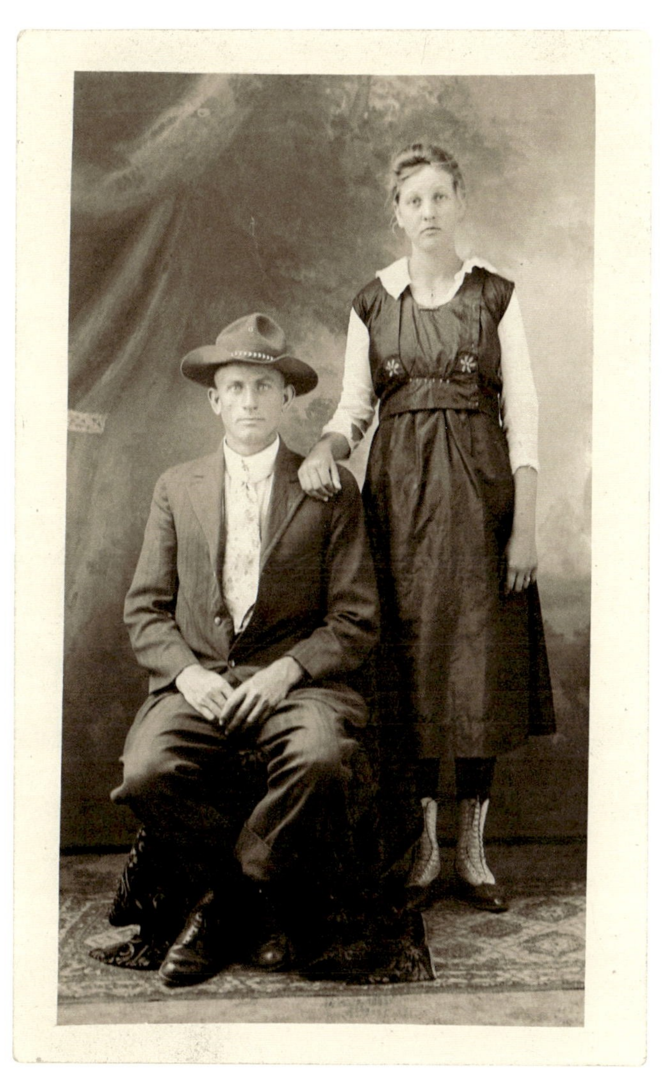

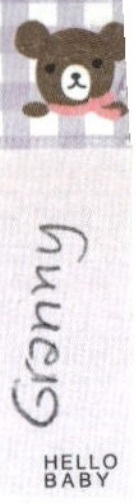
Granny
HELLO
BABY

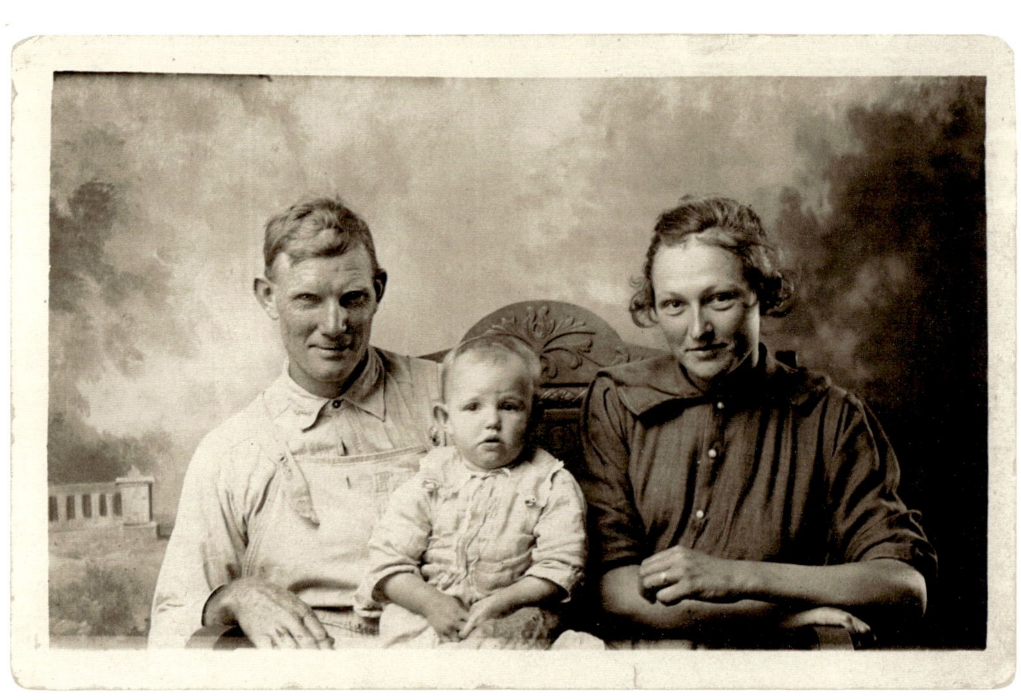

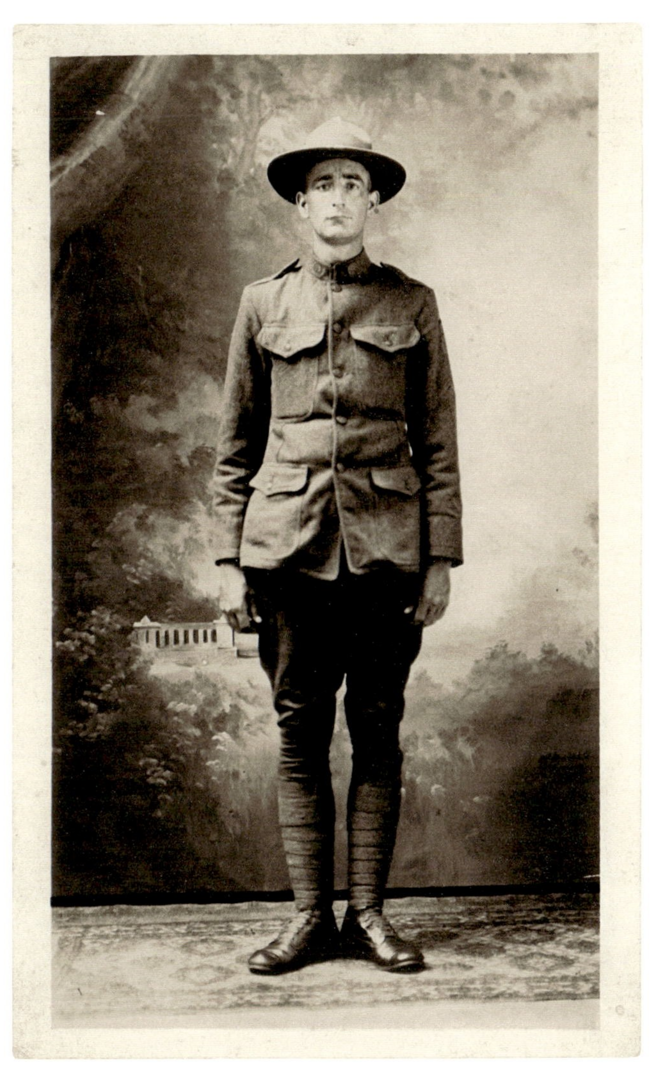

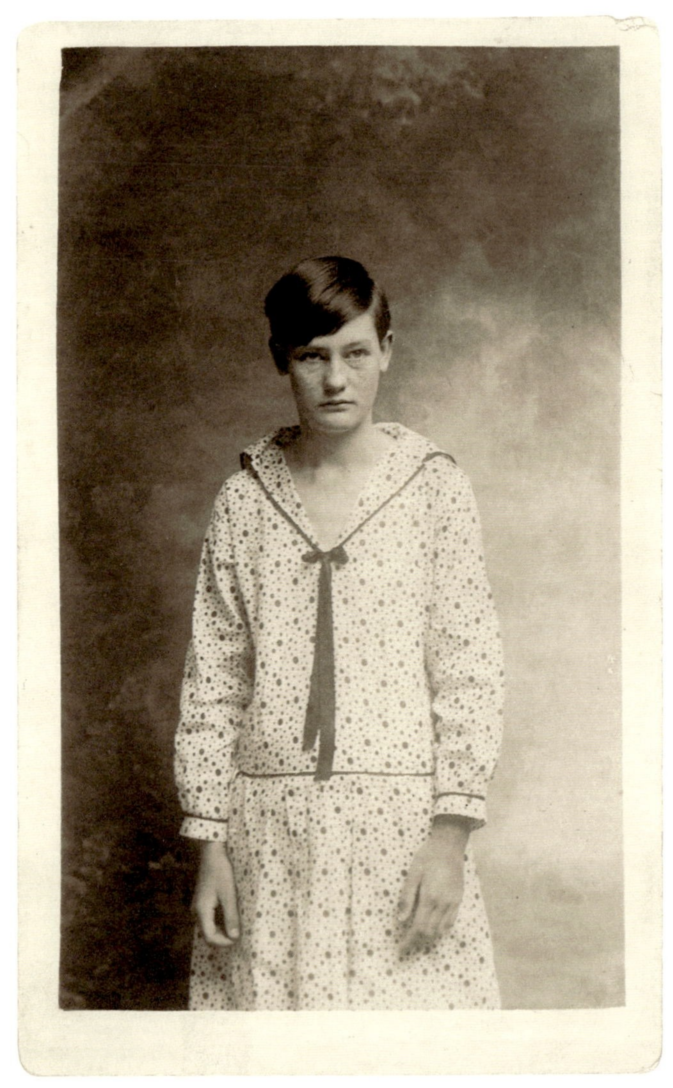

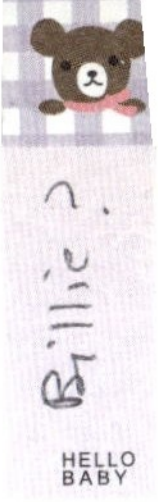
Billie ?
HELLO
BABY

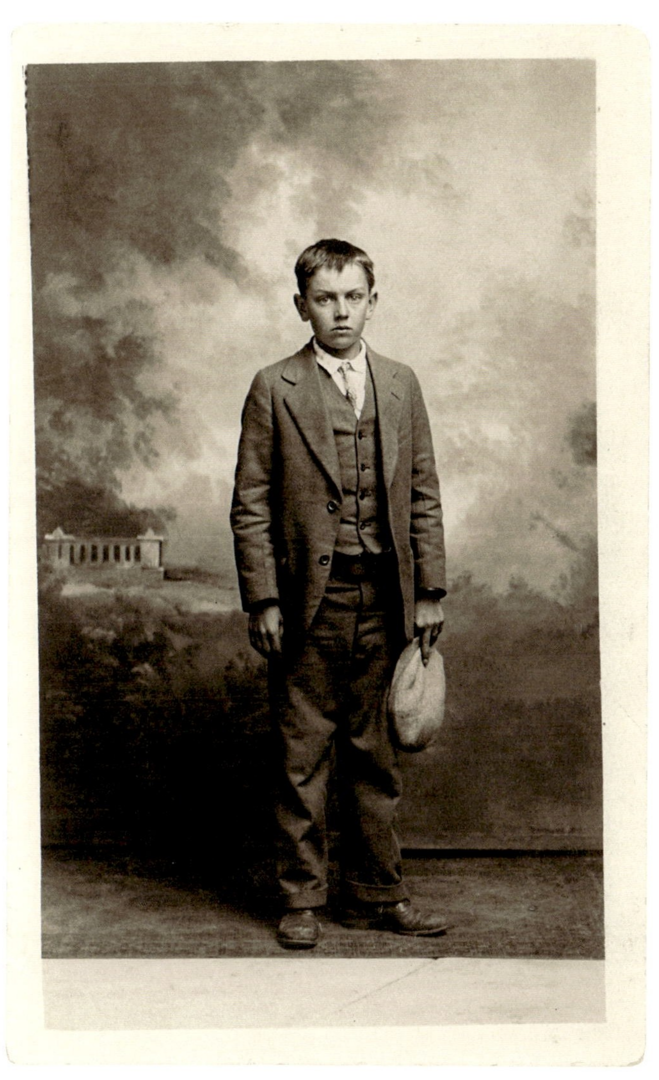

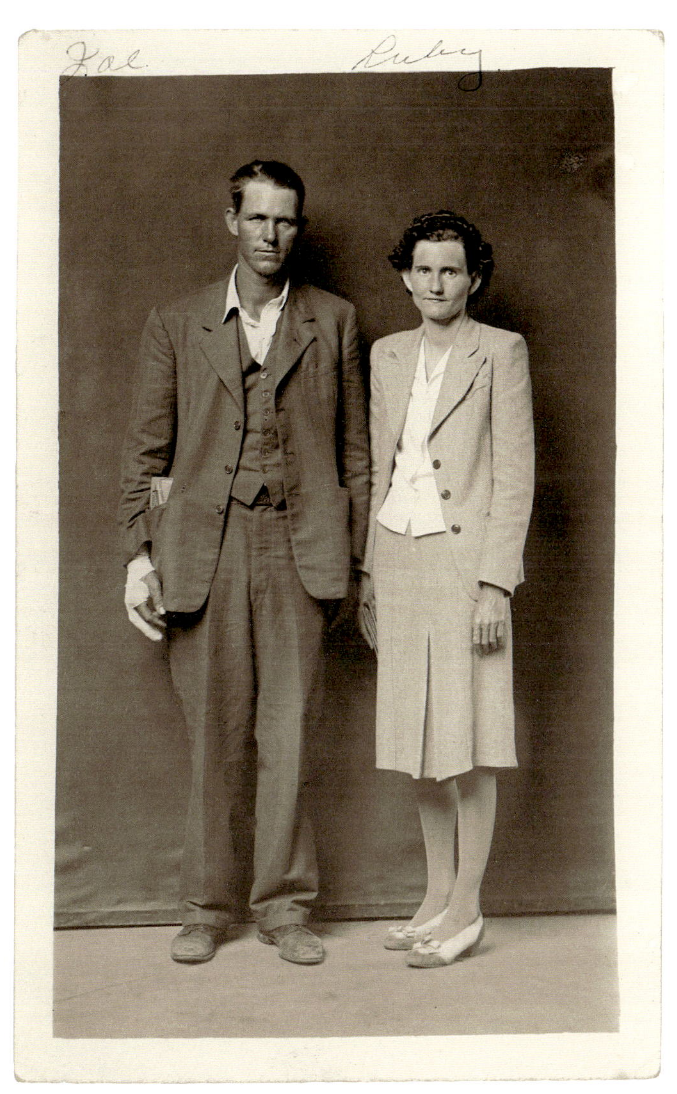
Ruby

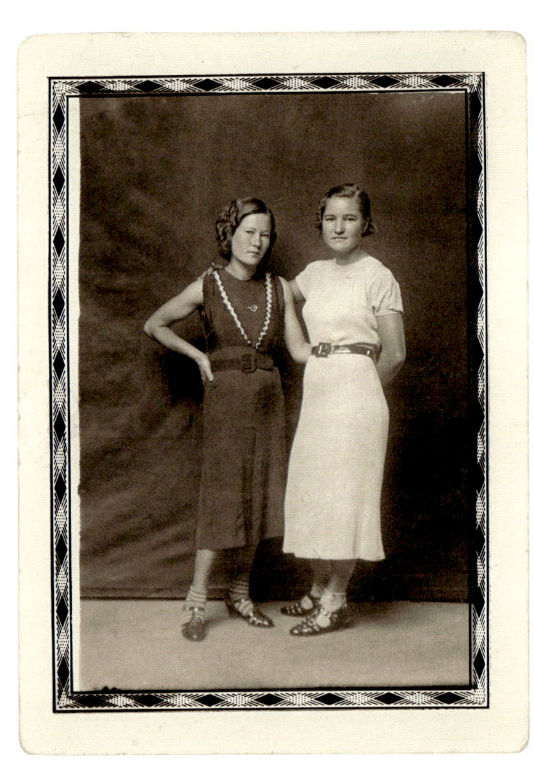

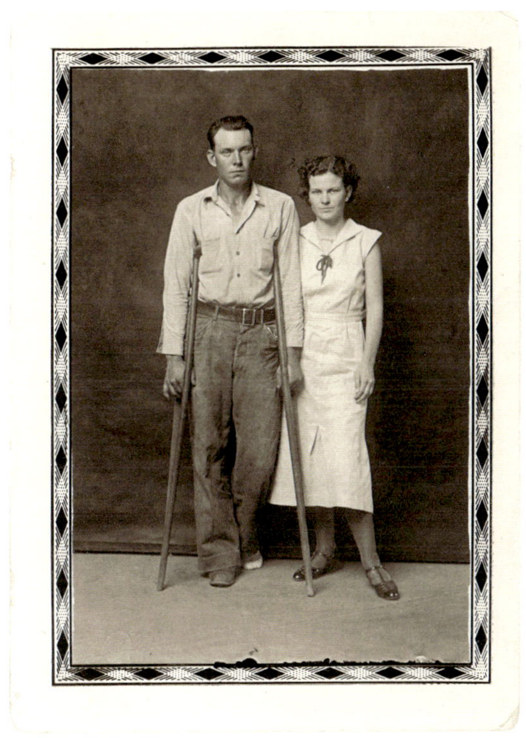

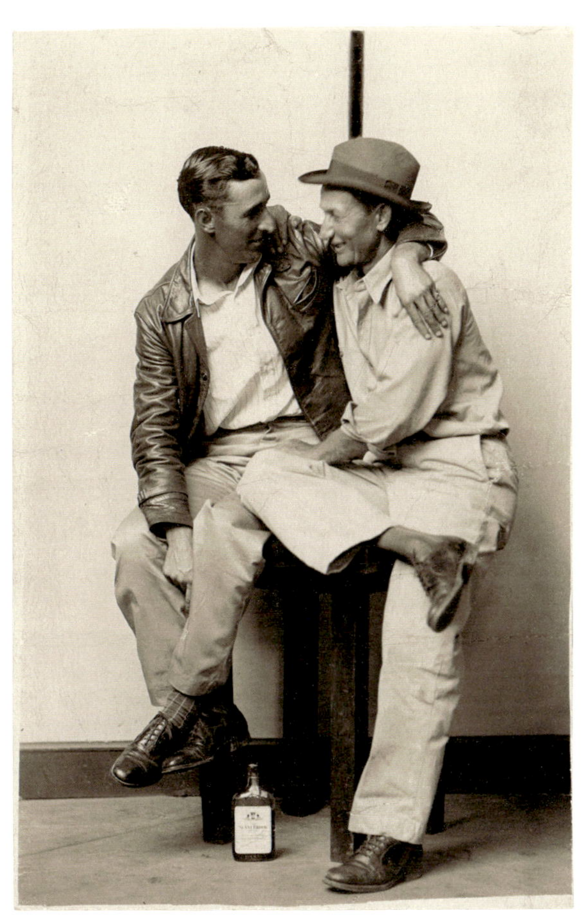

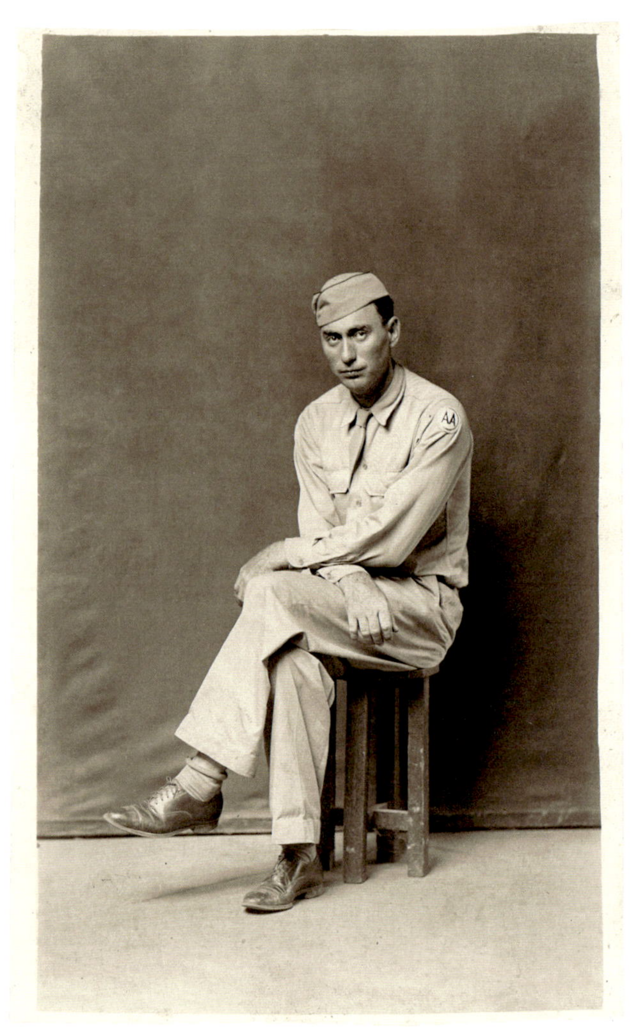
AA

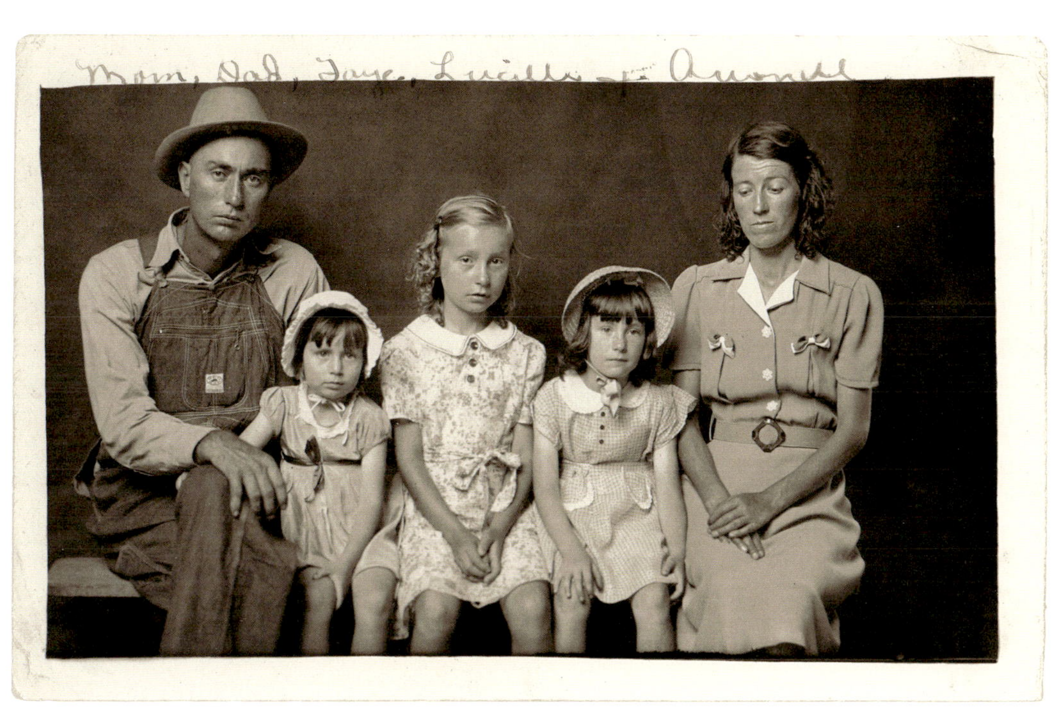
Mom, Dad, Faye, Lucille &

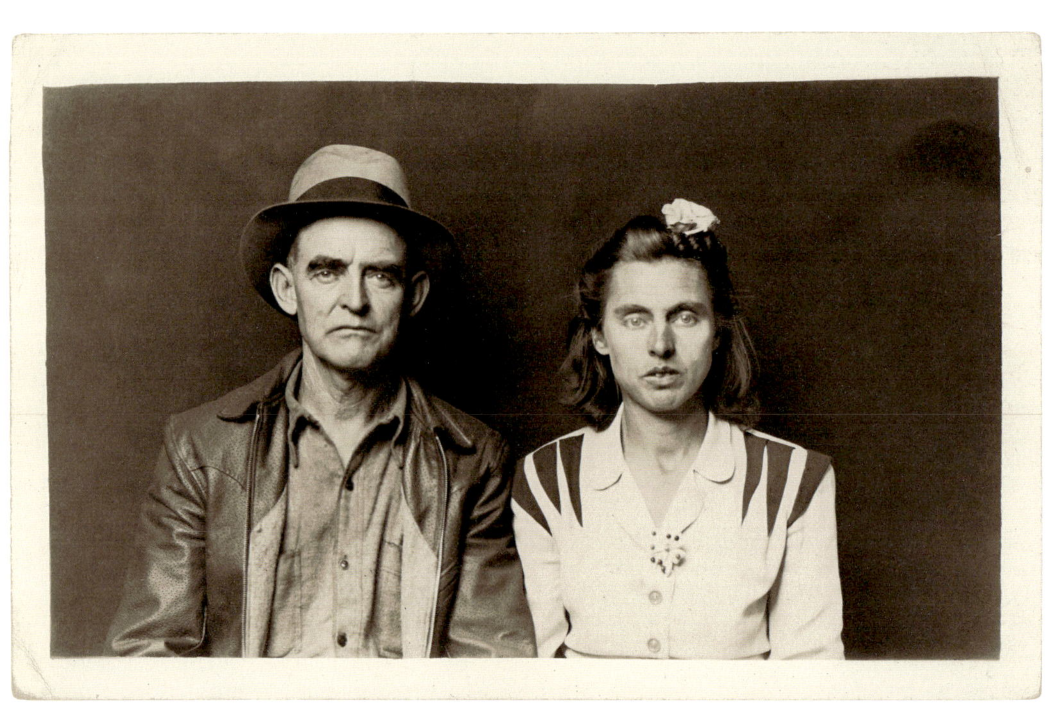

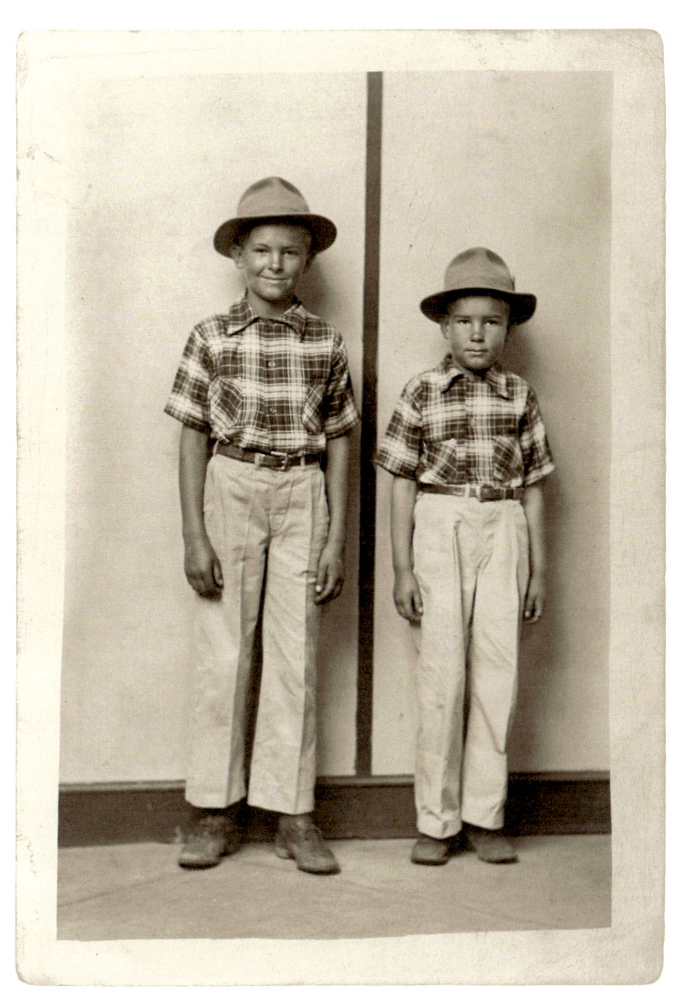

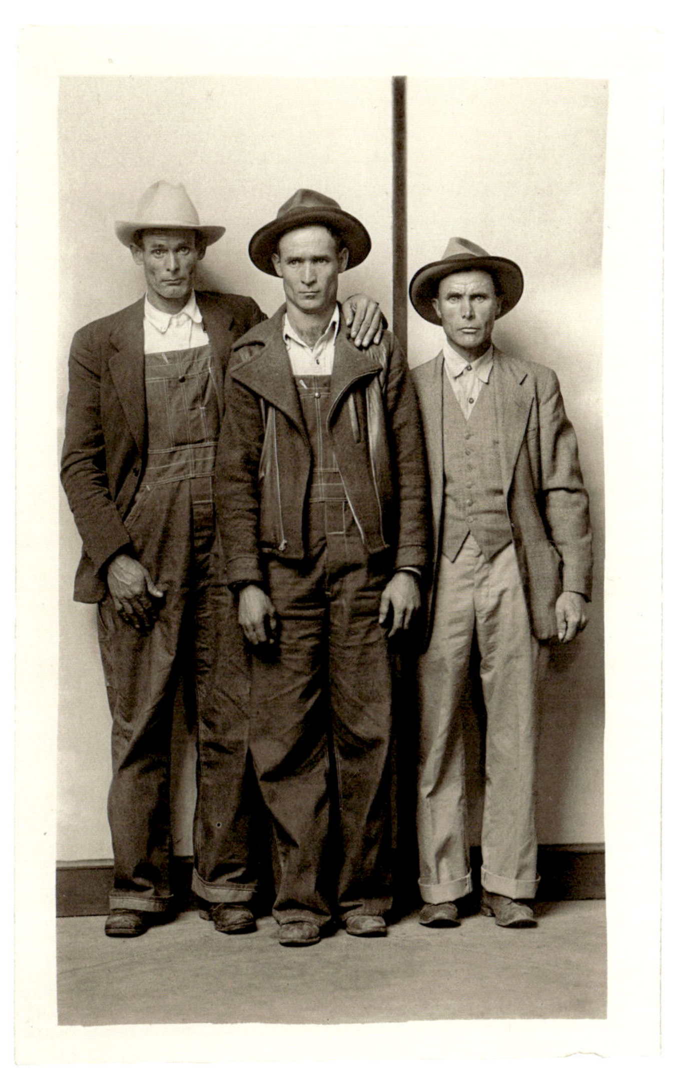

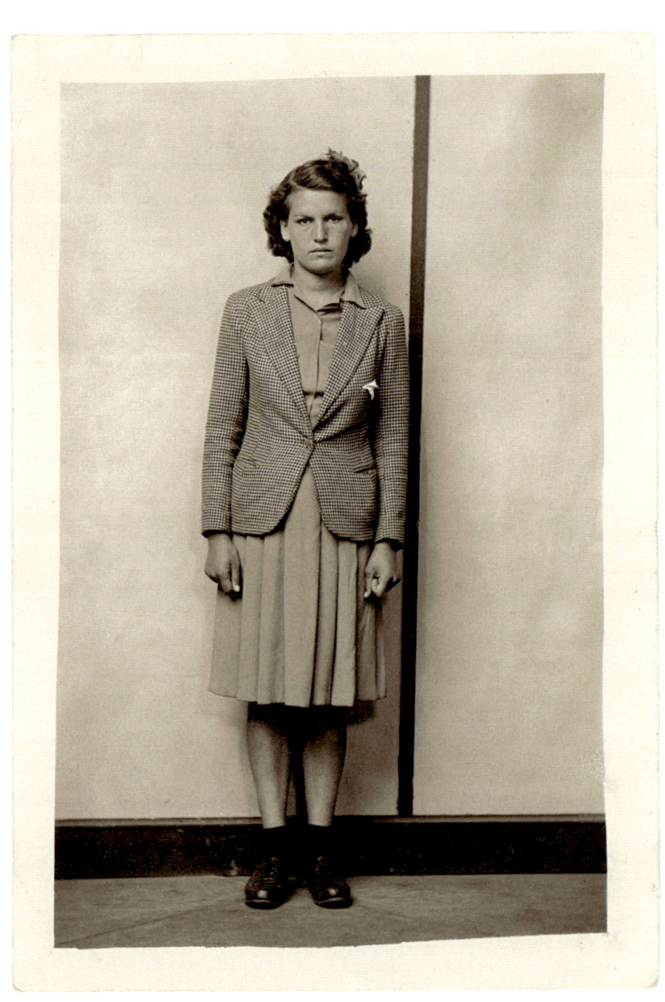

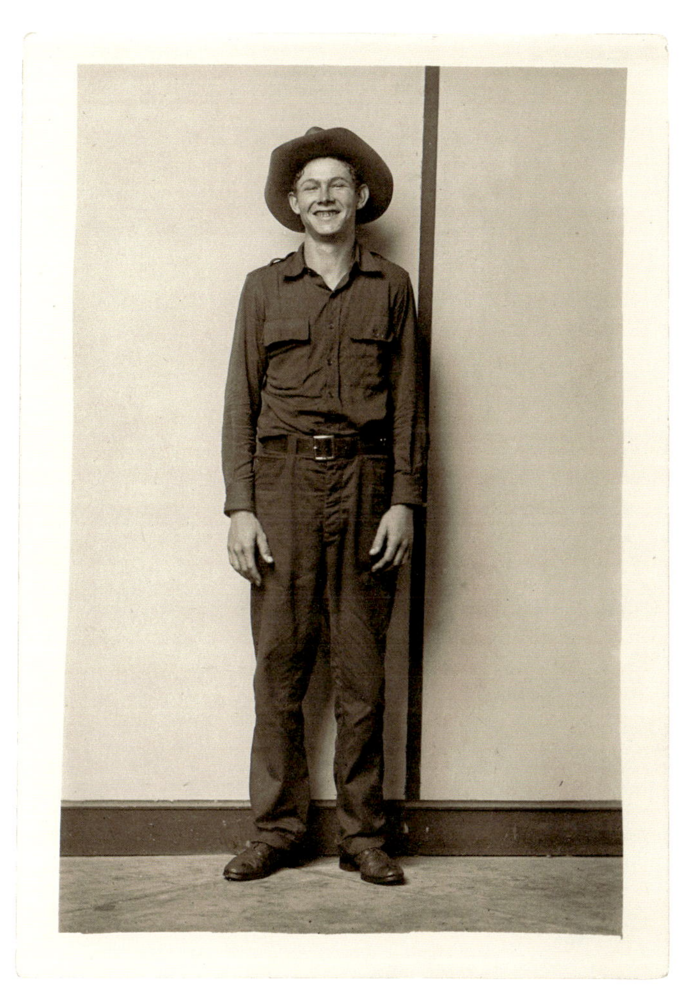

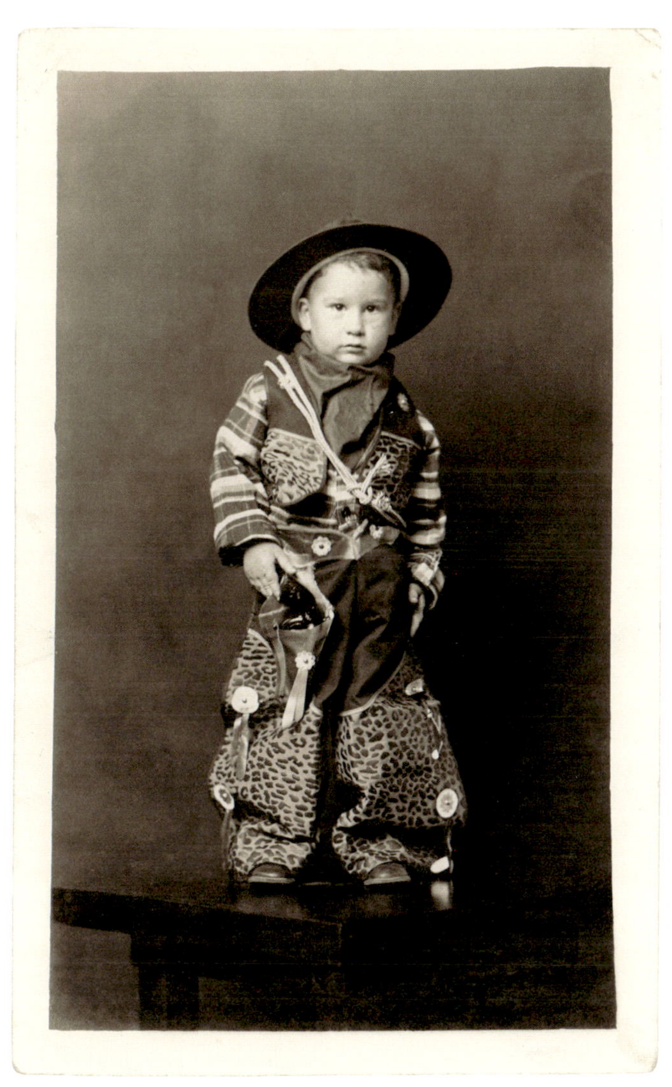

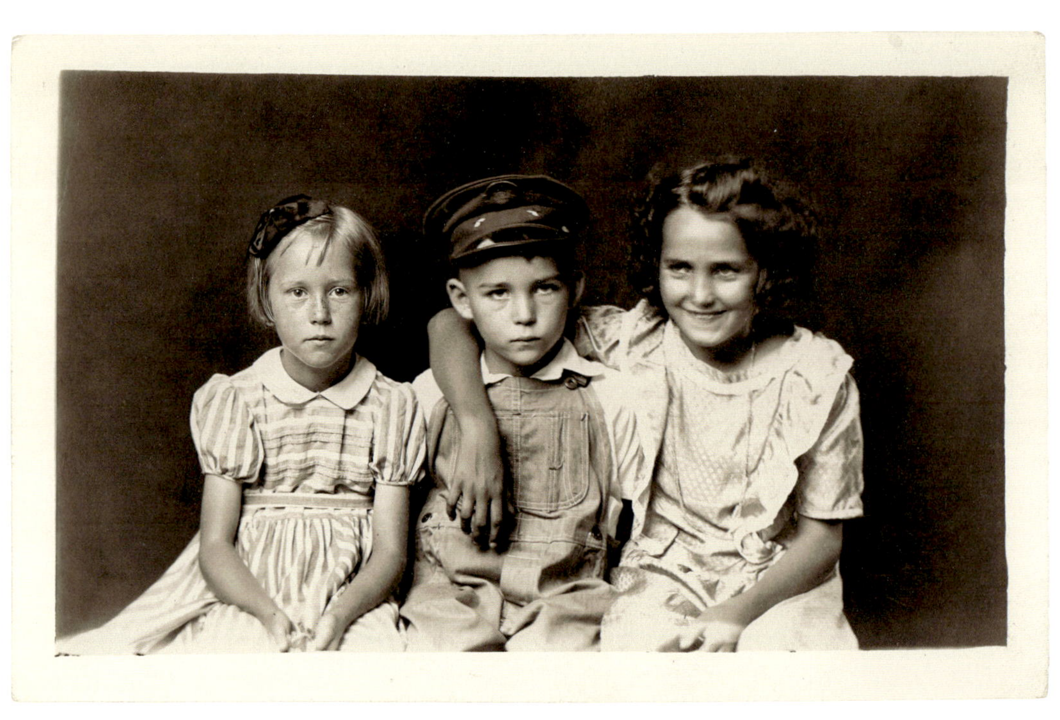

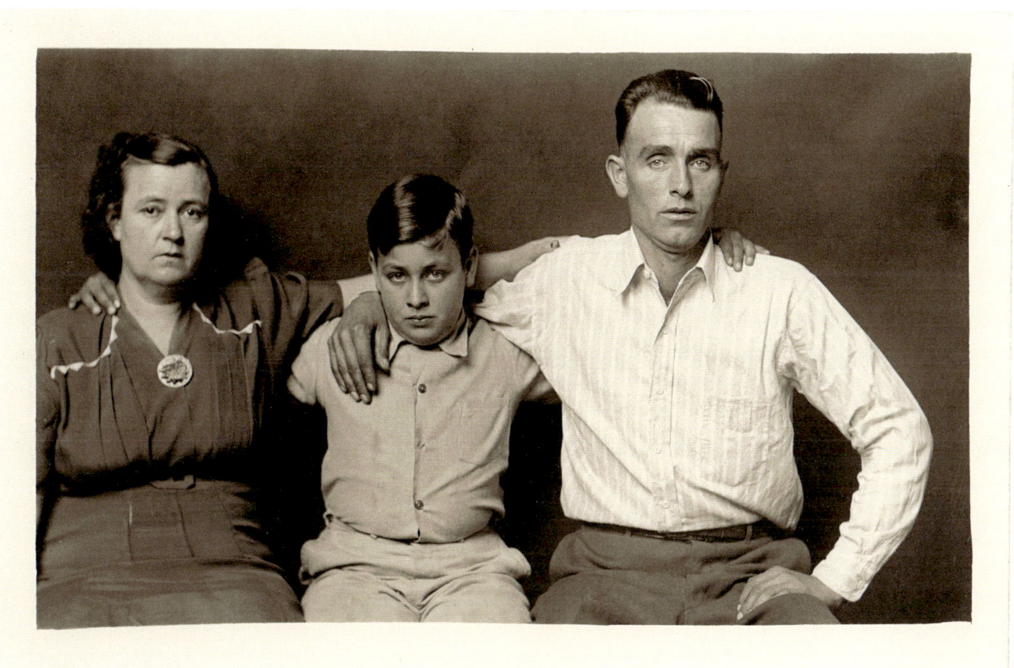

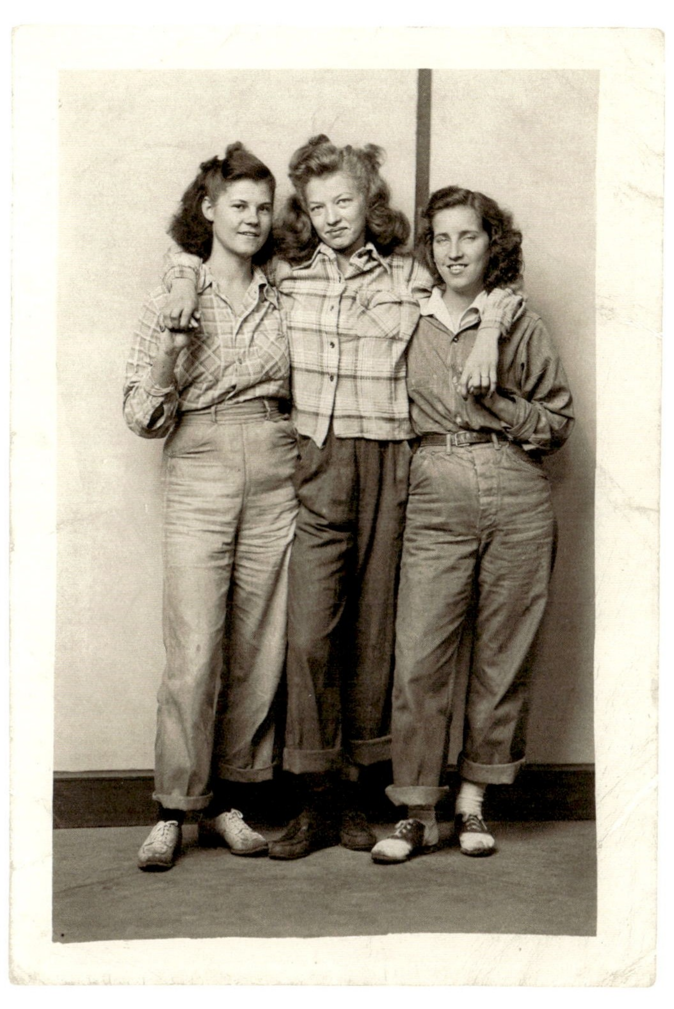

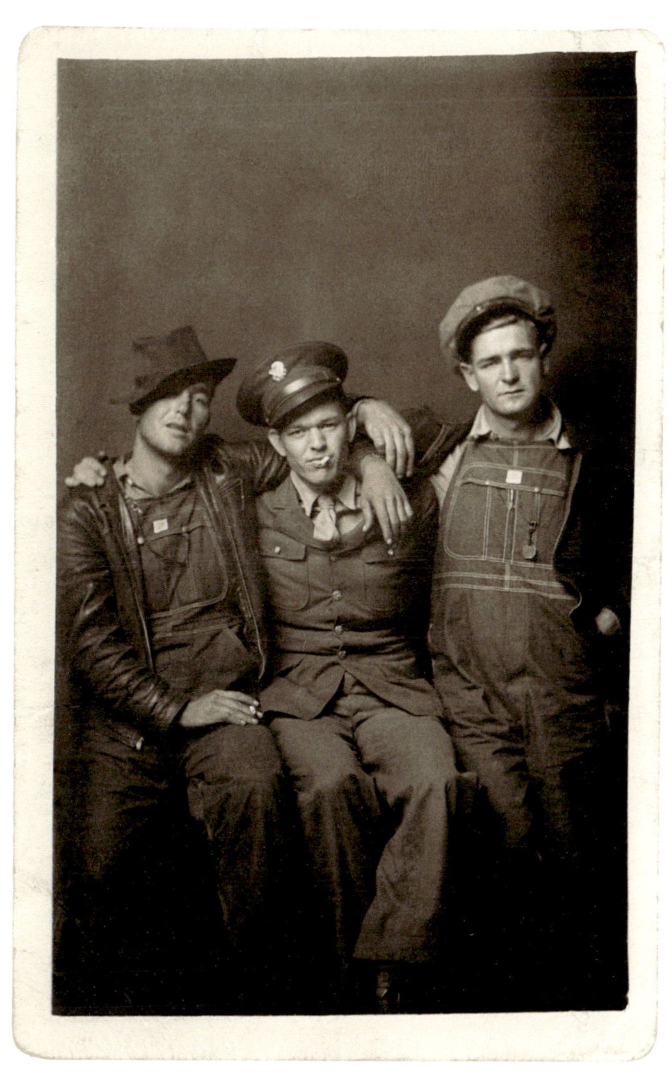

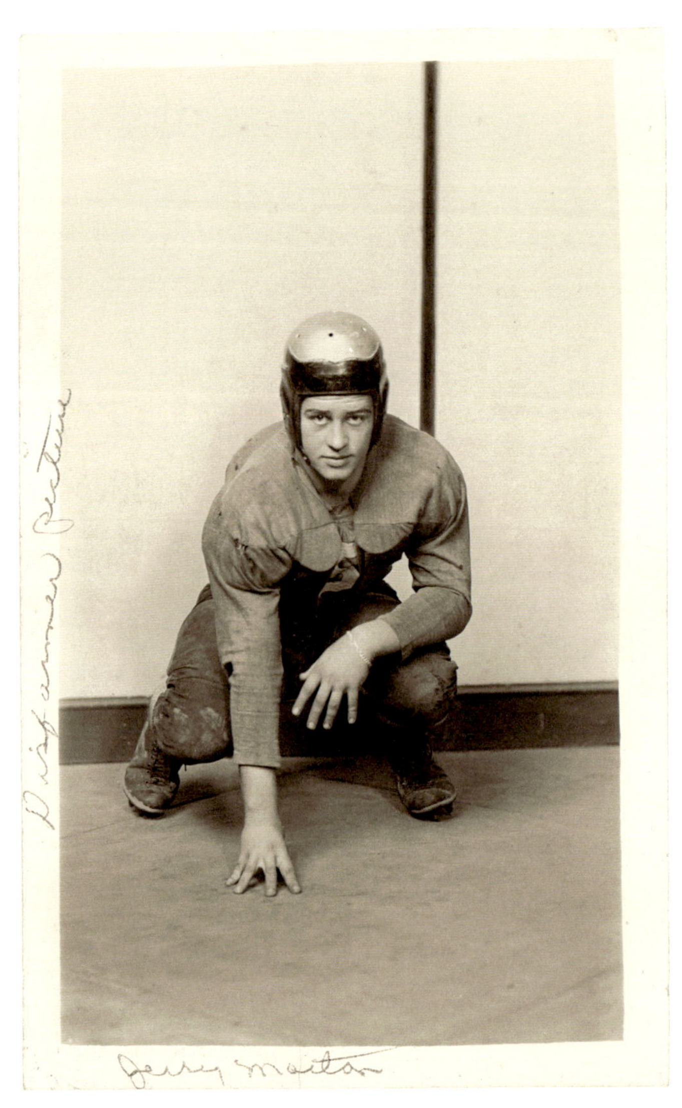

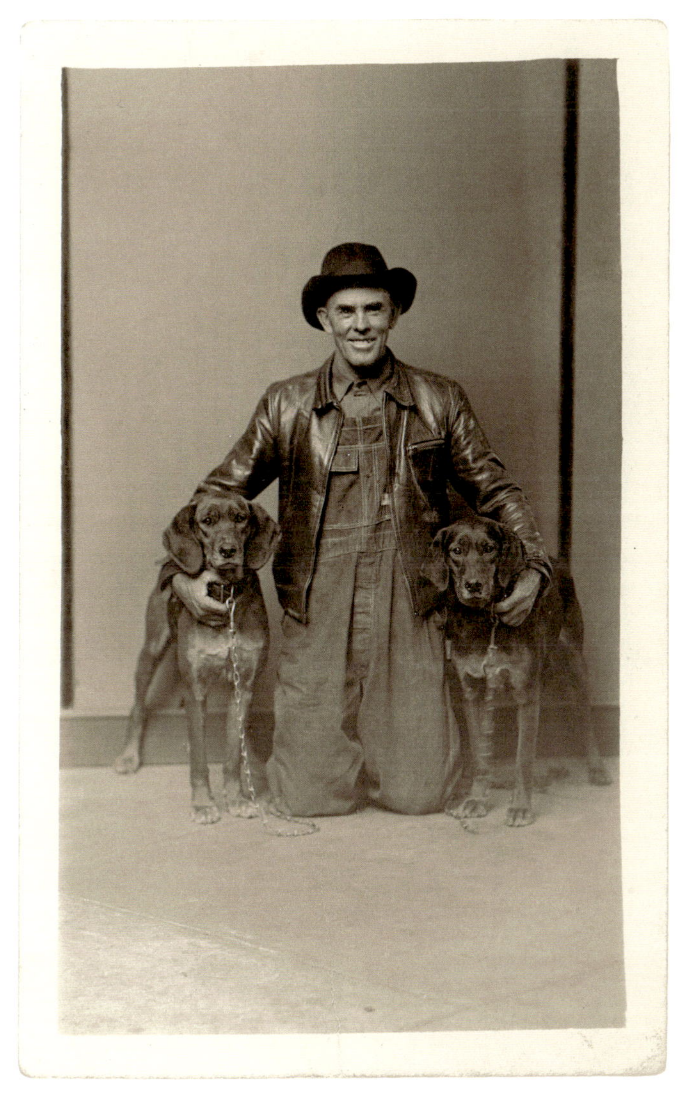

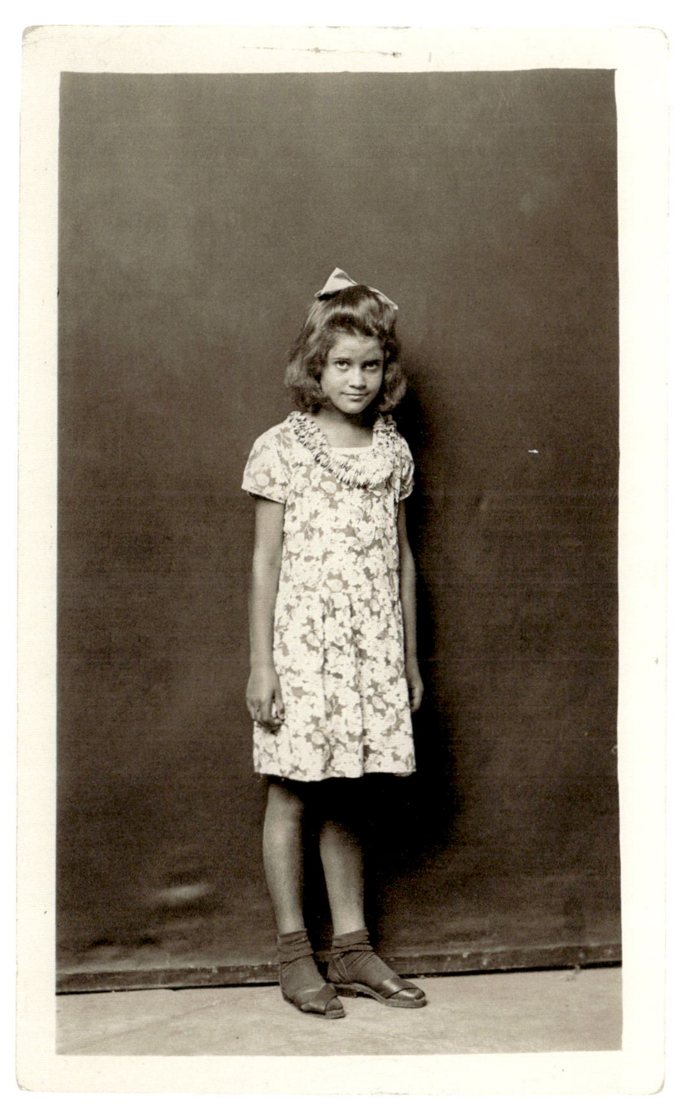

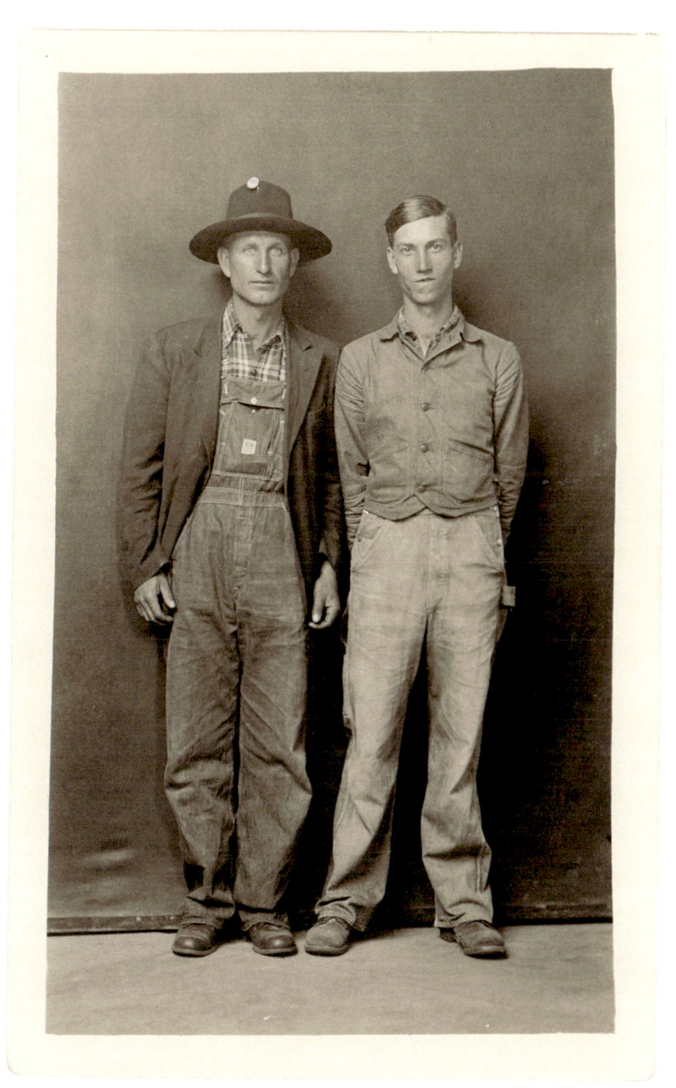

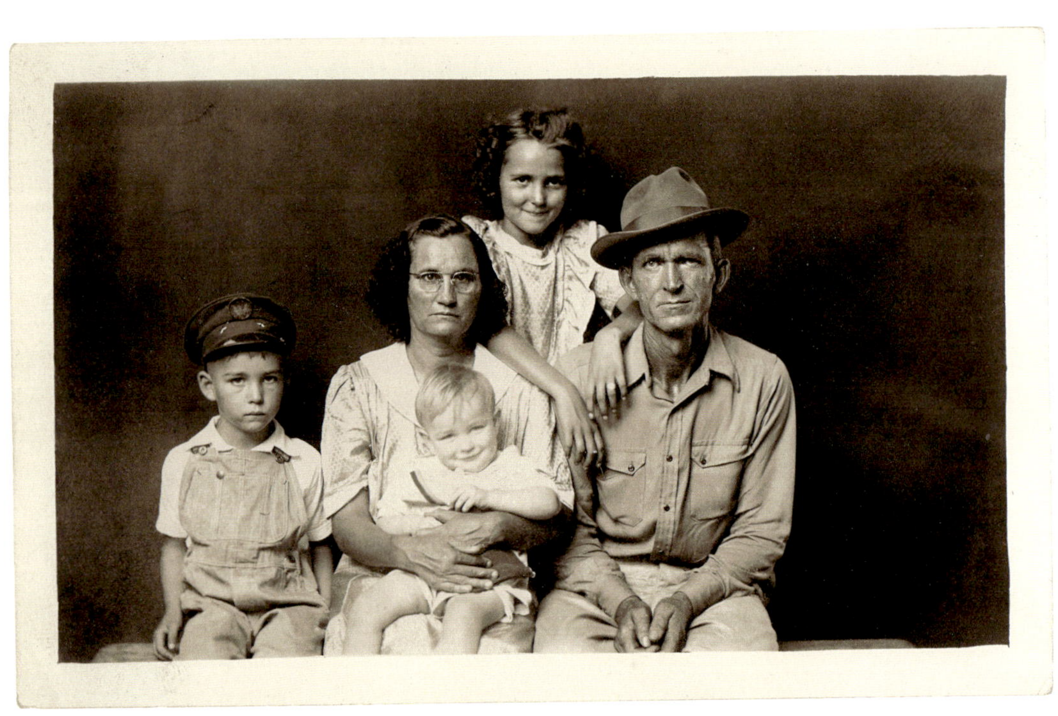

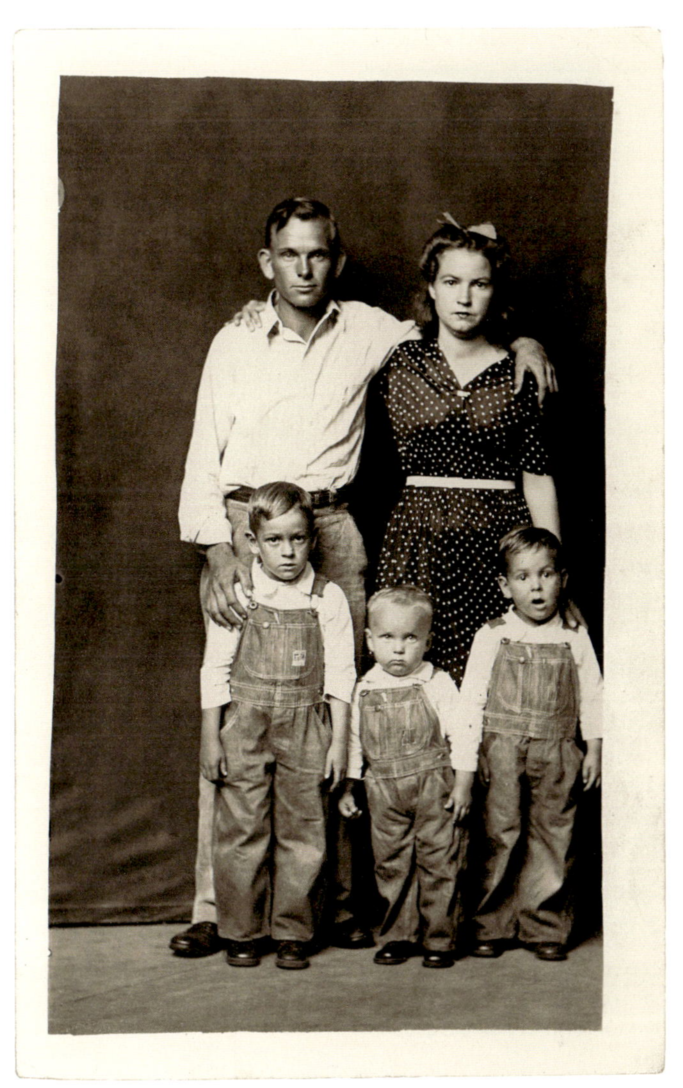

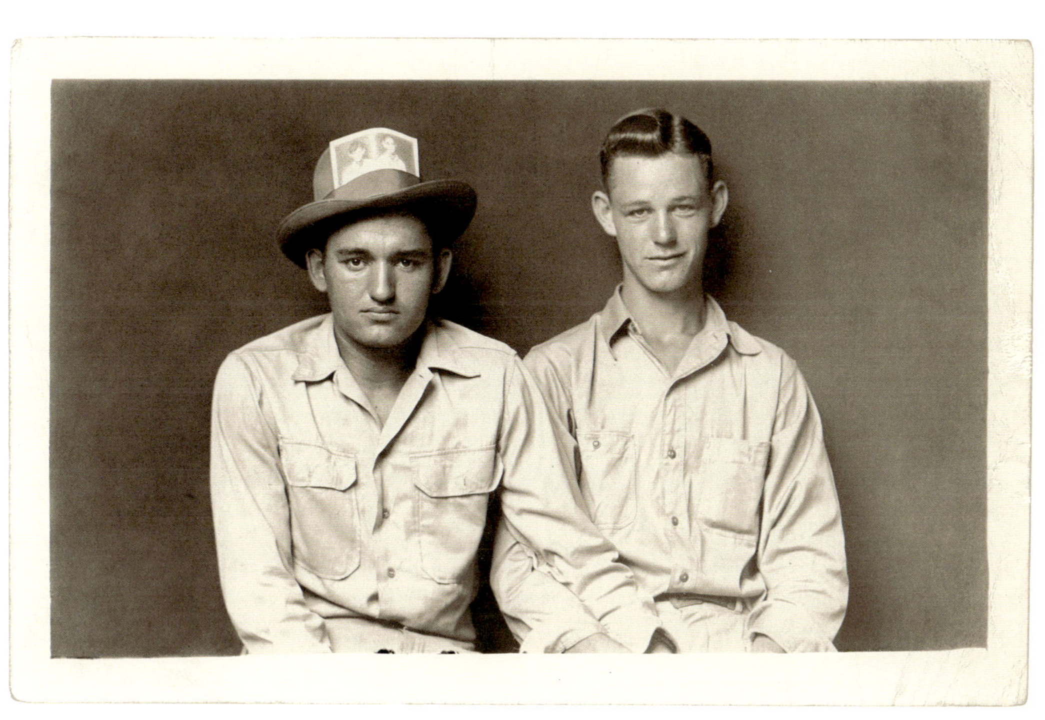

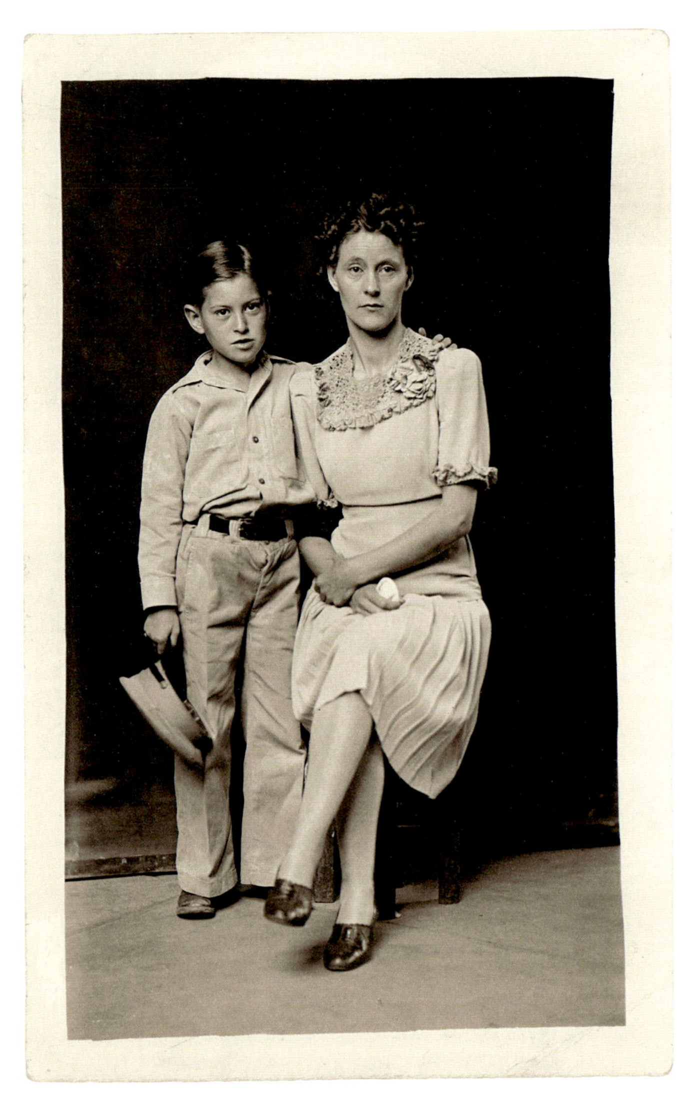

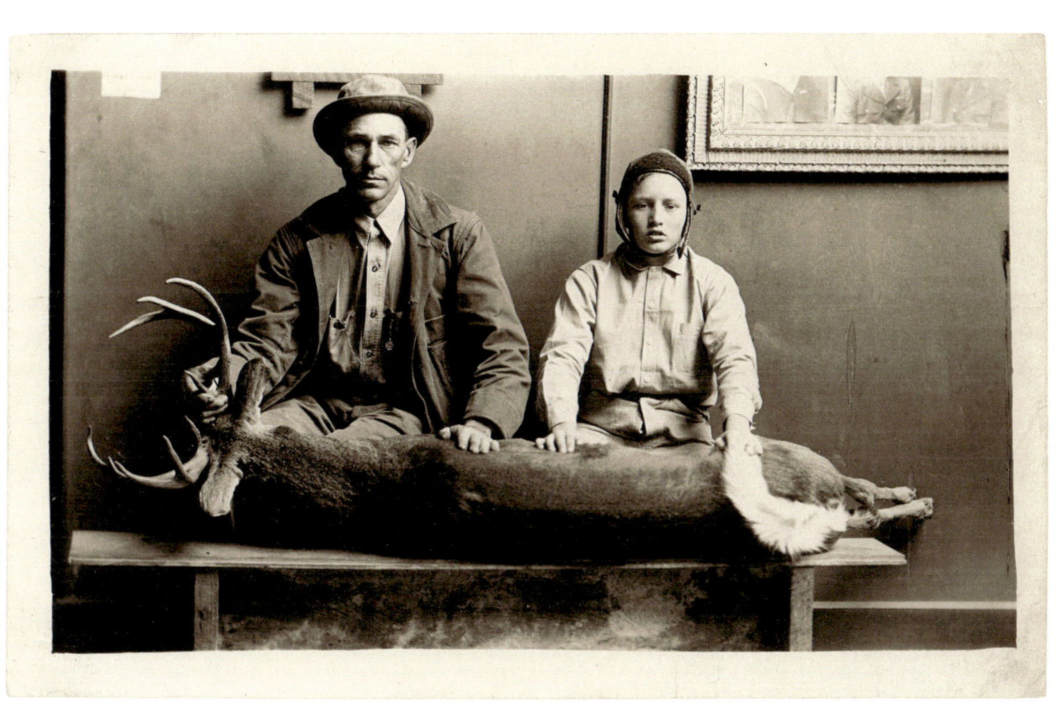

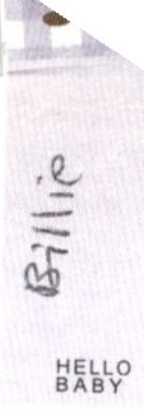
Billie
HELLO
BABY

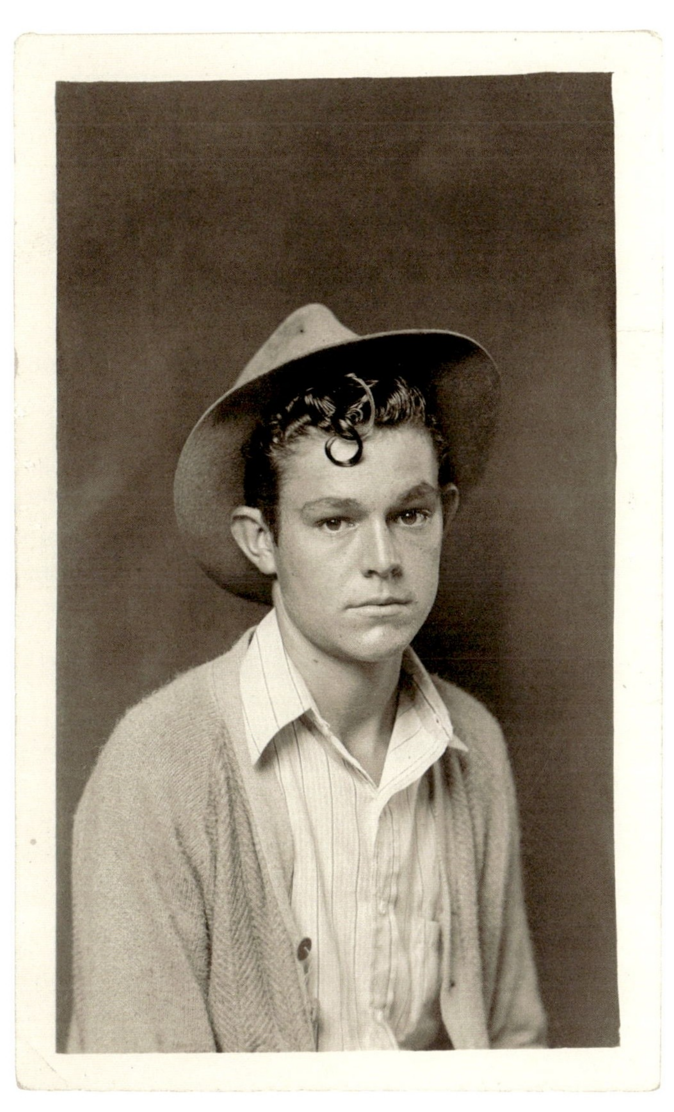

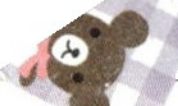

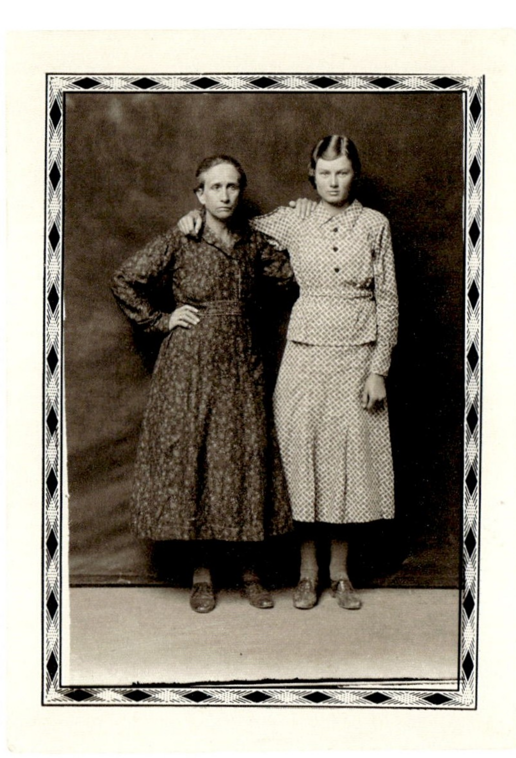

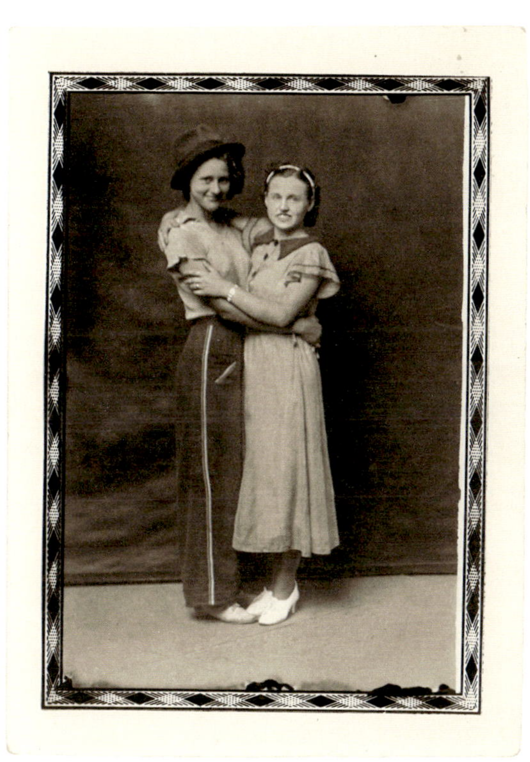

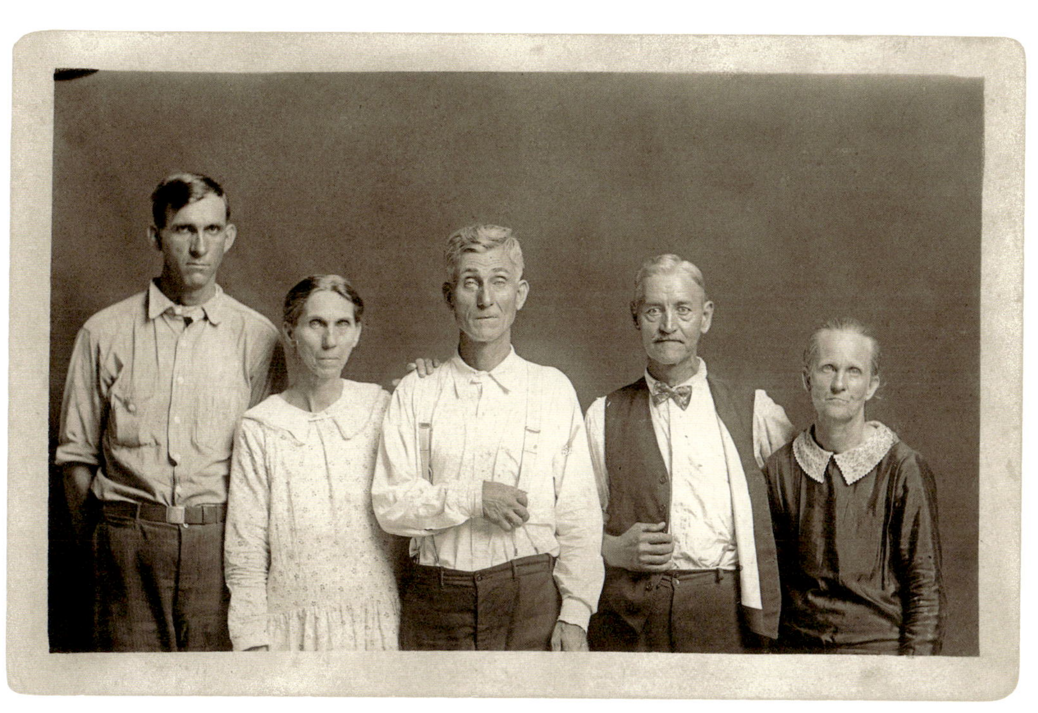

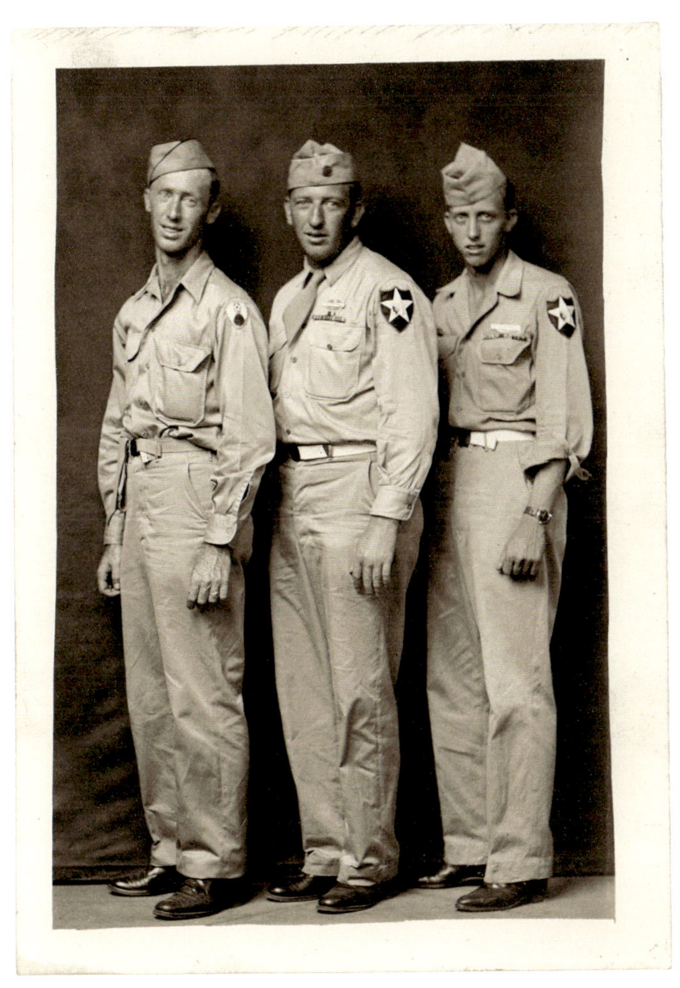

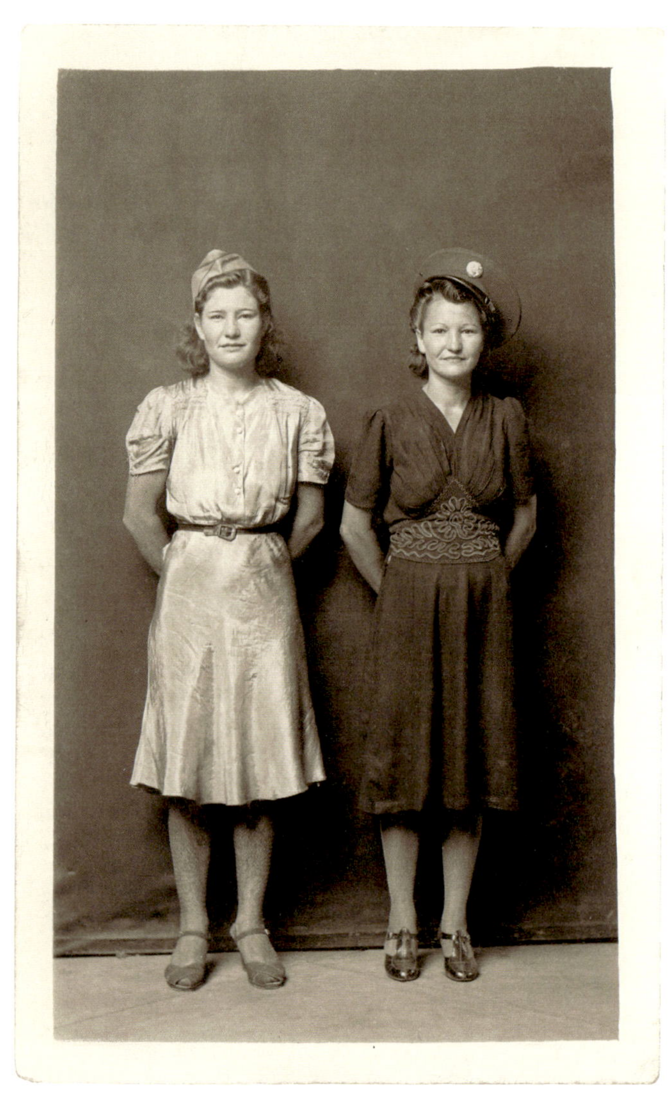

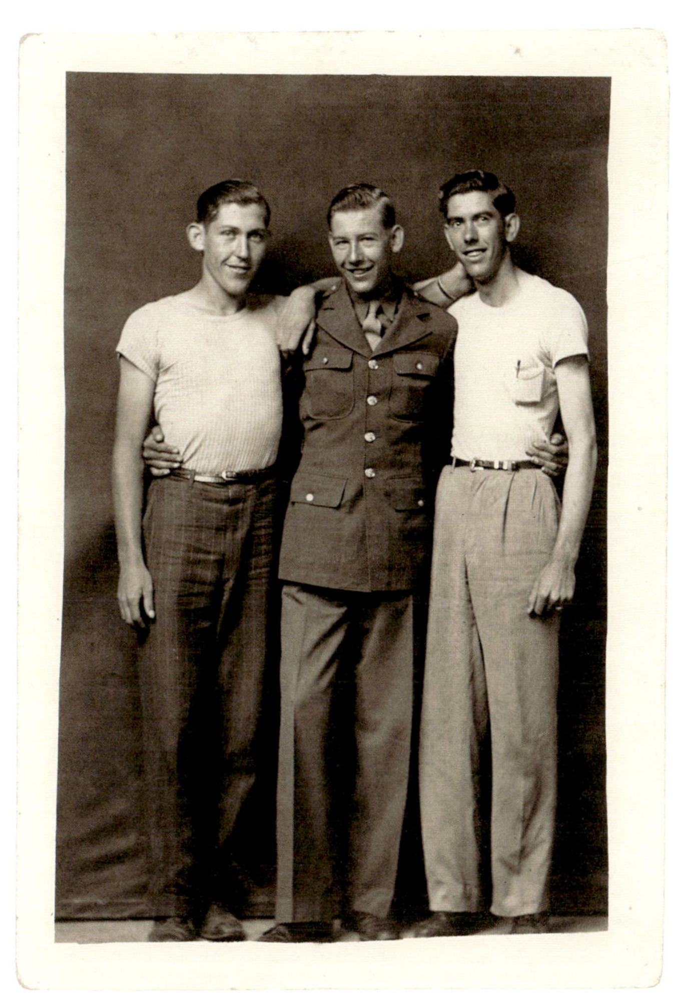

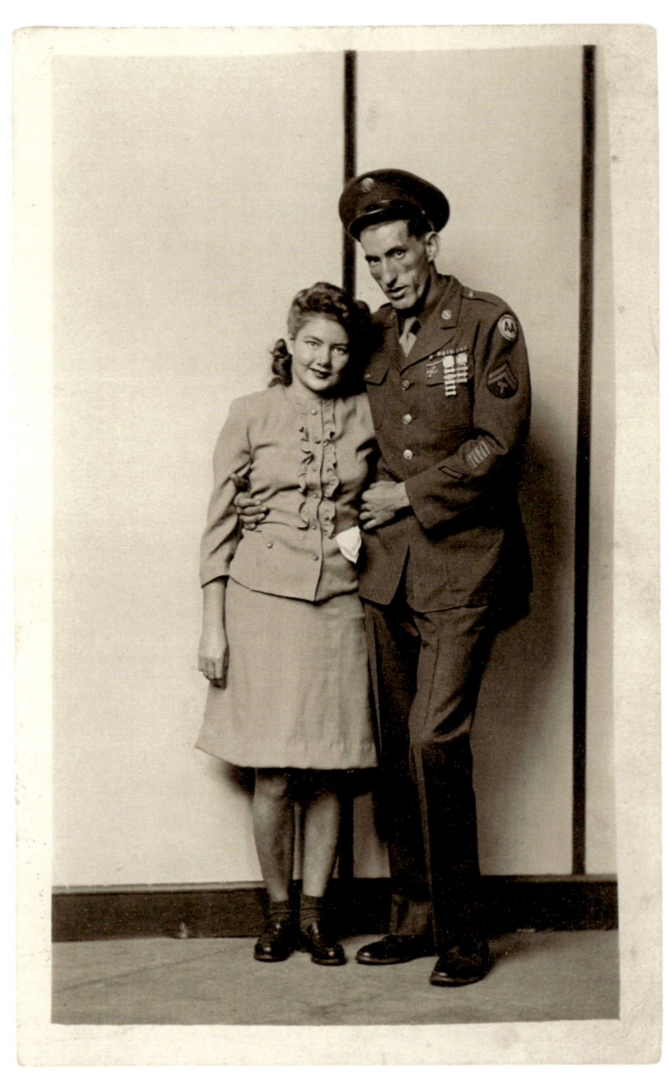

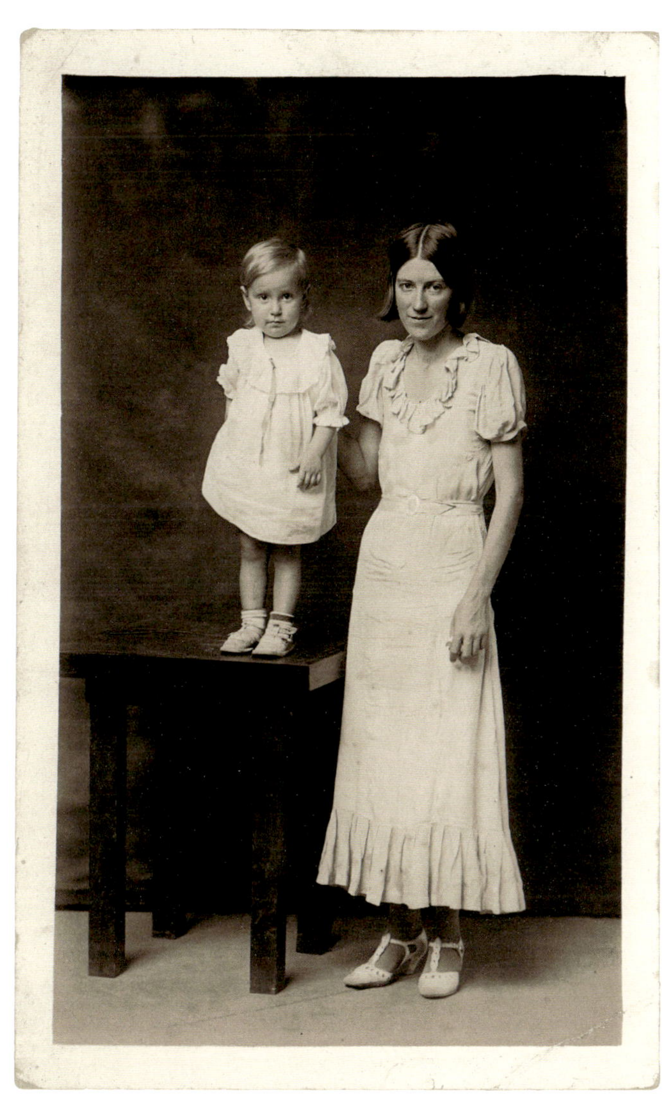

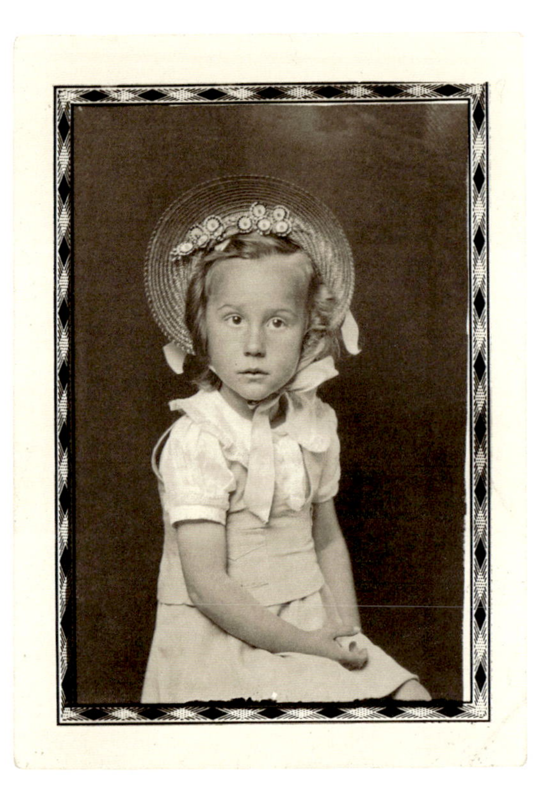

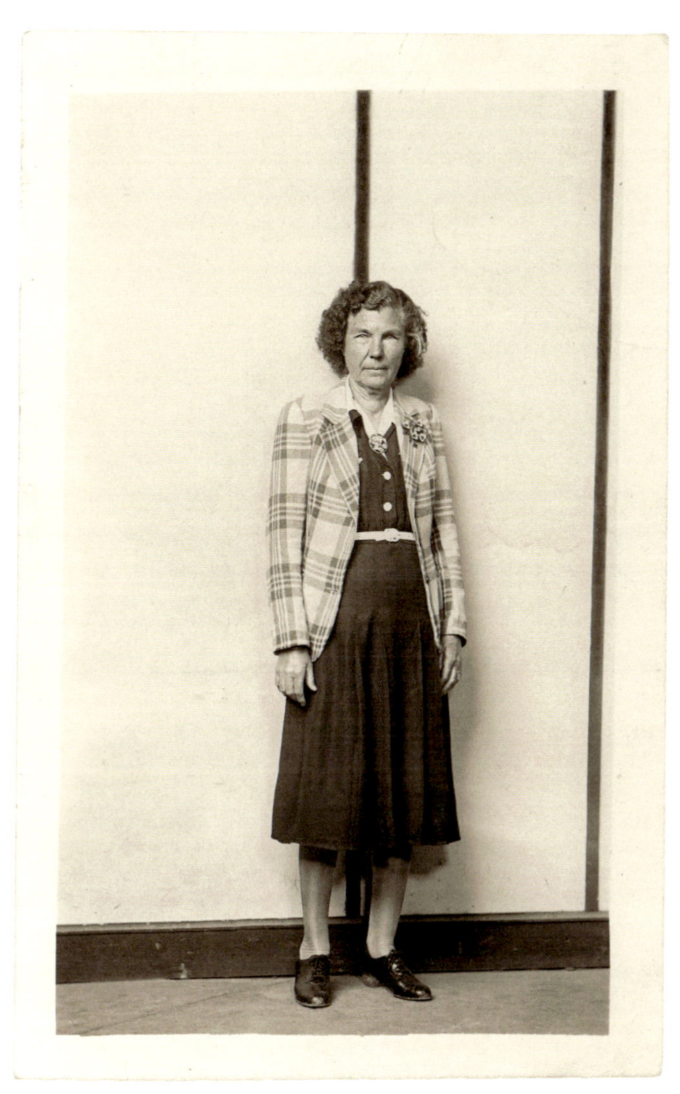

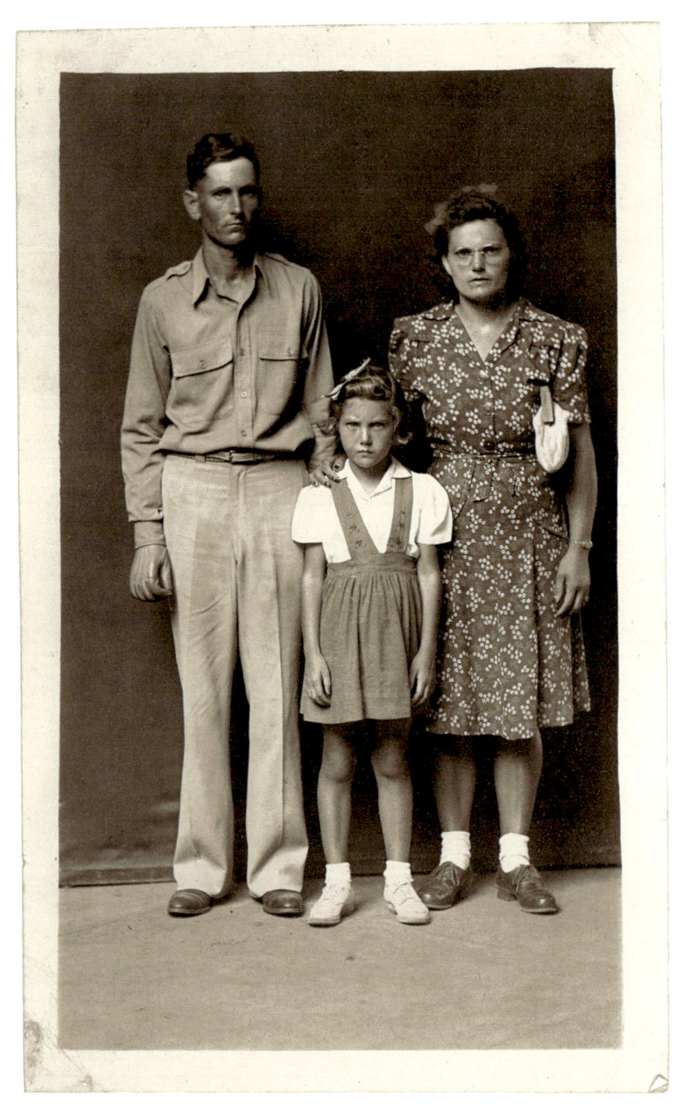

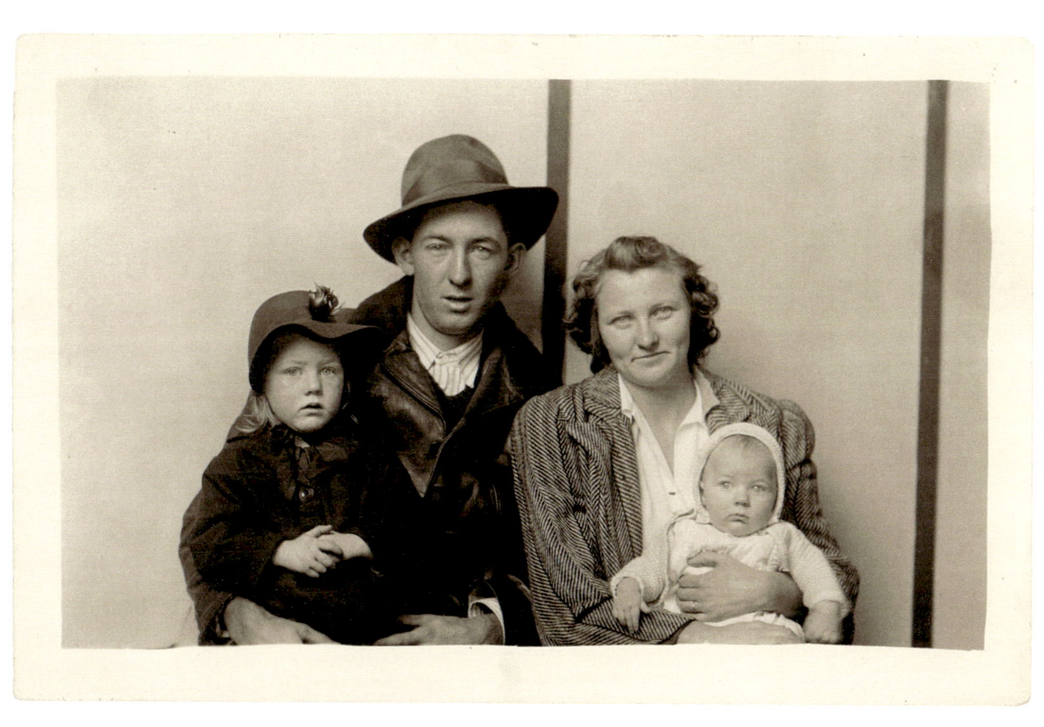

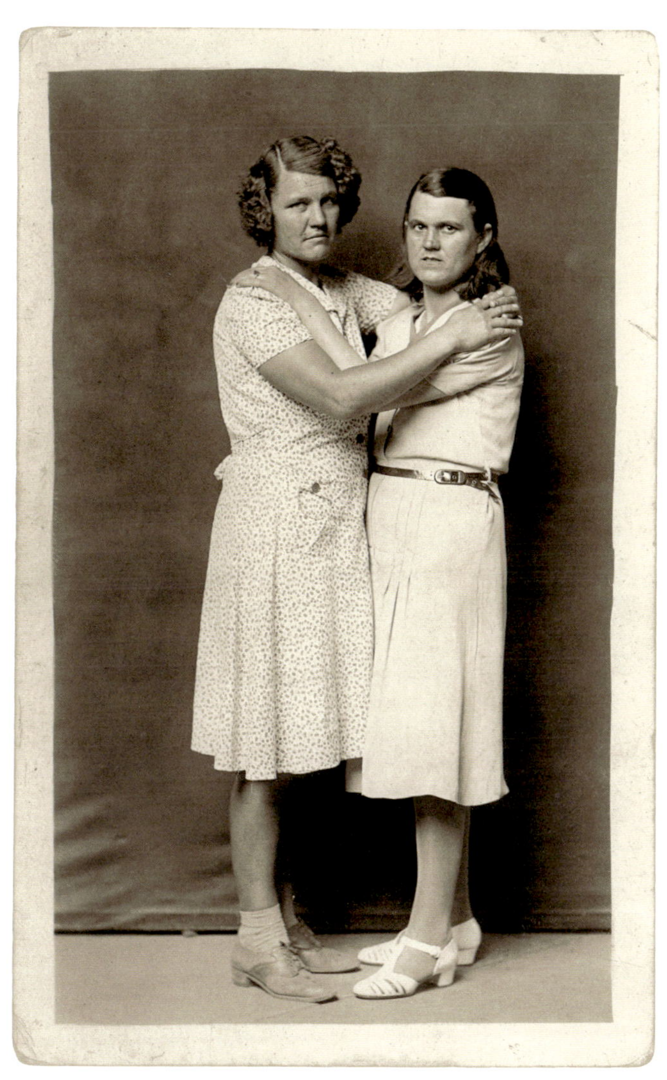

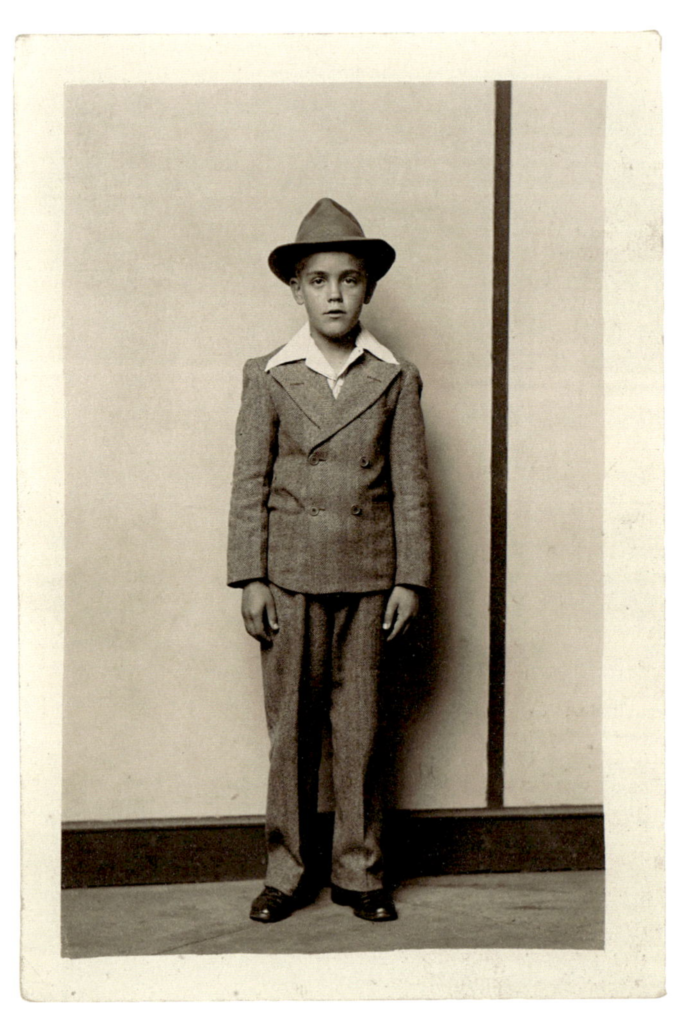

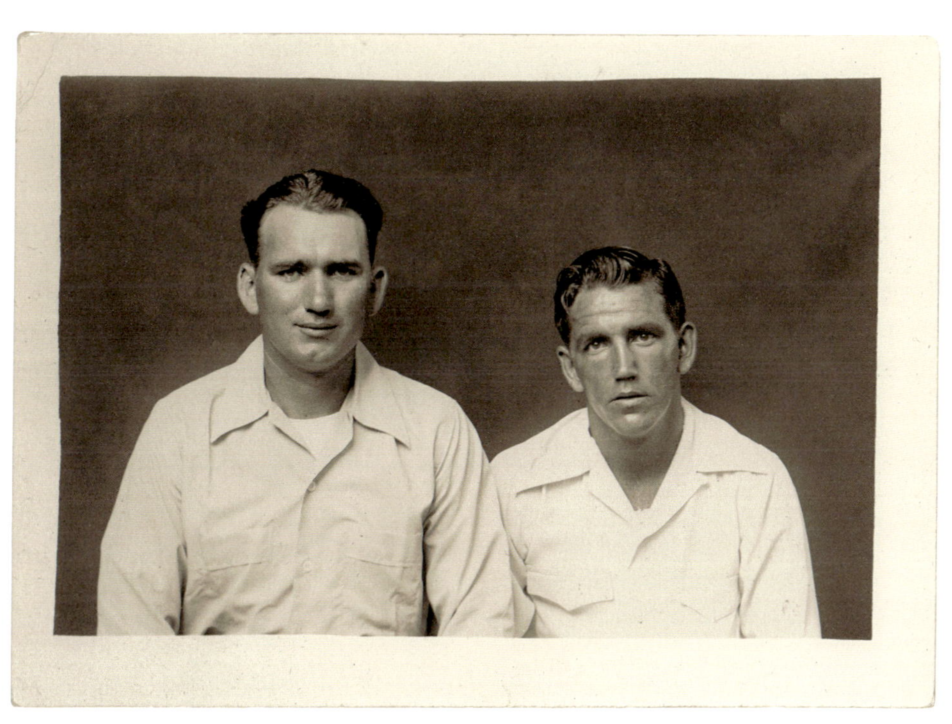

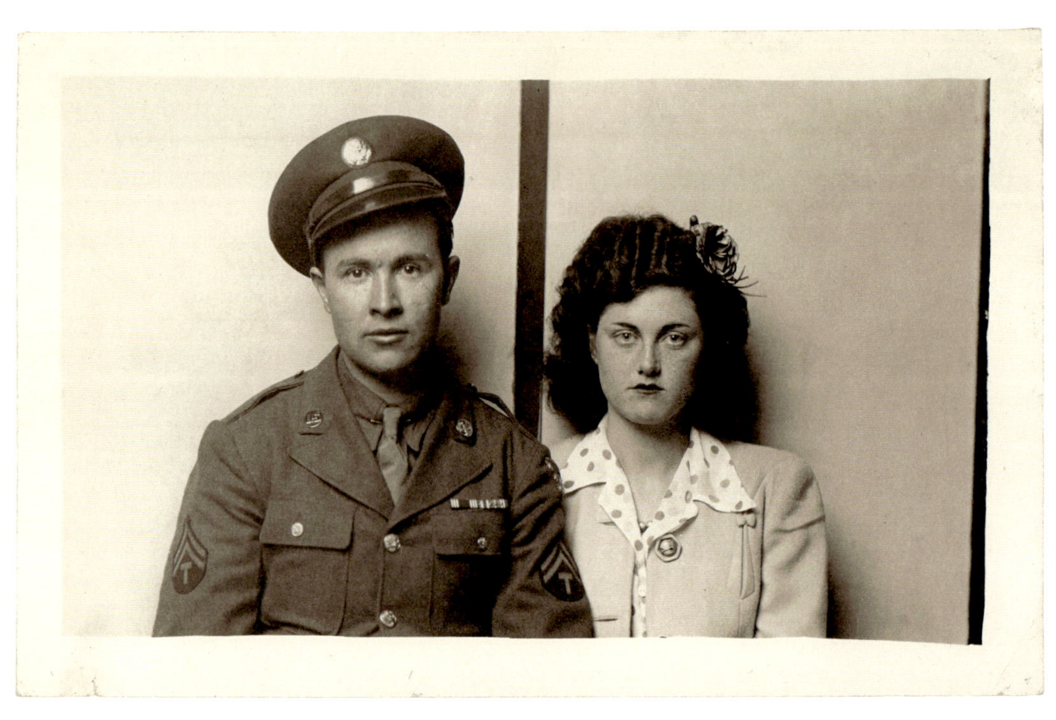

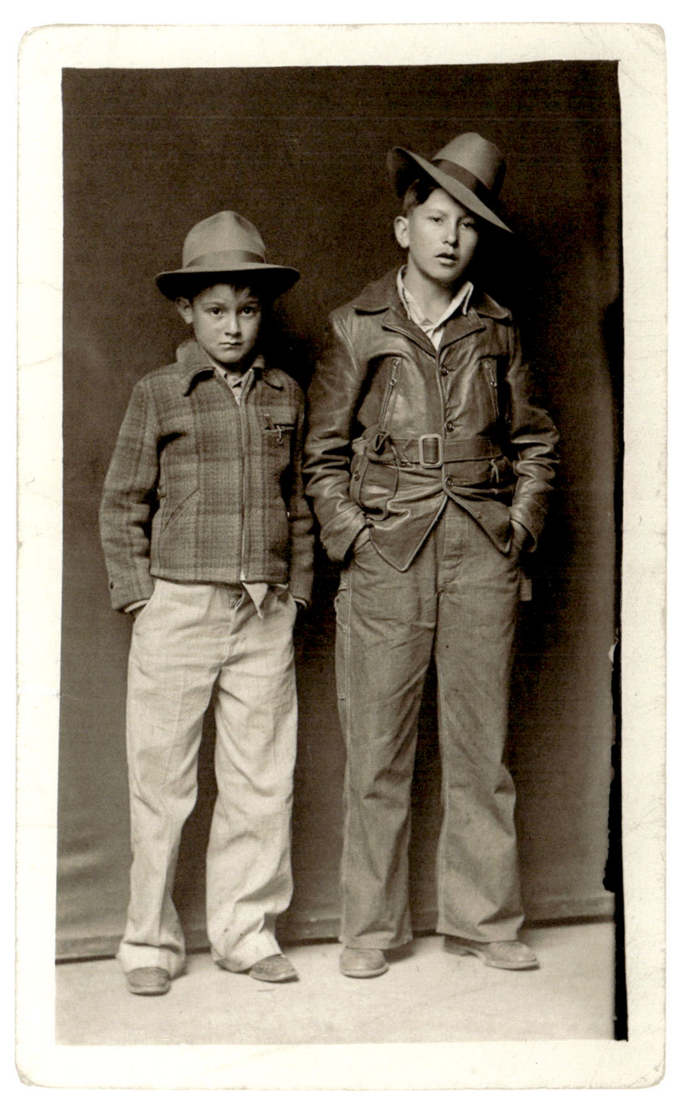

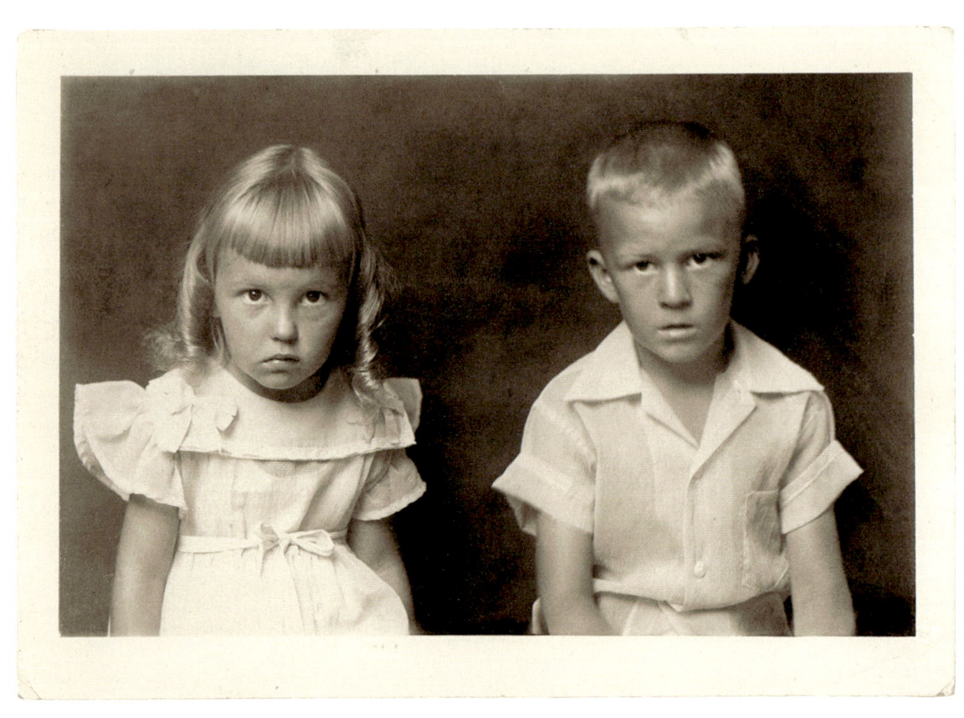

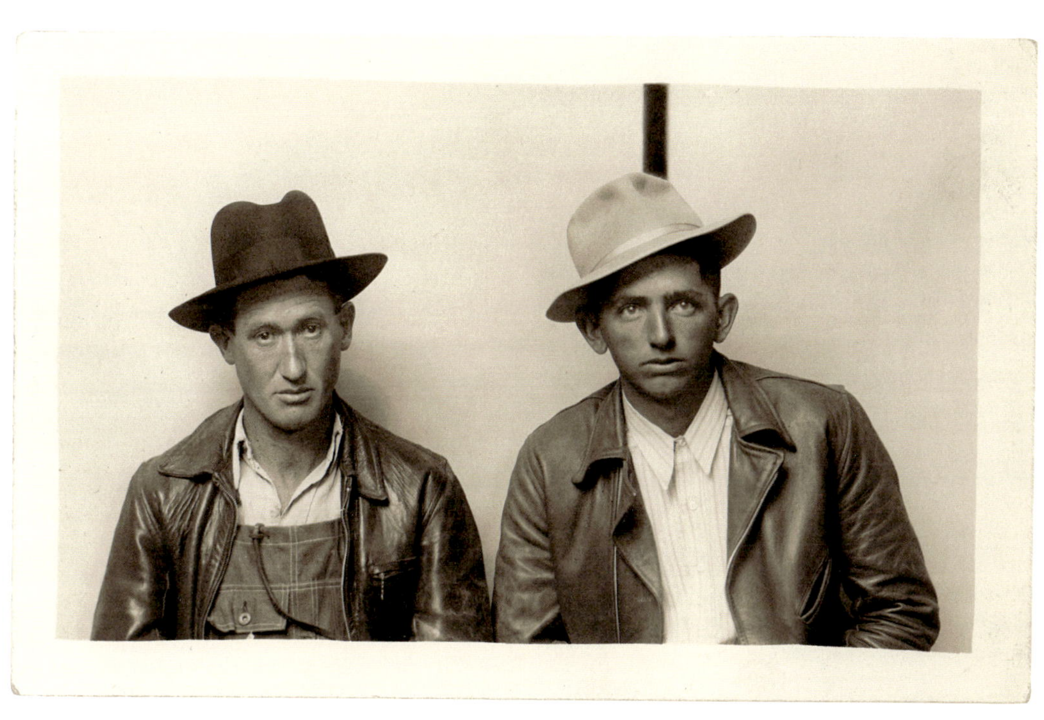

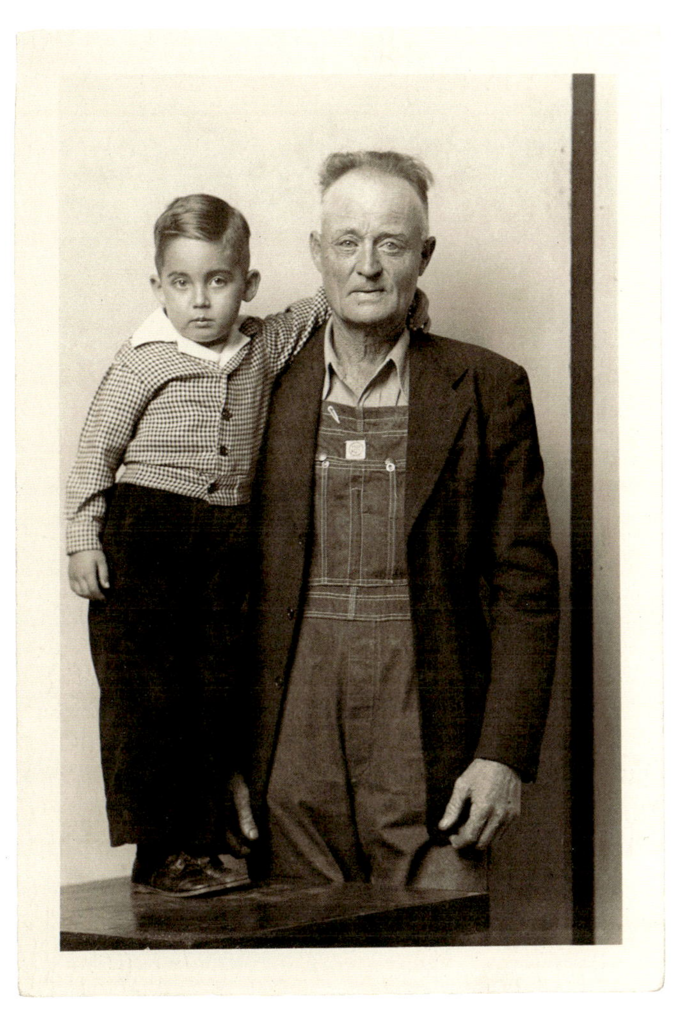

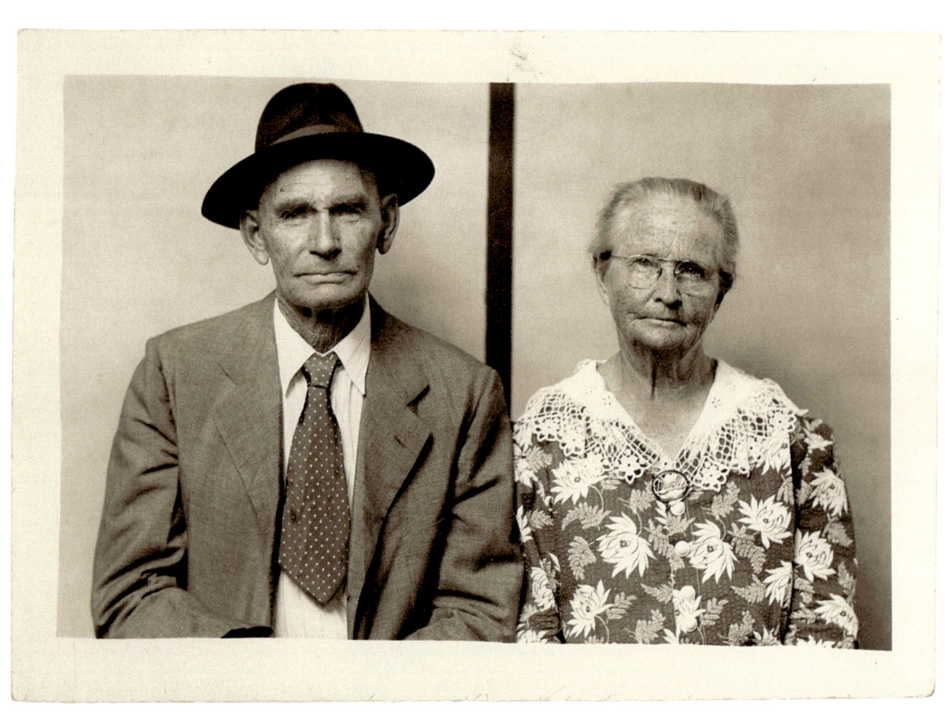

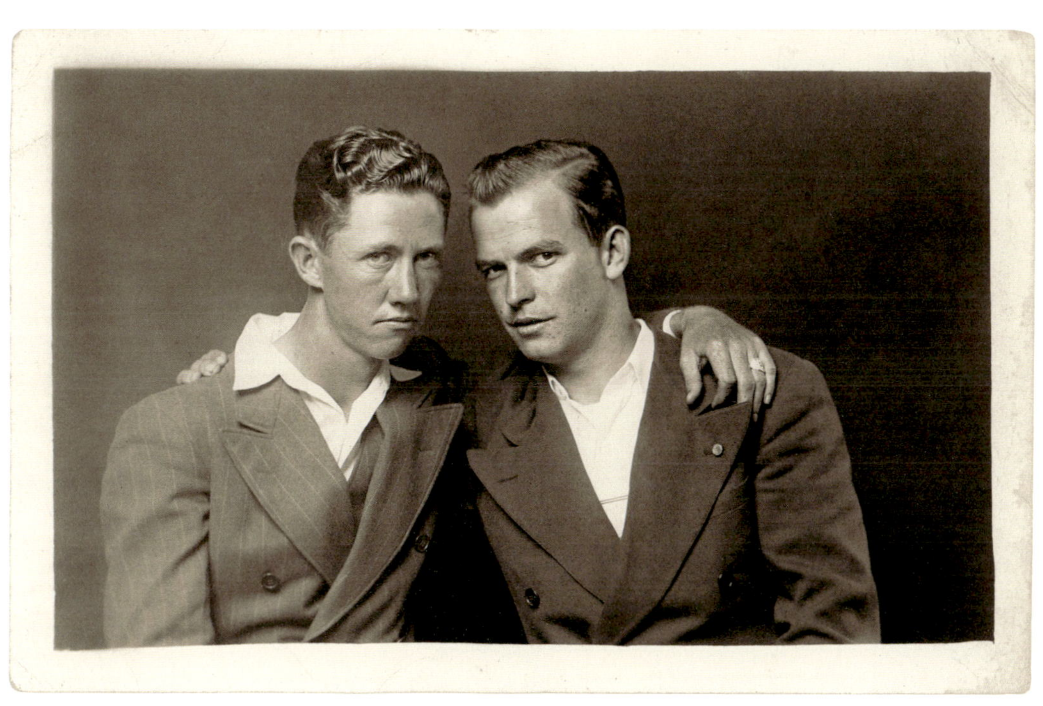

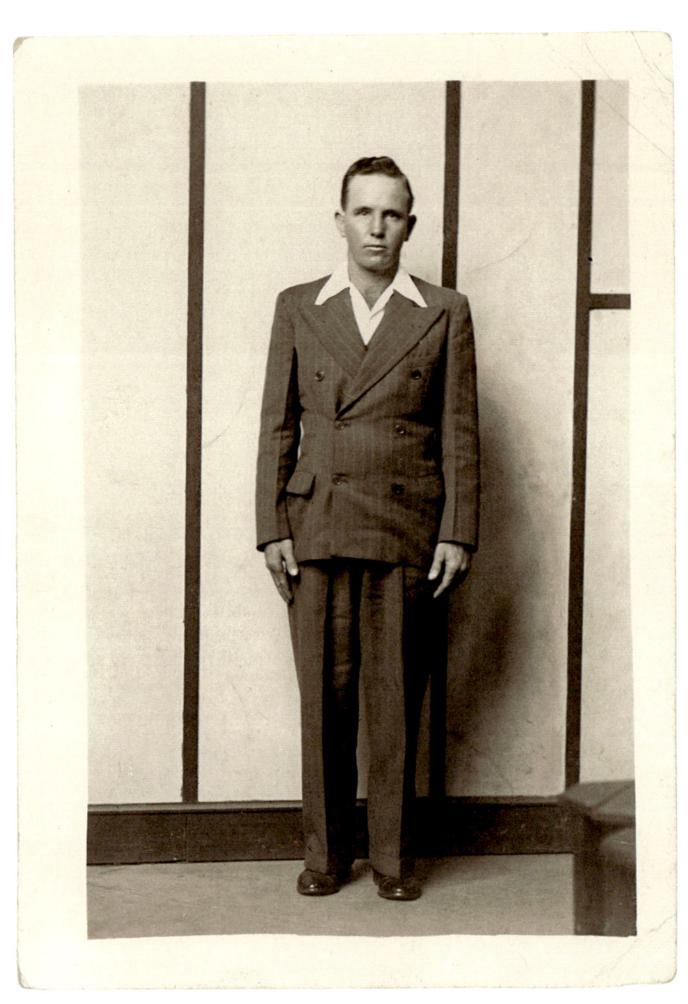

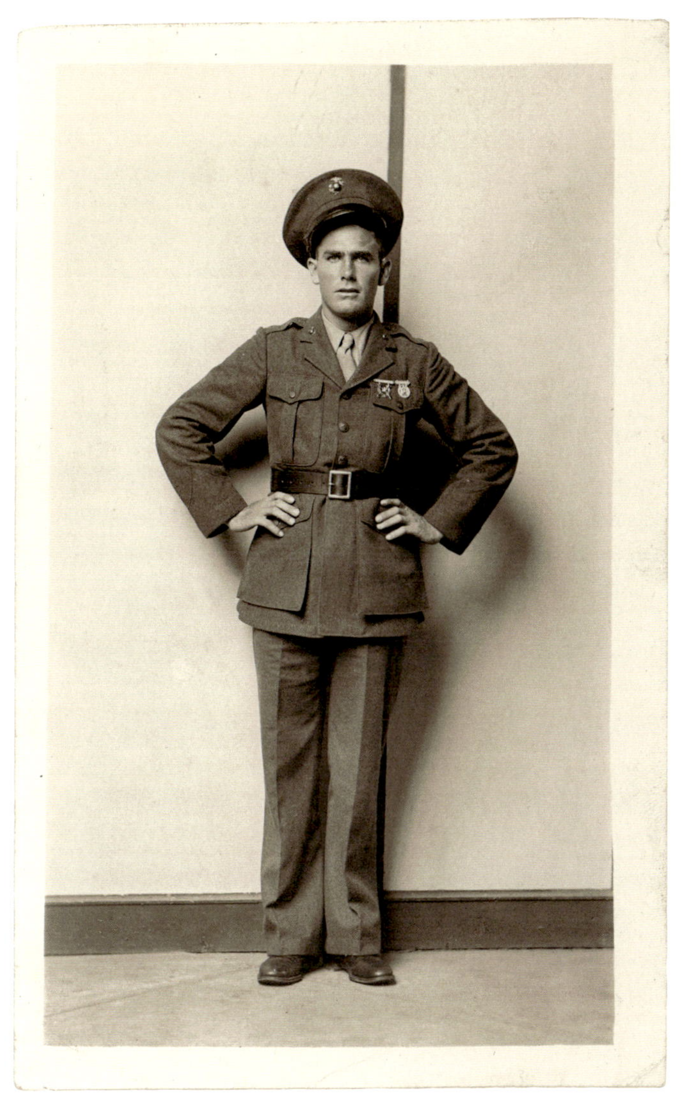

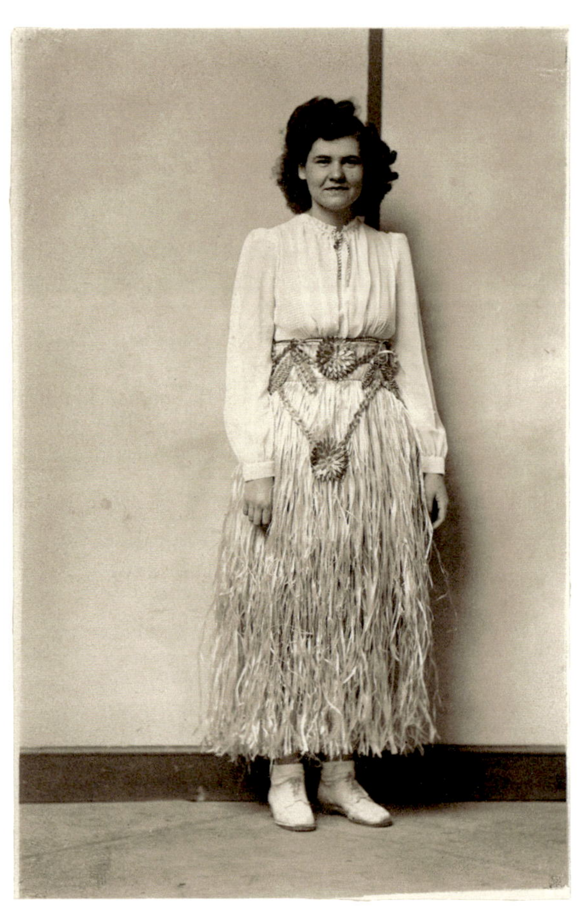

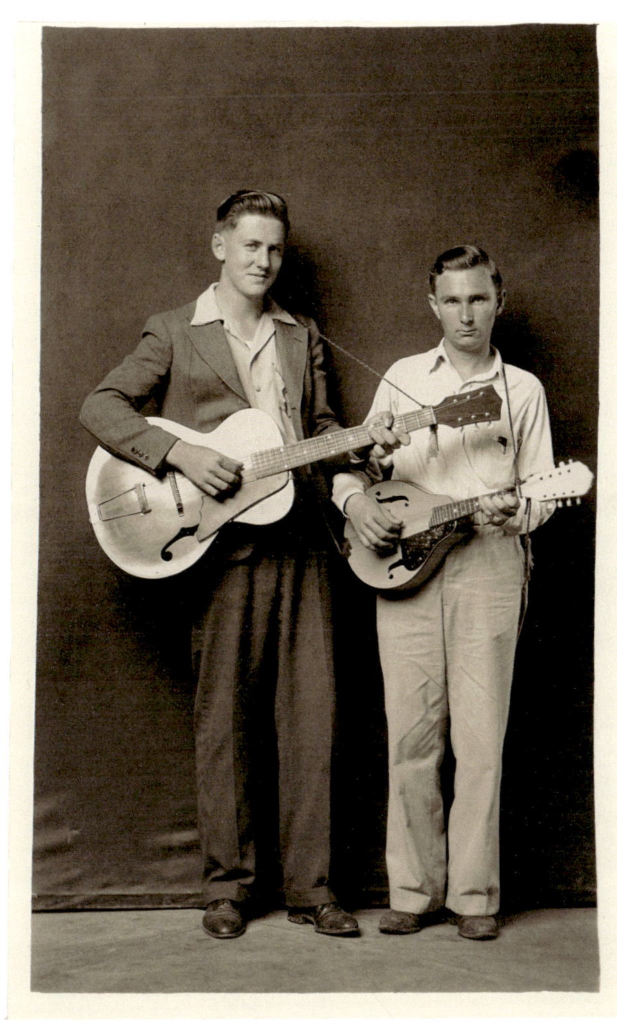

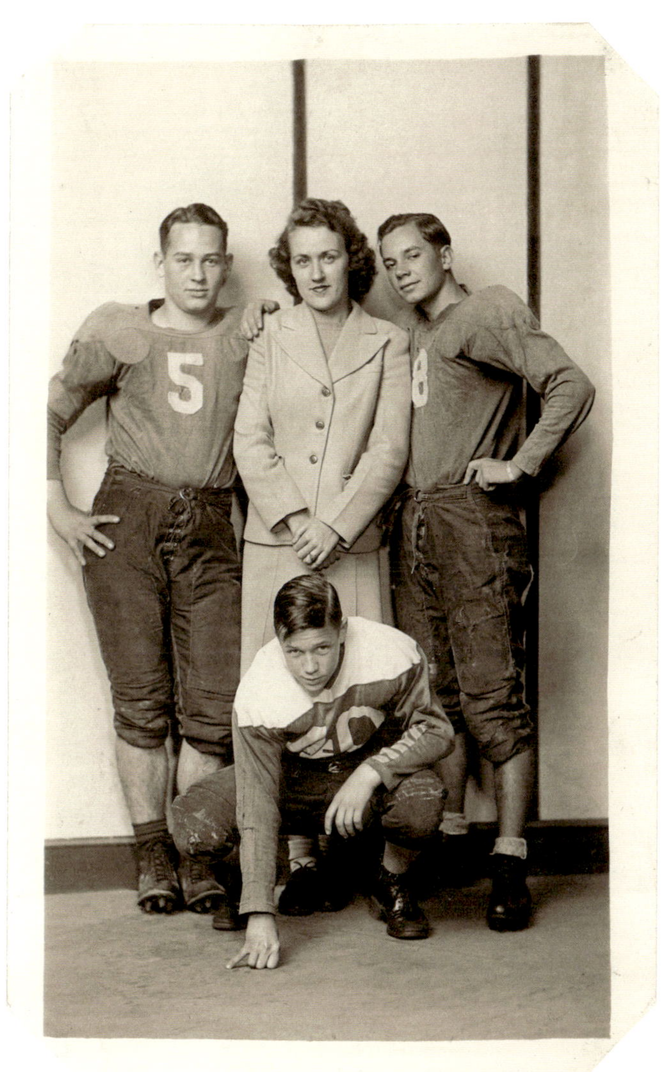
5
8

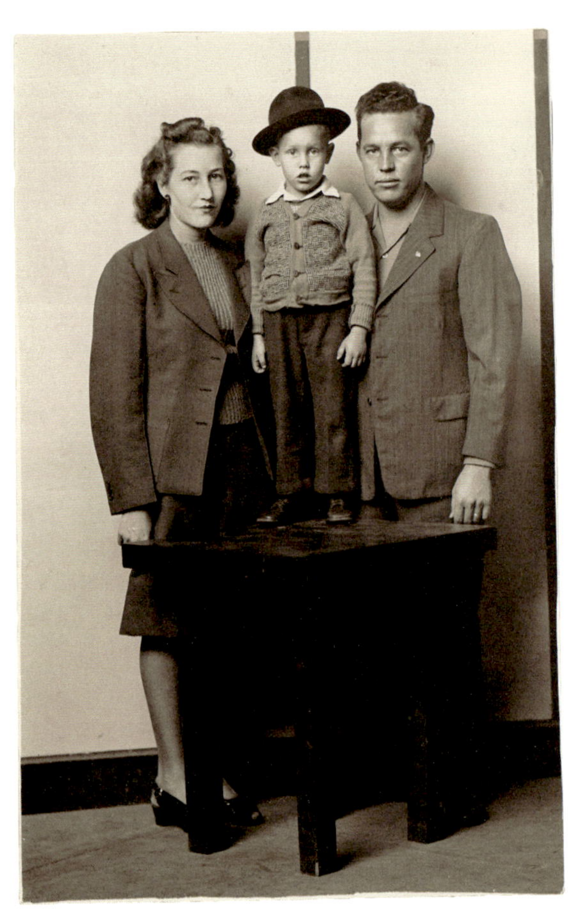

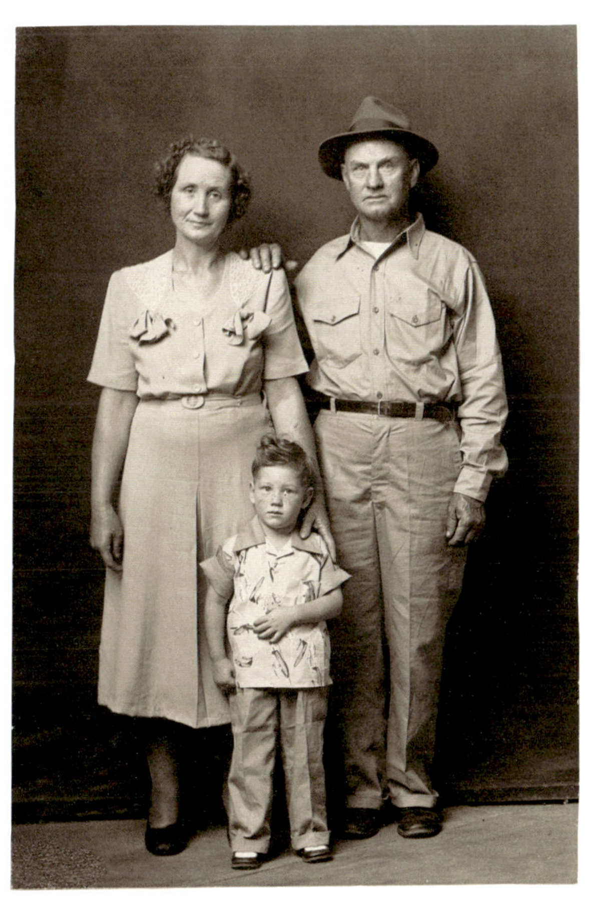

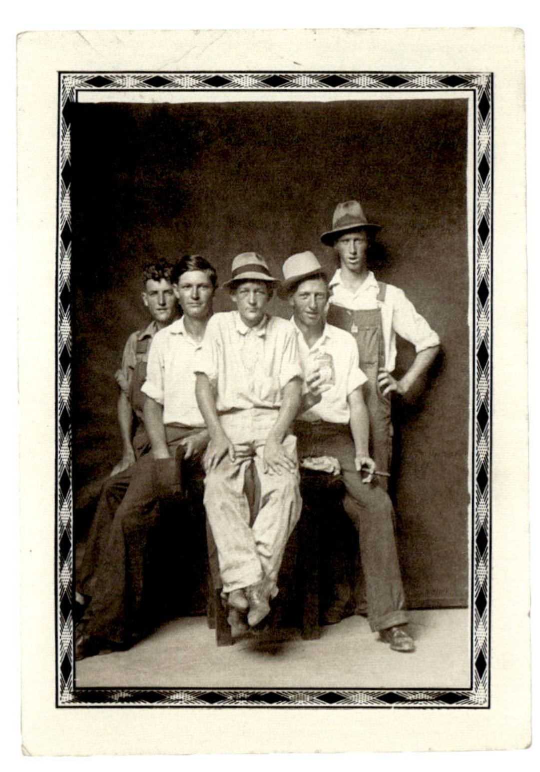

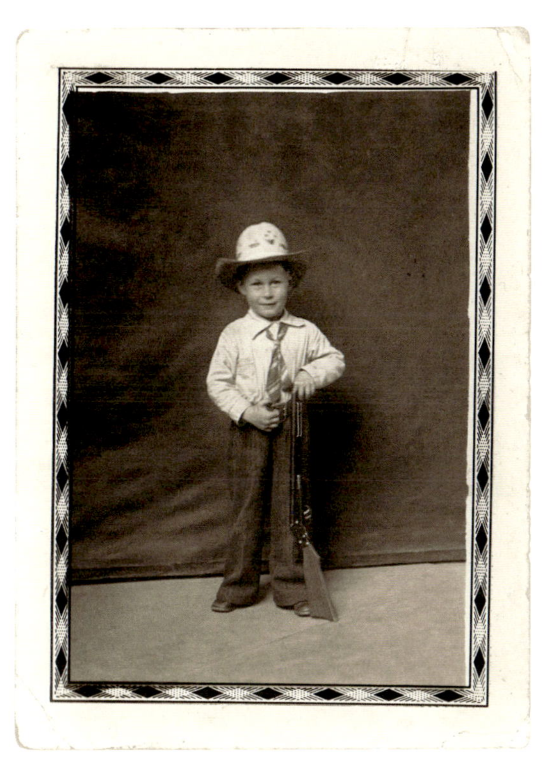

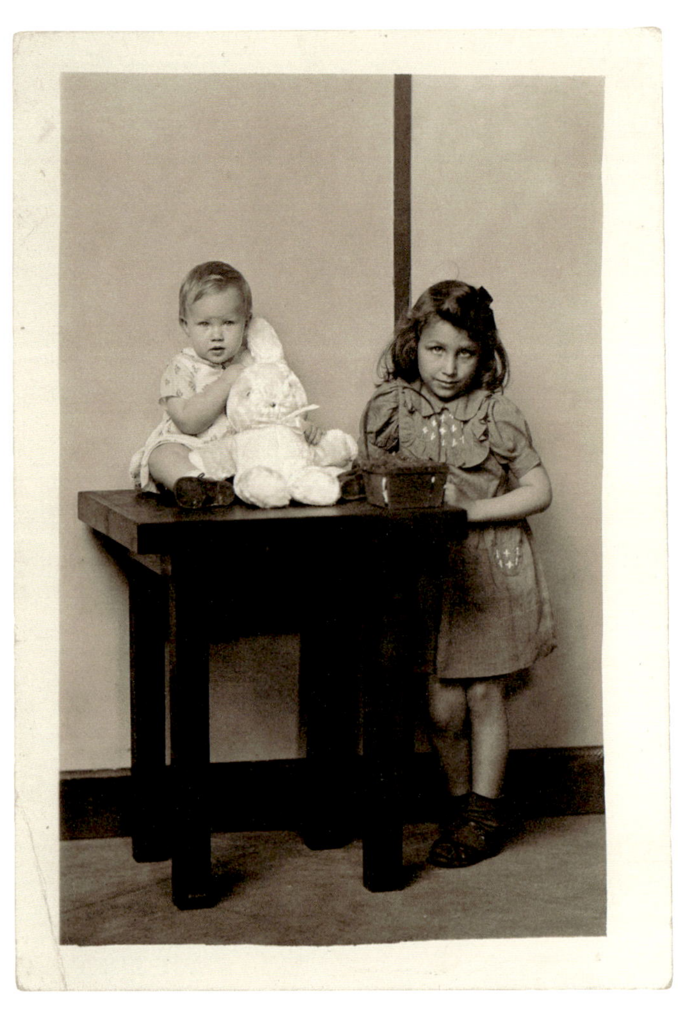

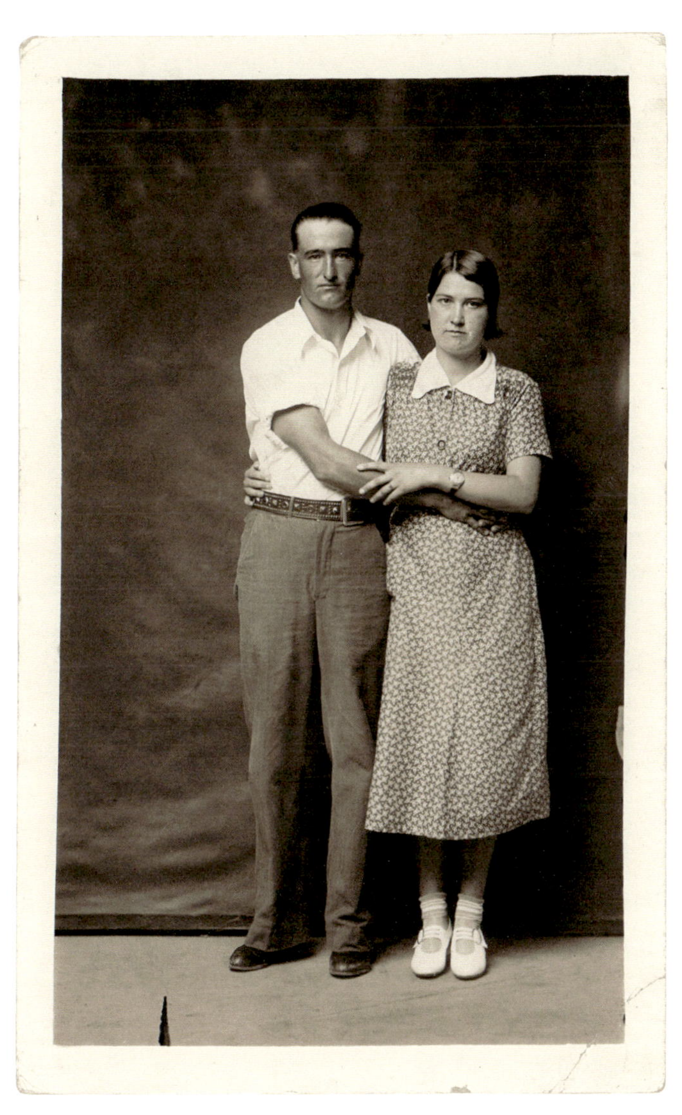

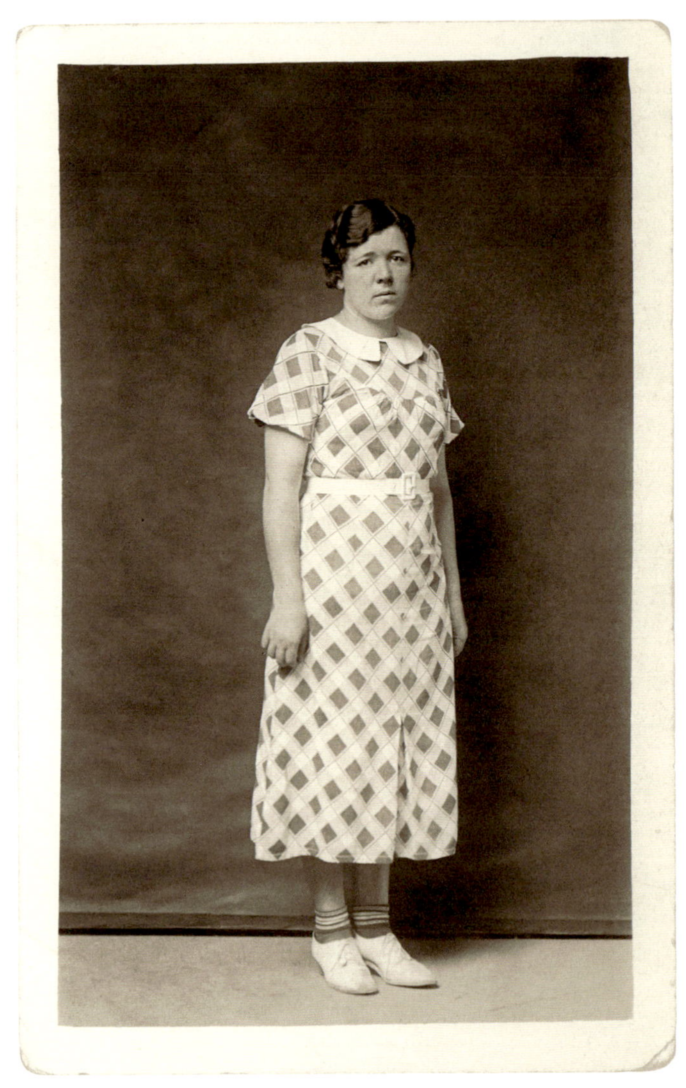

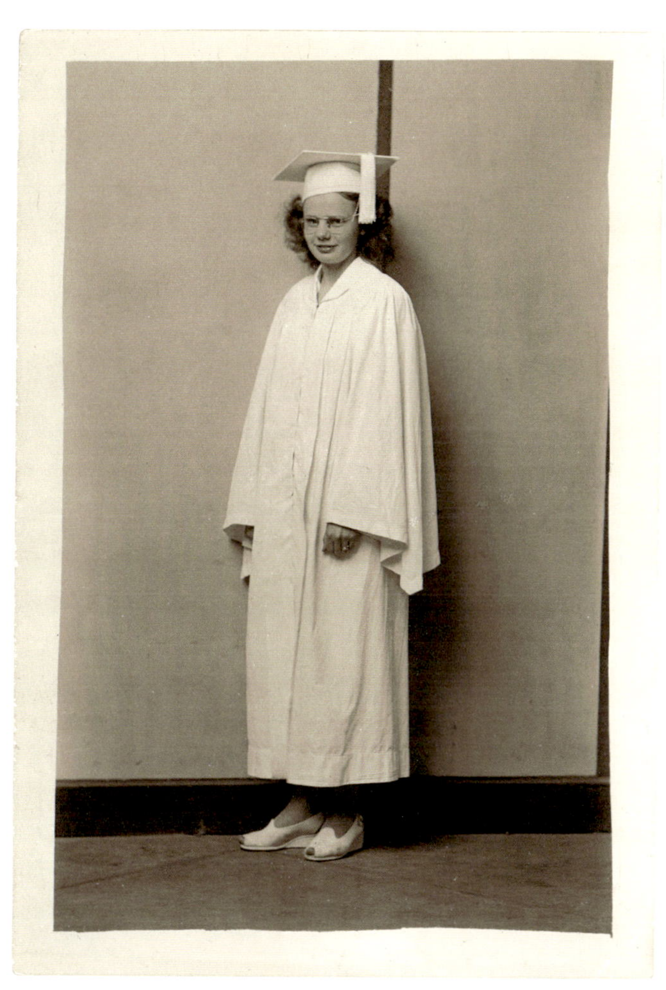

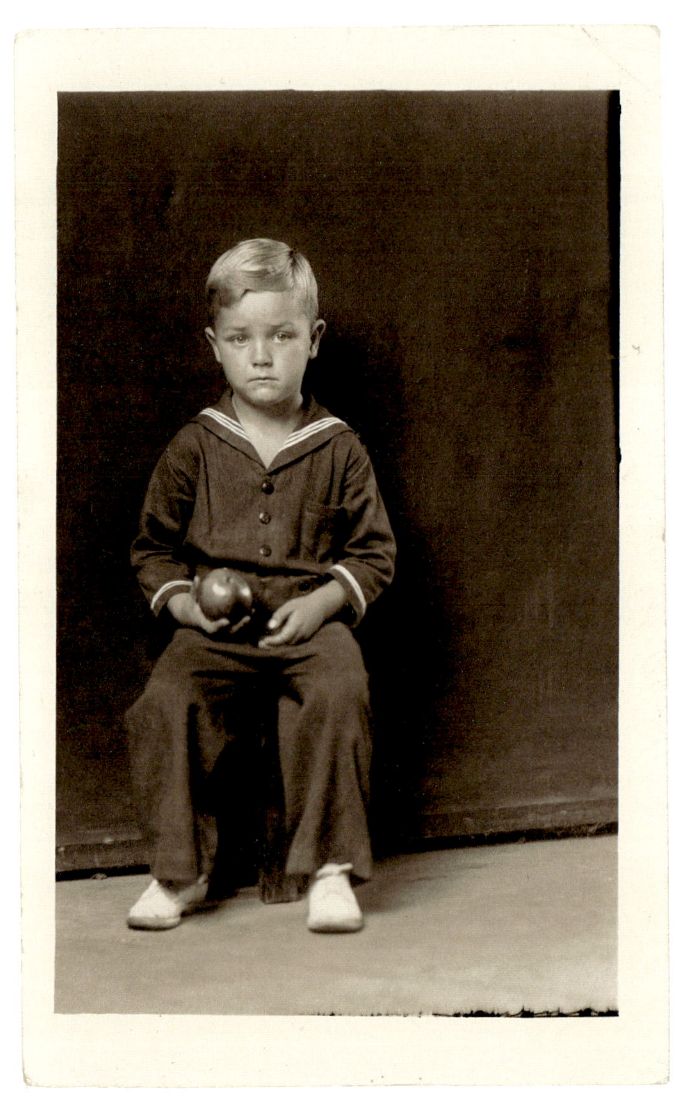

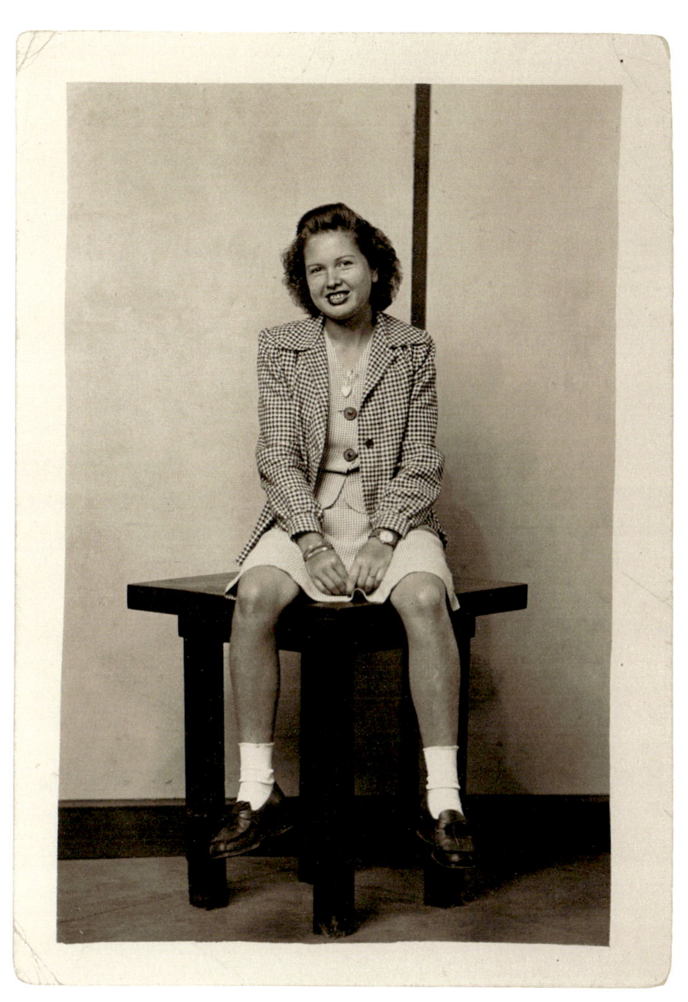

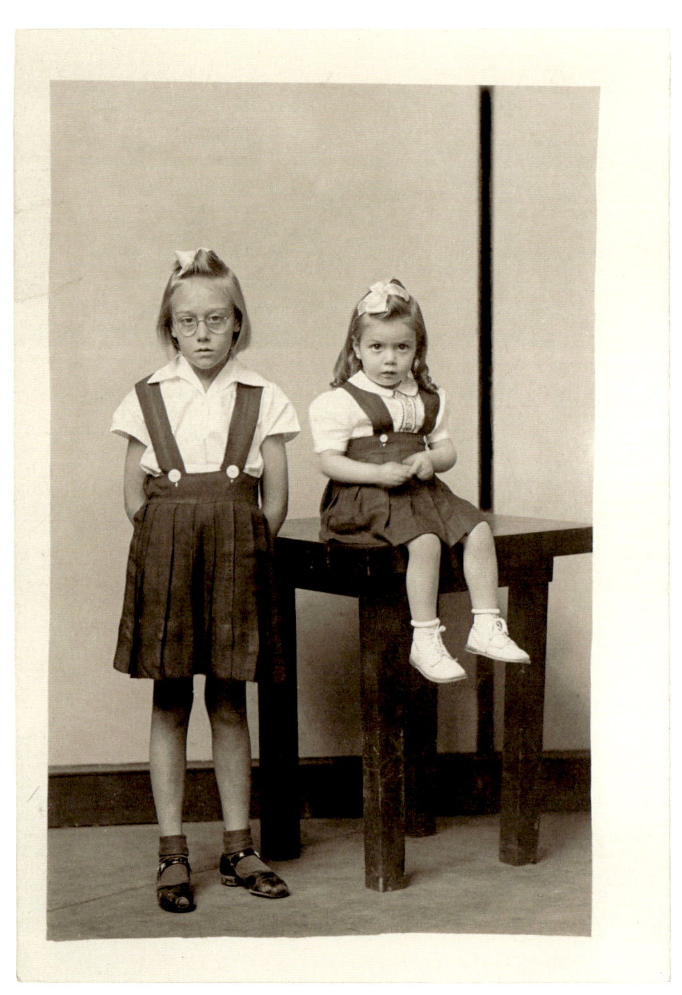

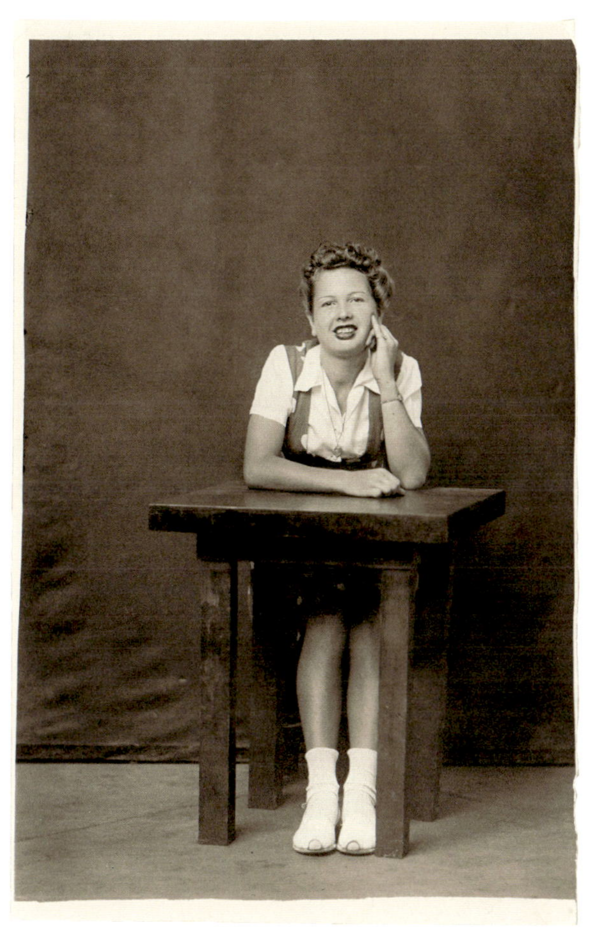

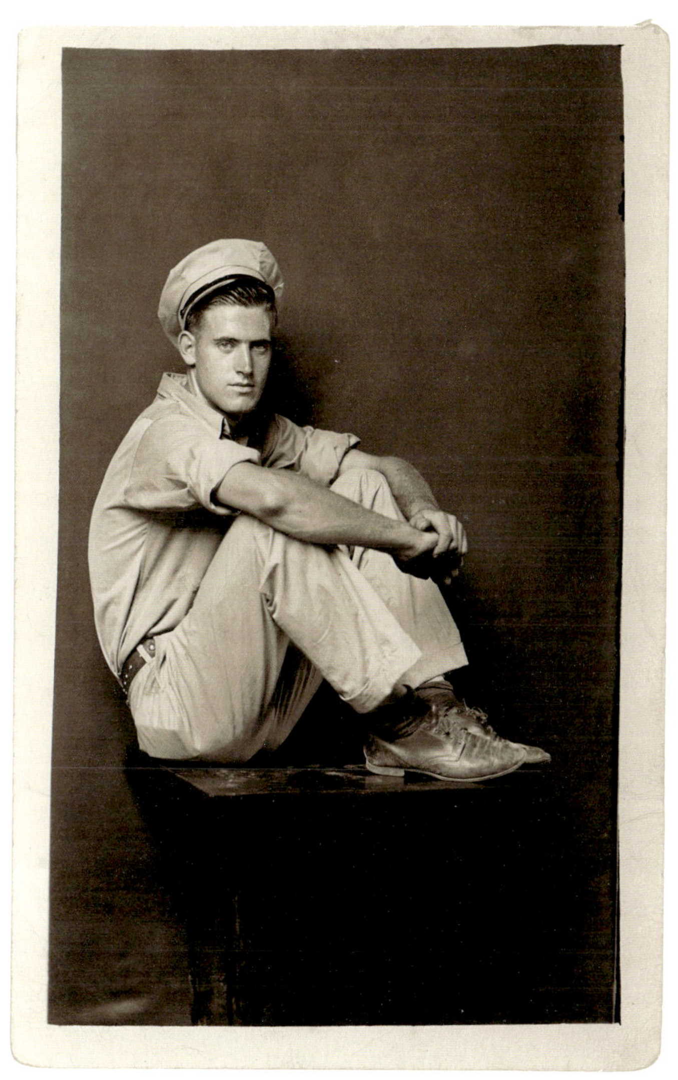

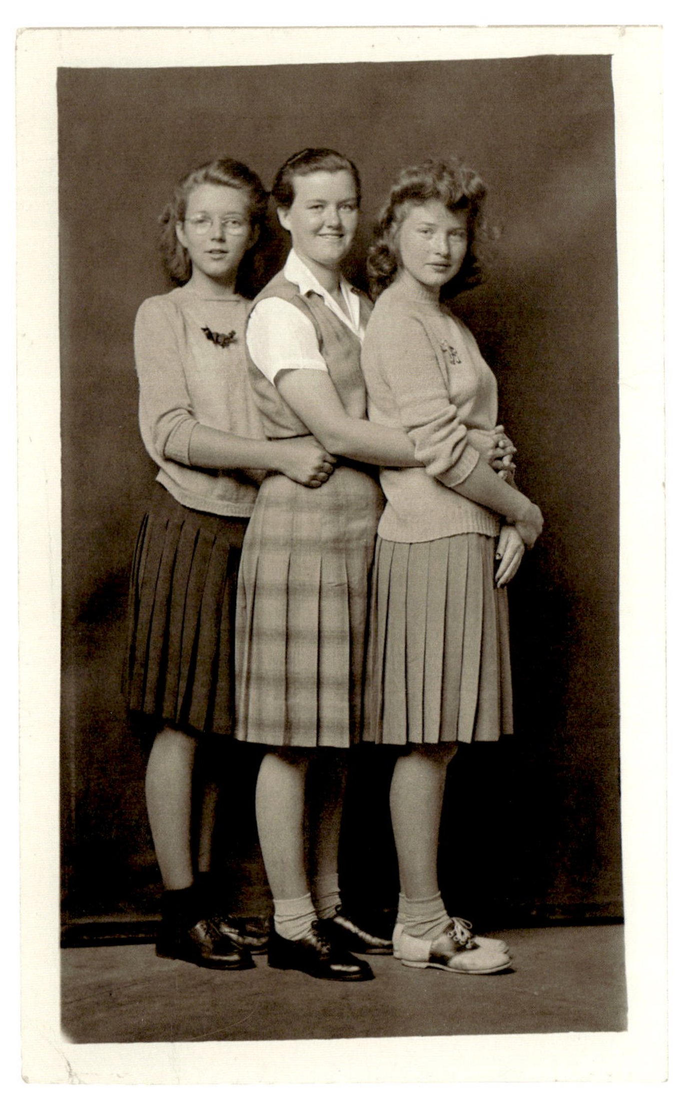

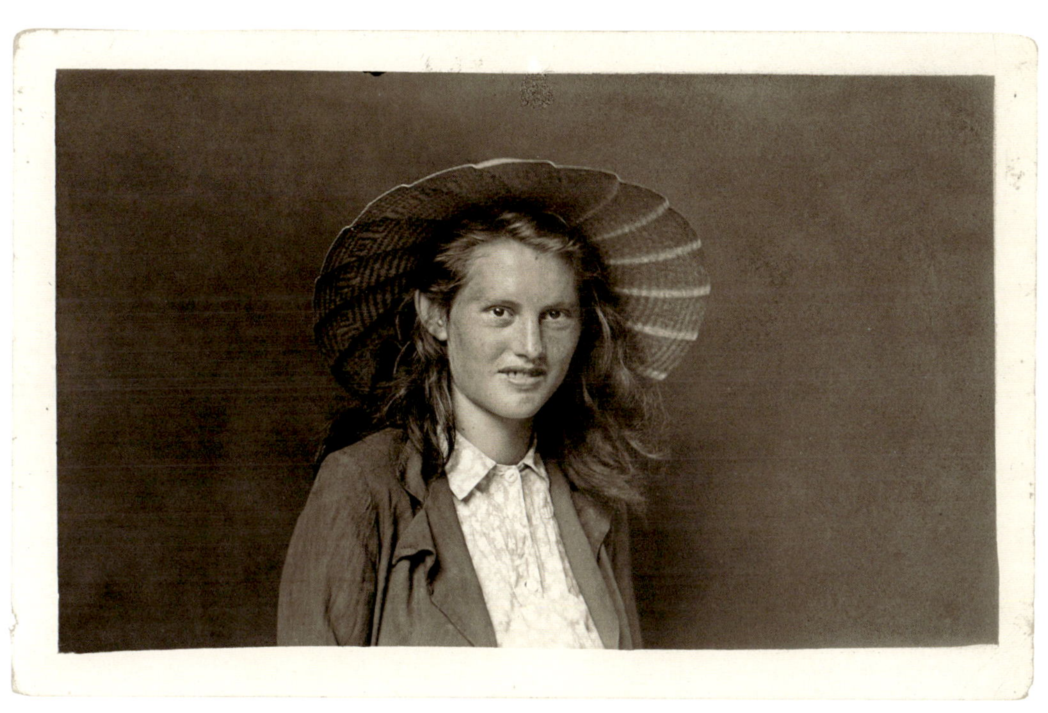

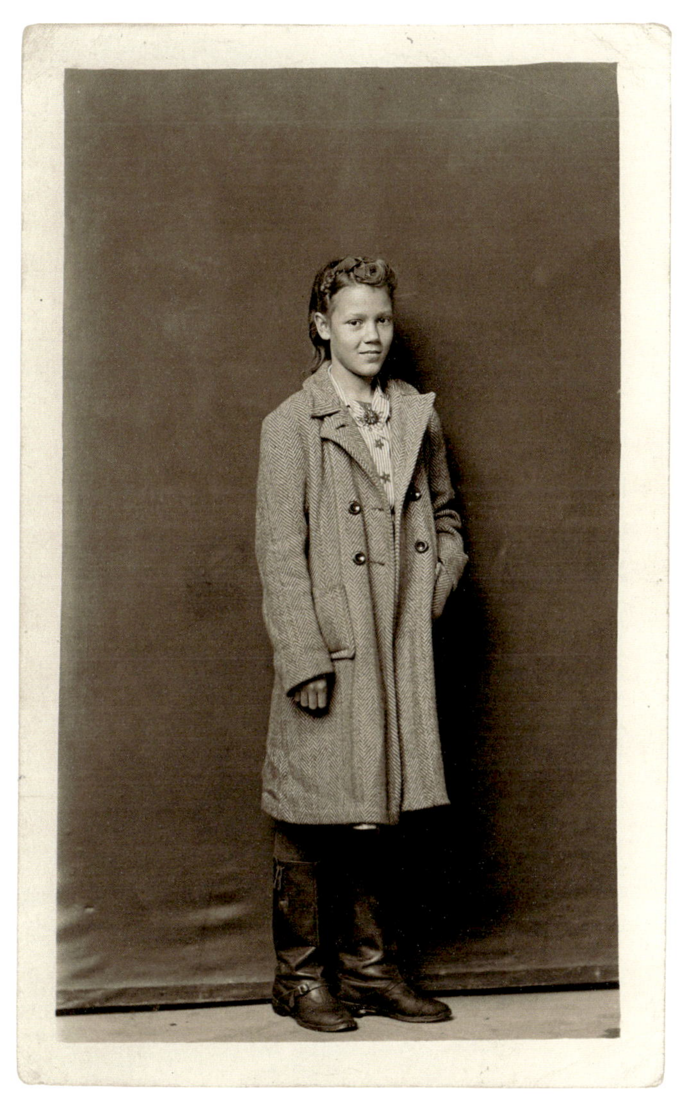

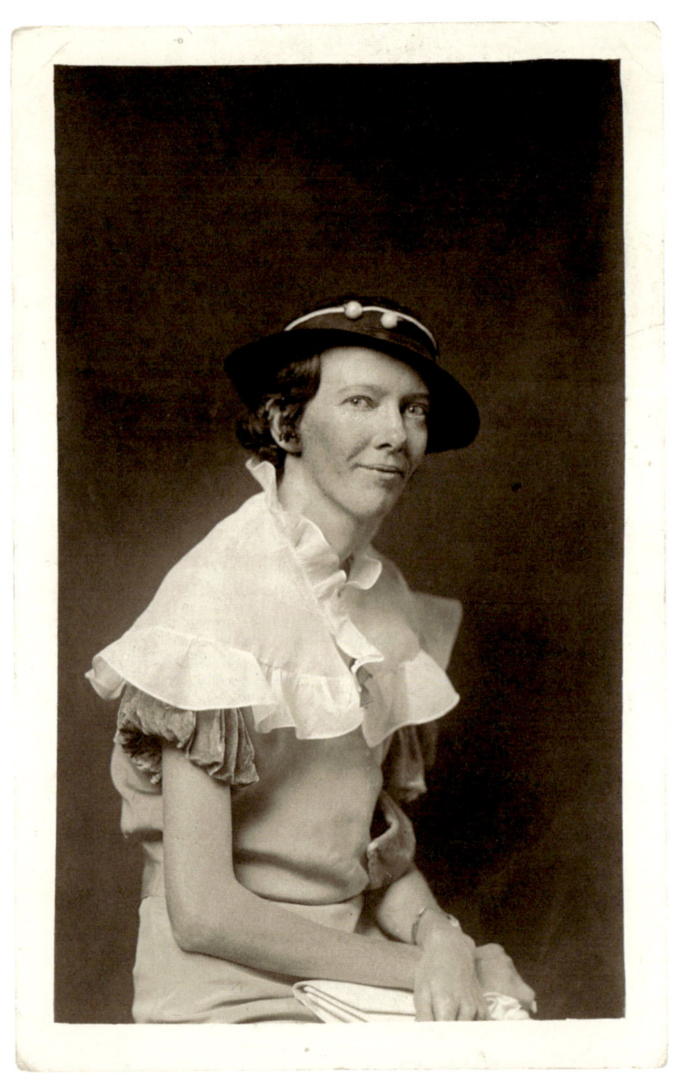

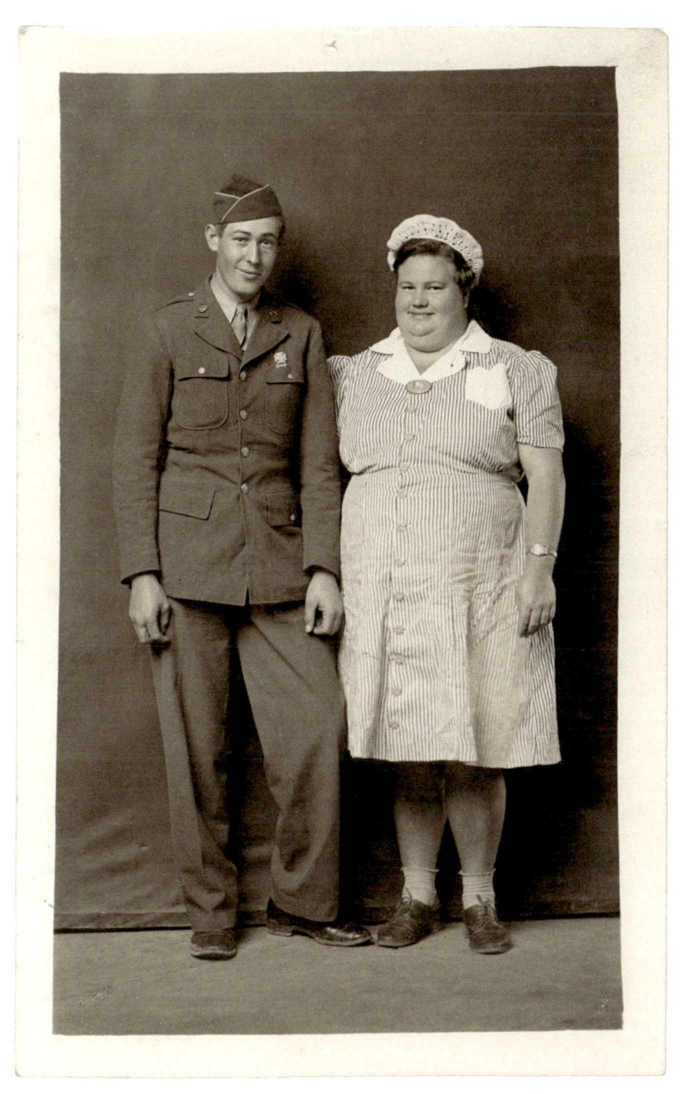

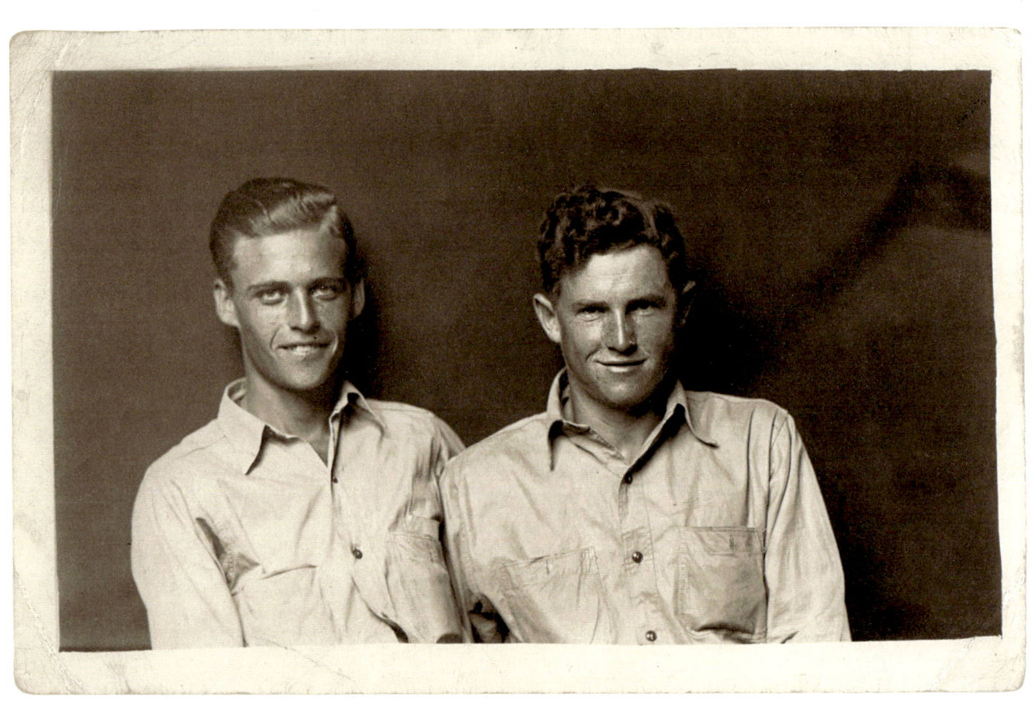

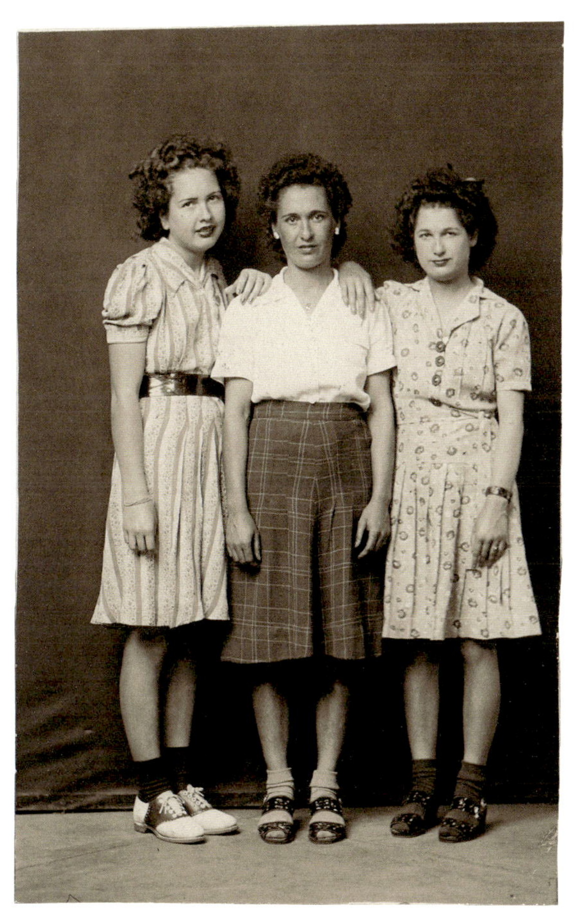

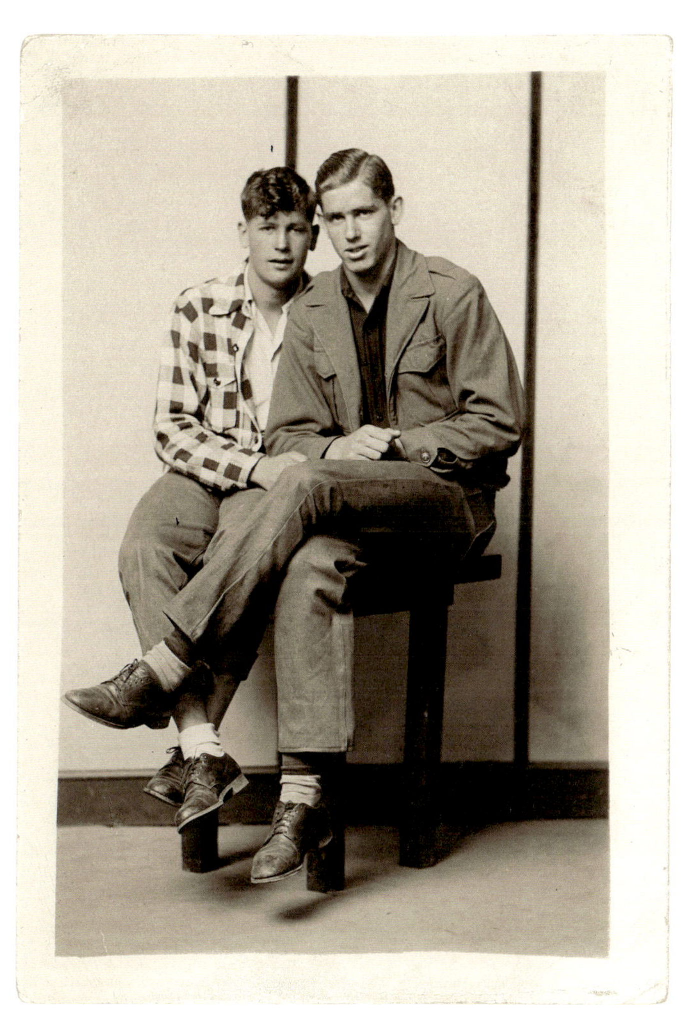

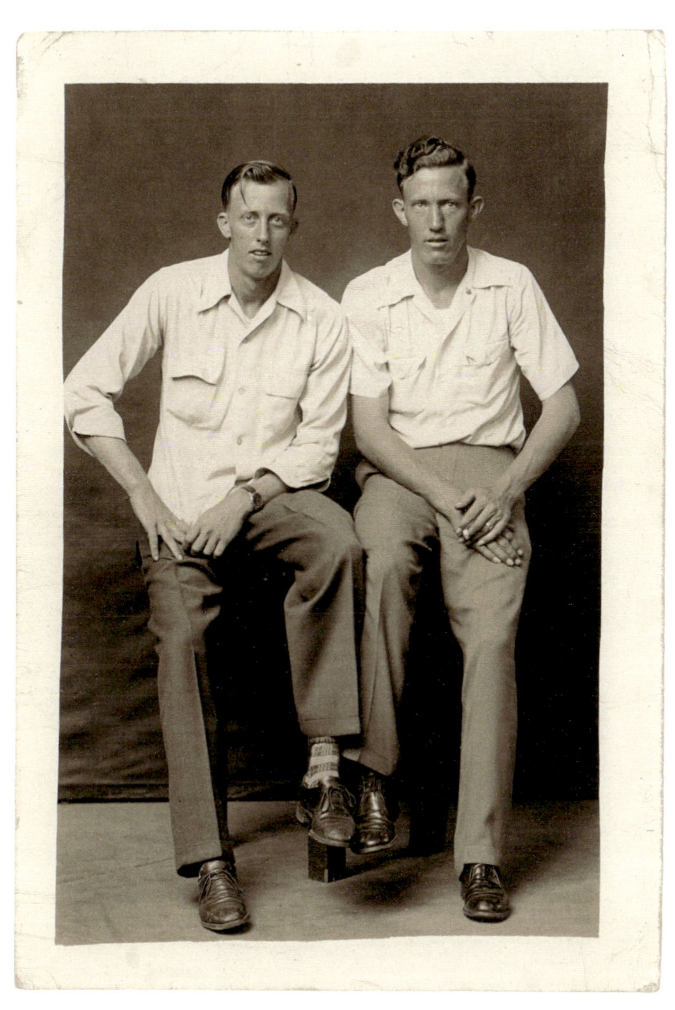

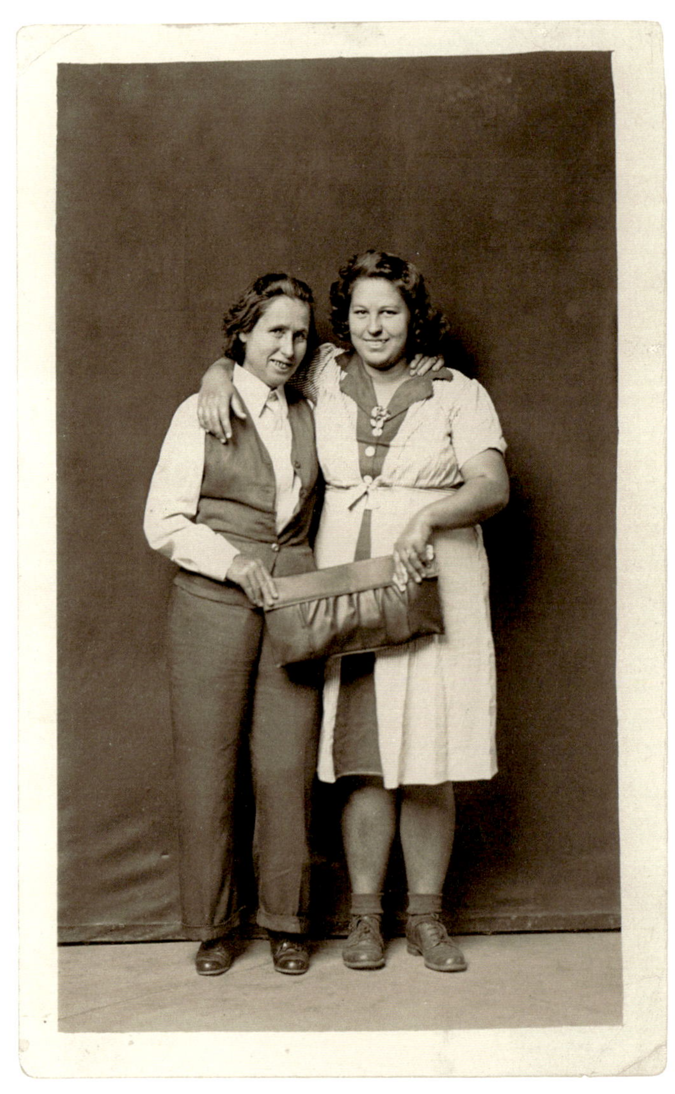

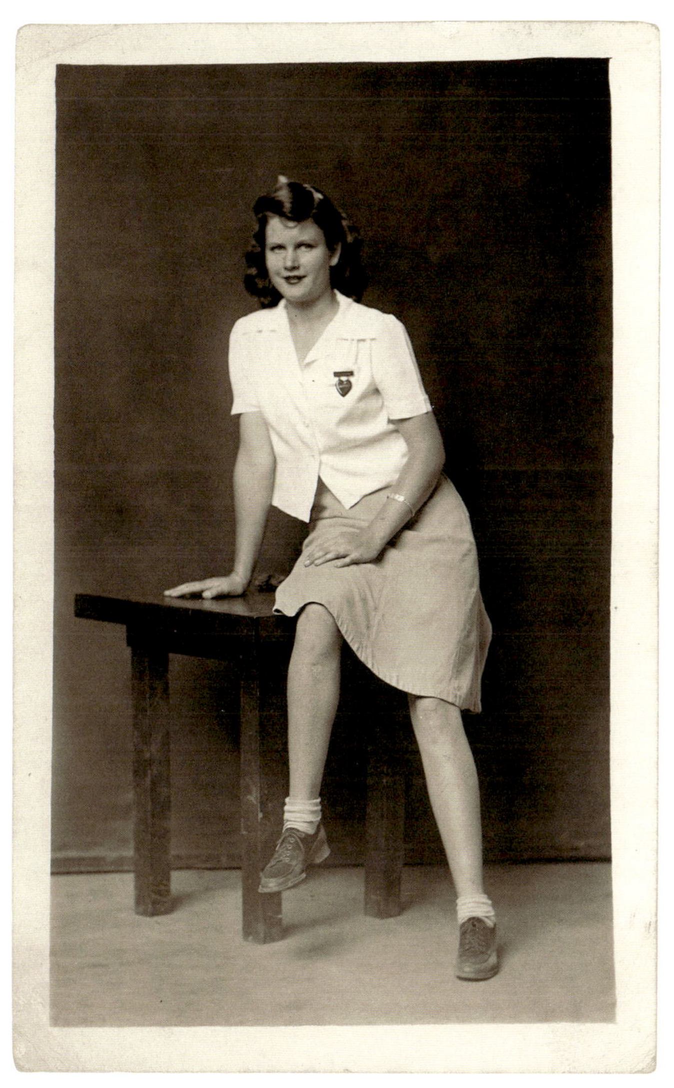

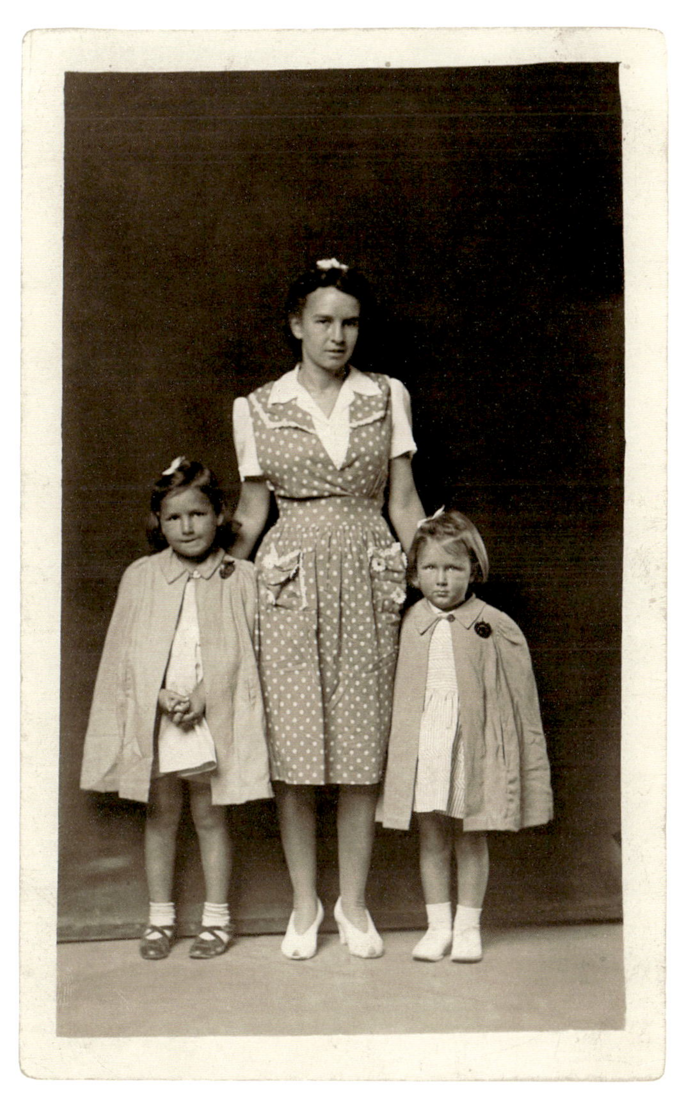

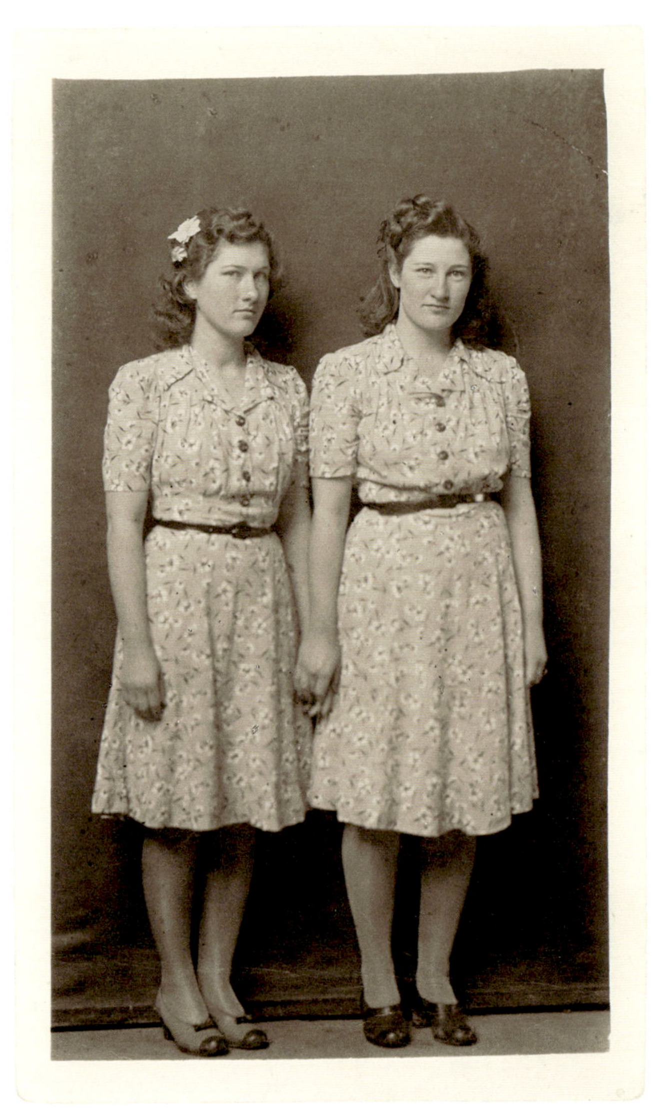

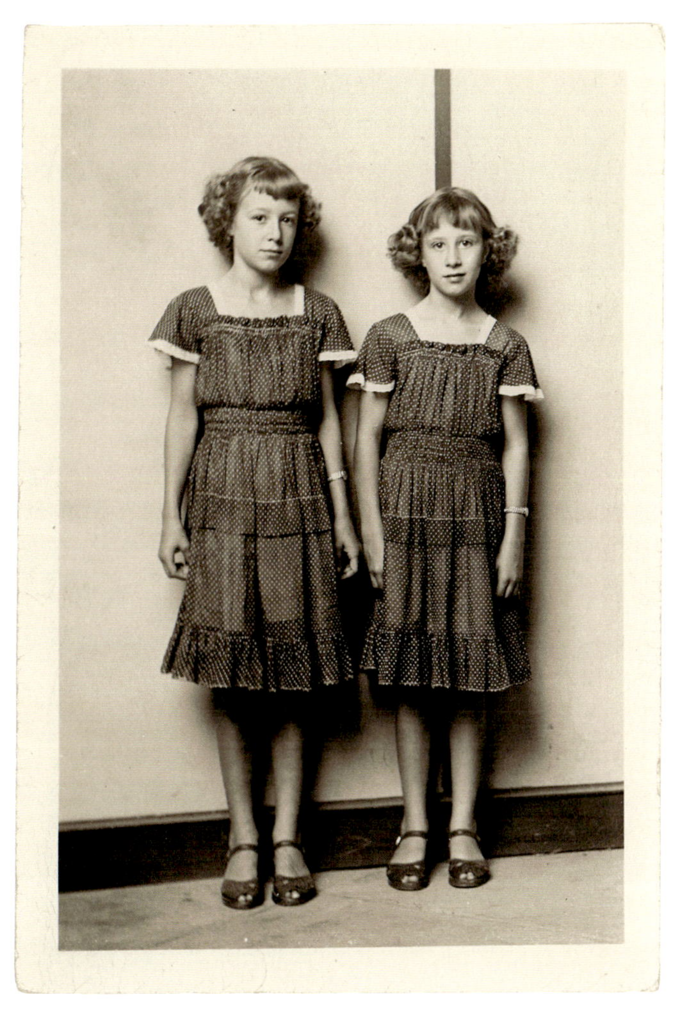

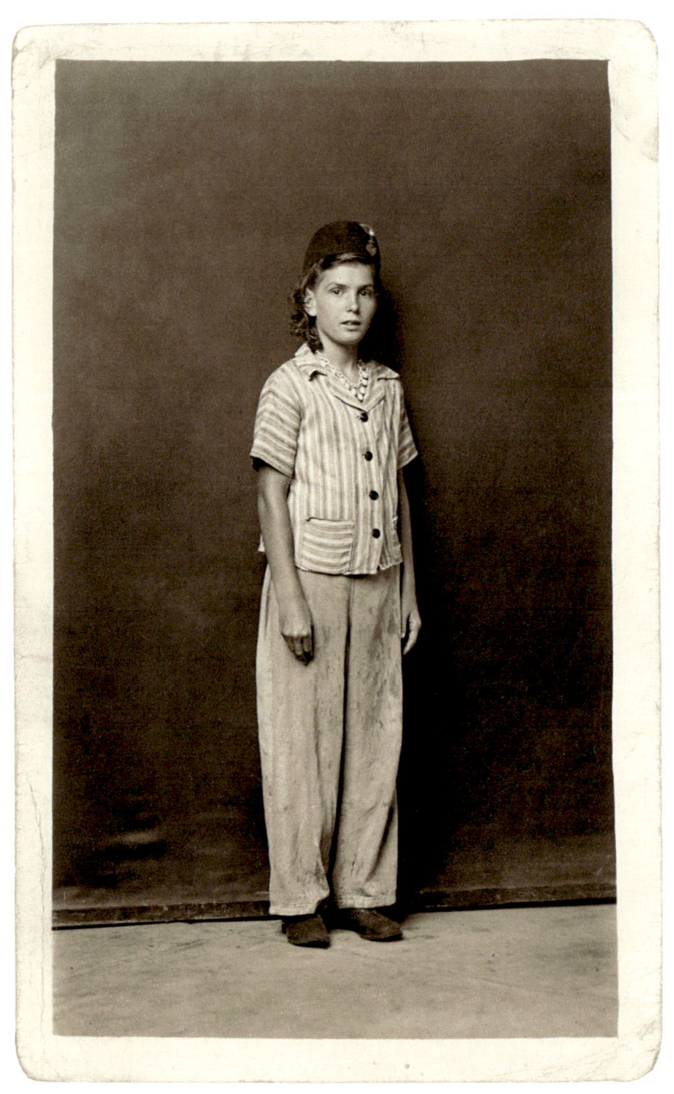

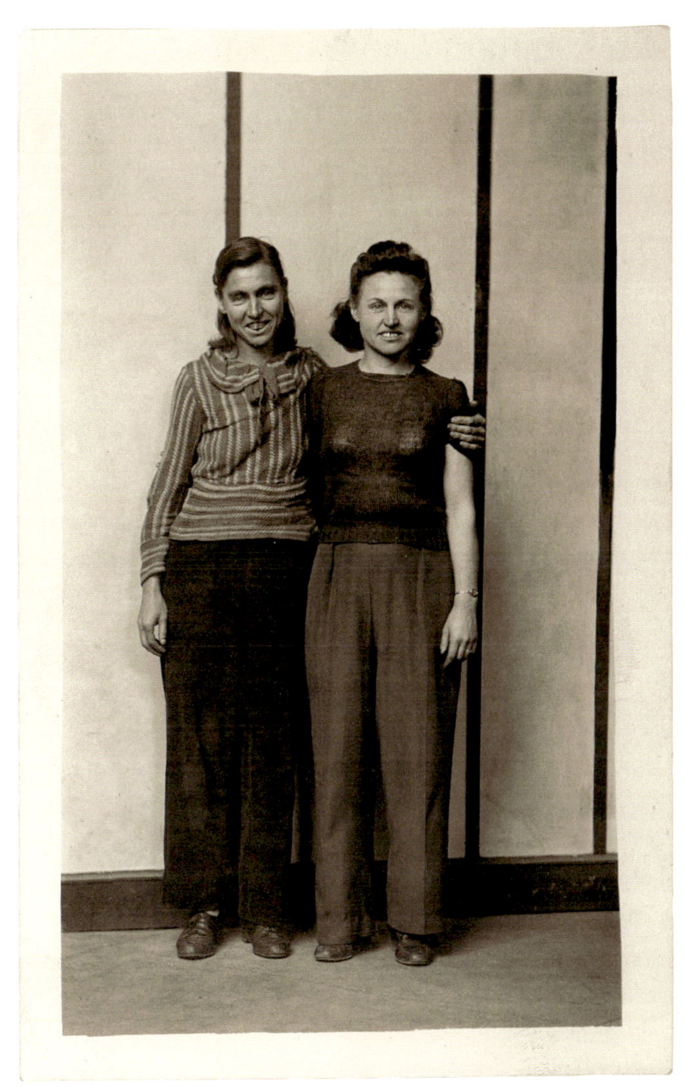

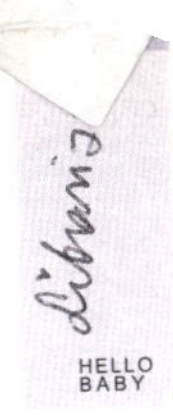
HELLO
BABY

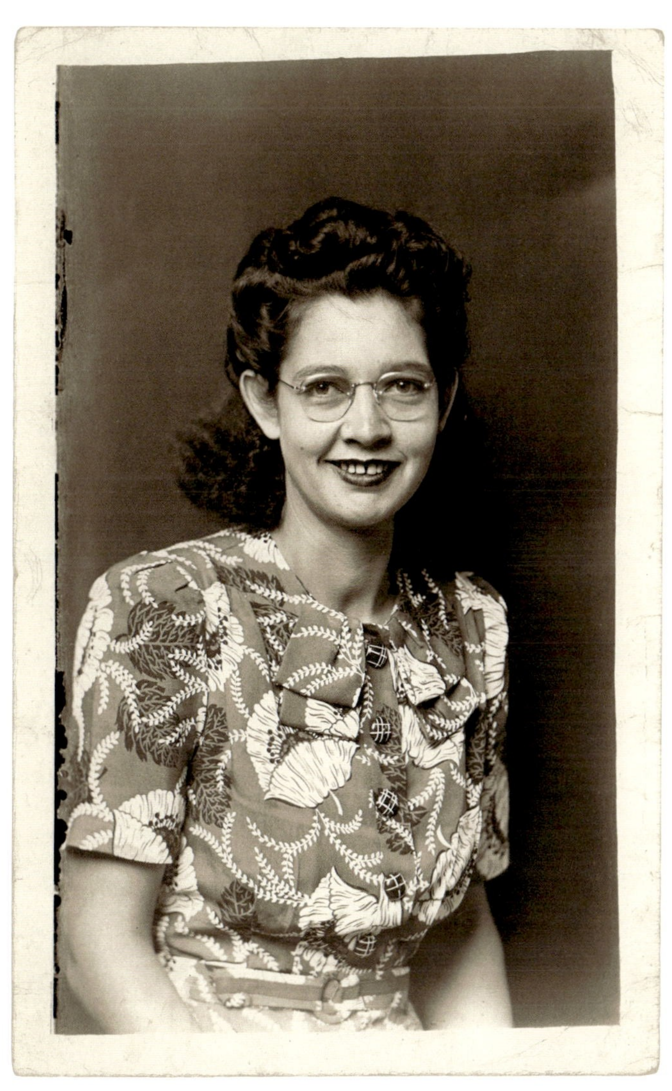

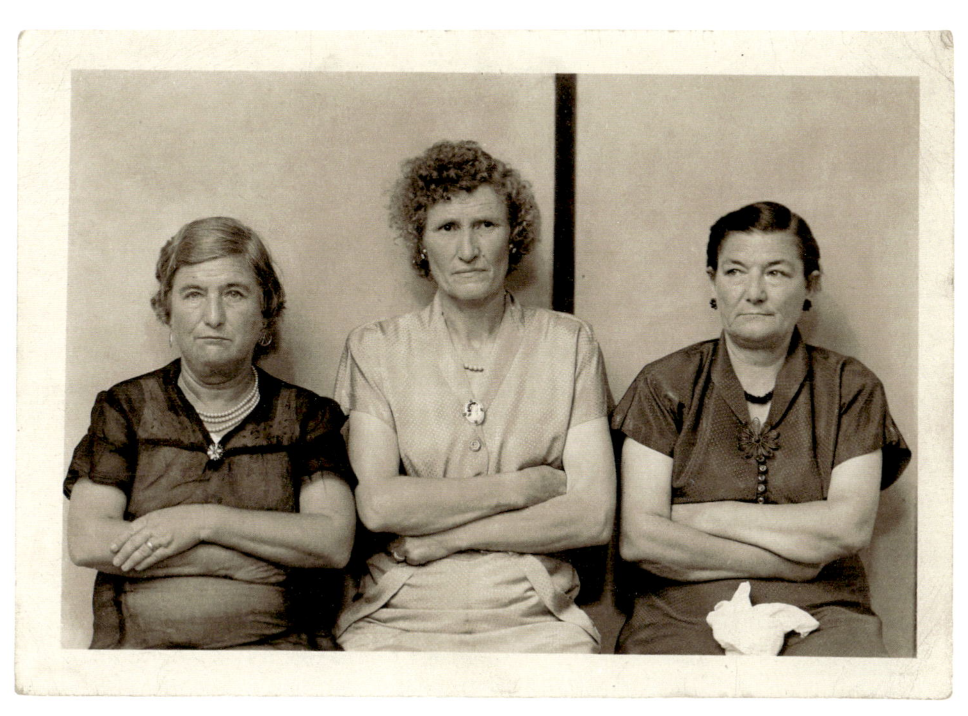

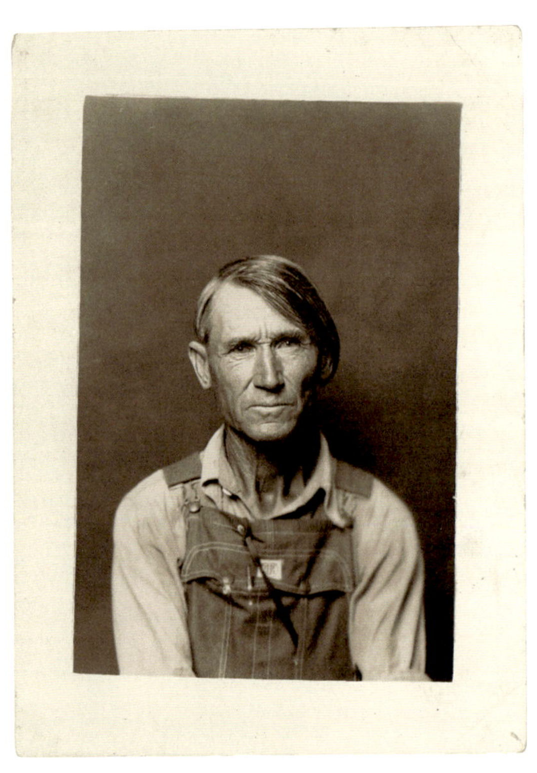

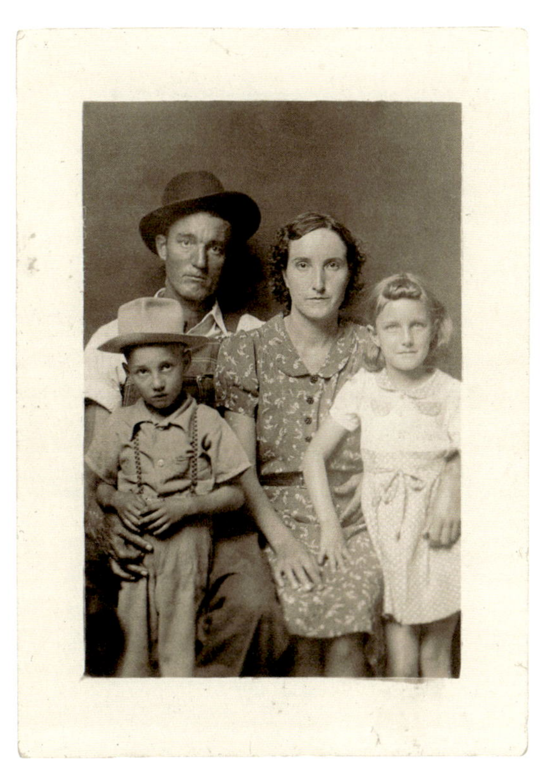

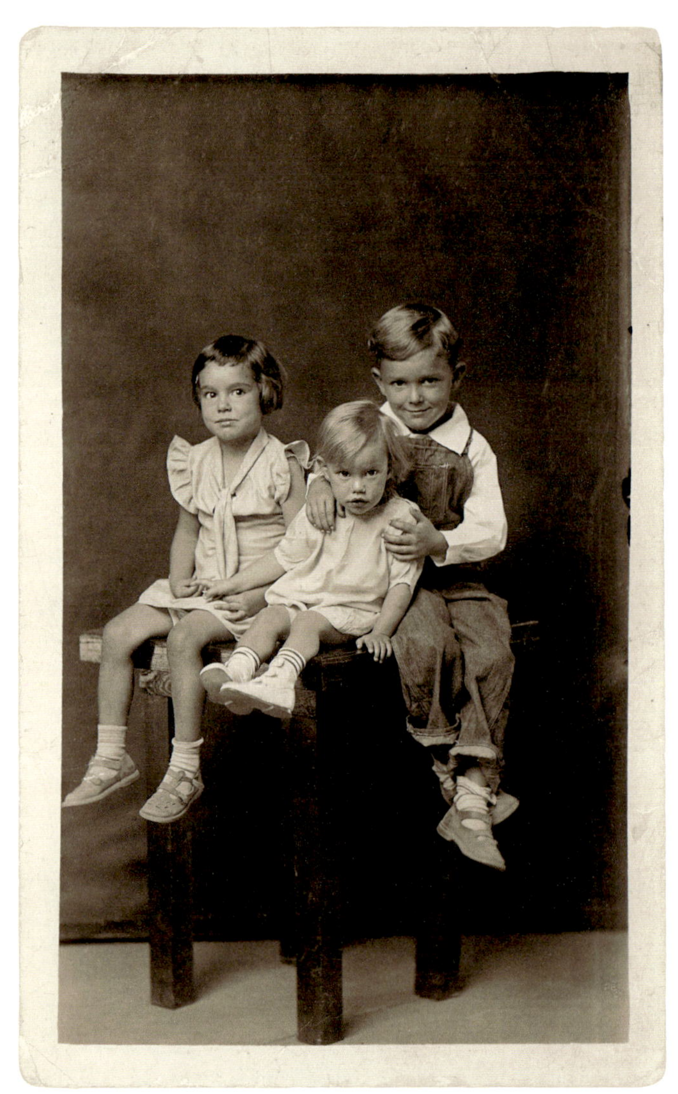

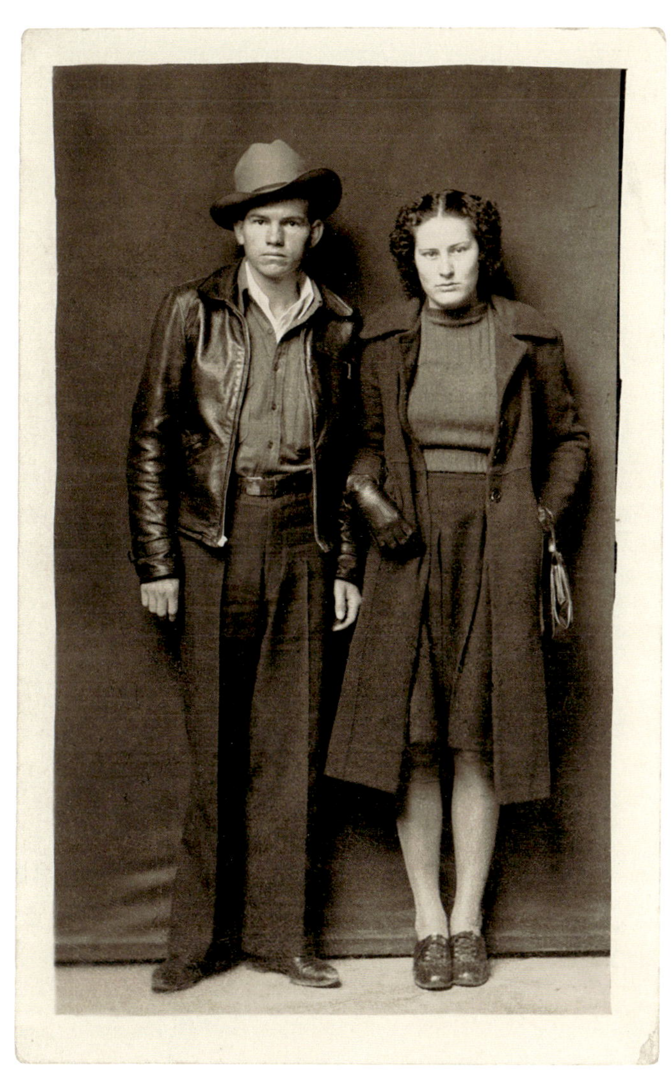

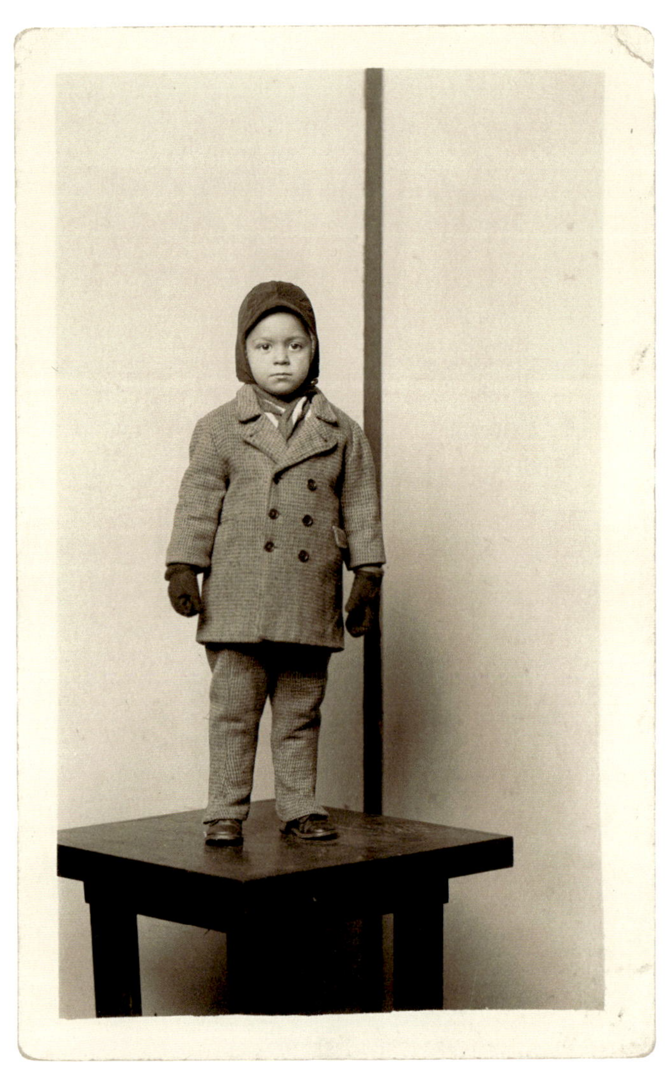

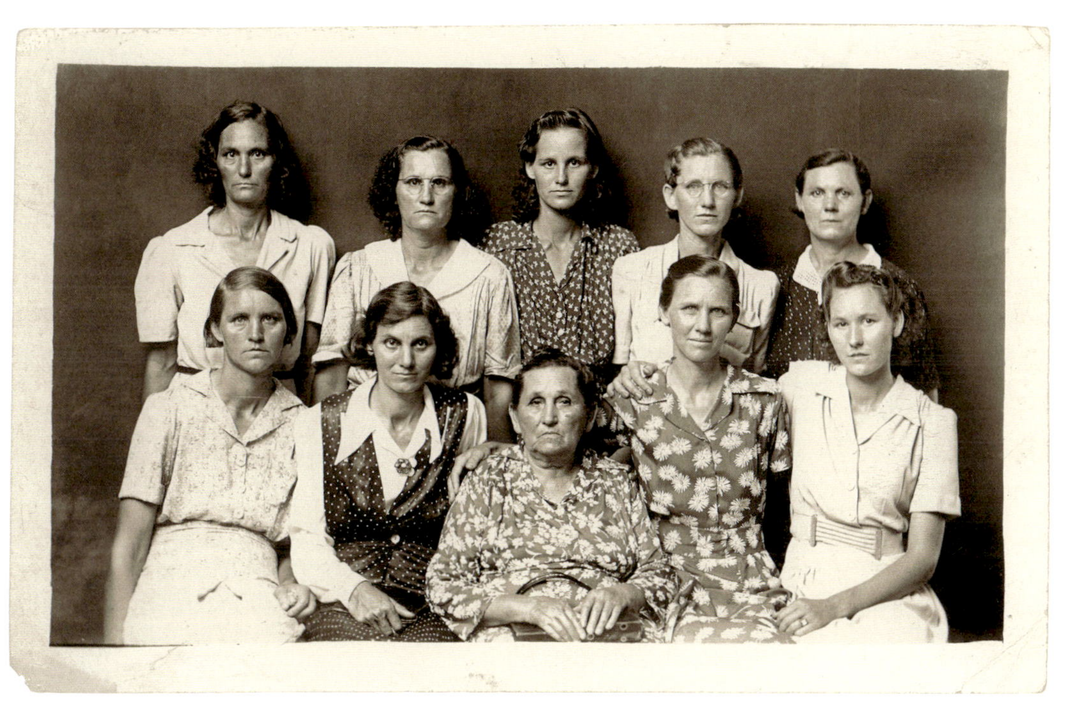

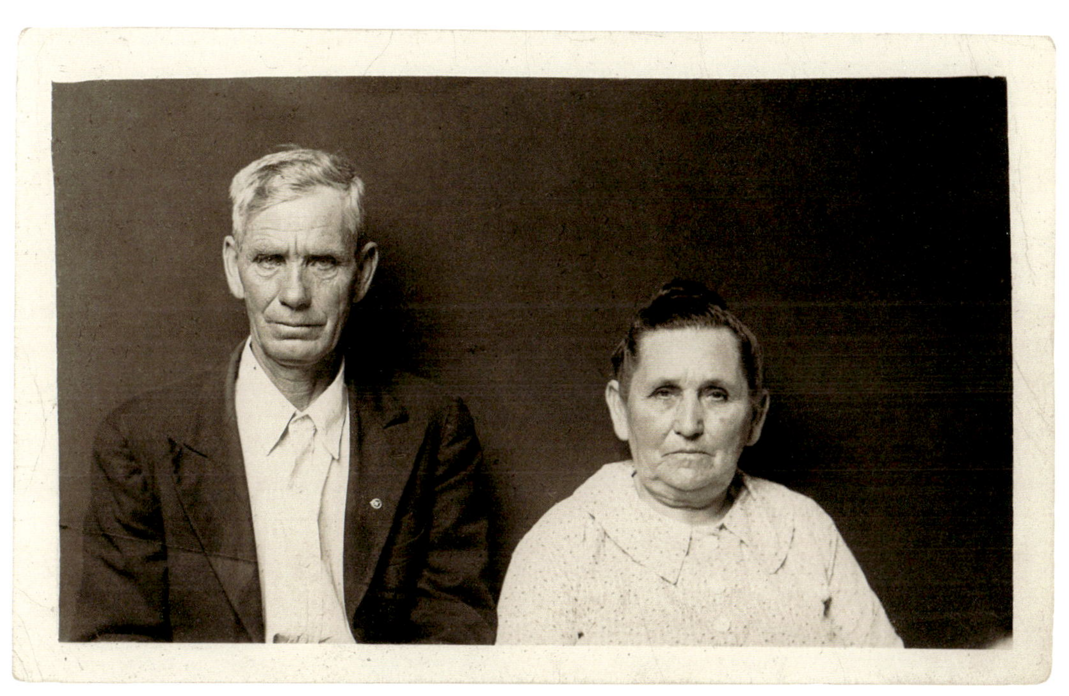

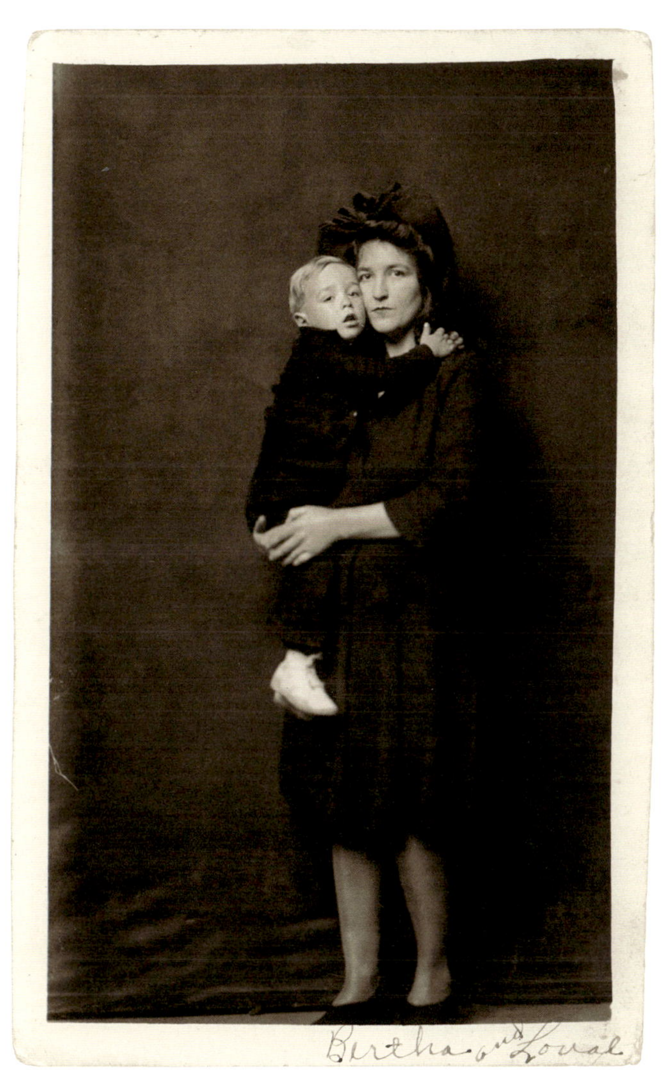
Bertha and Loval

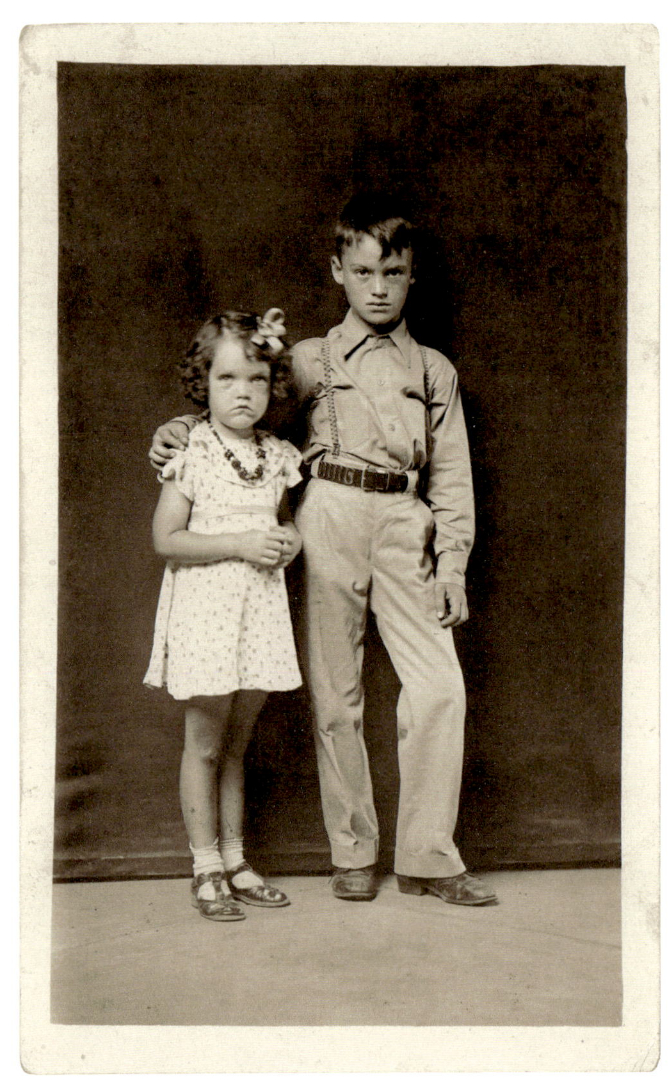

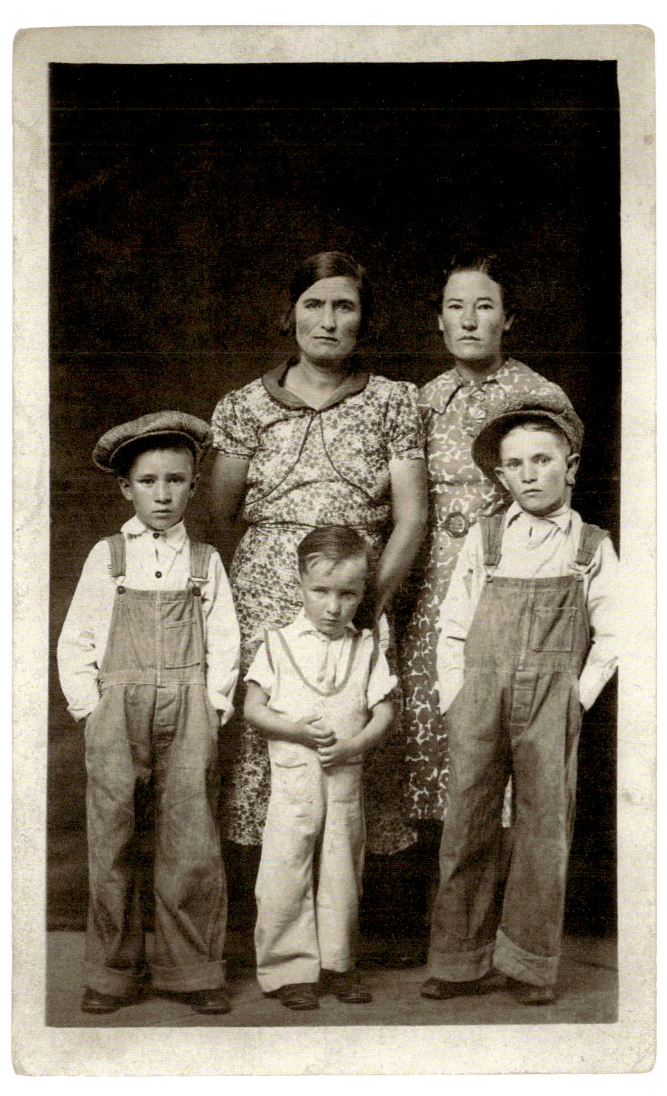

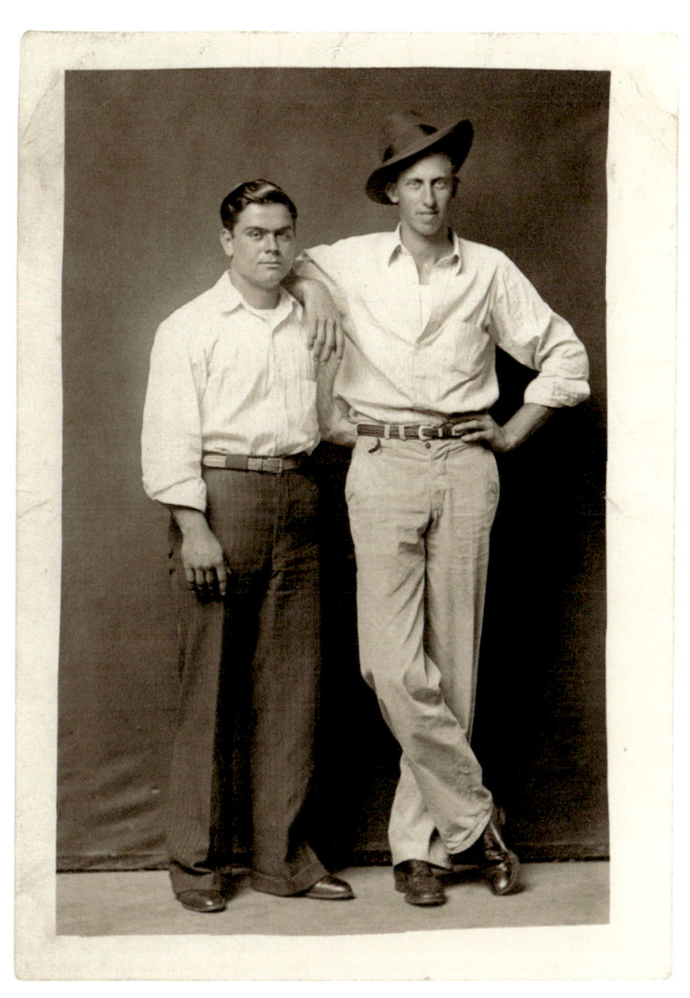

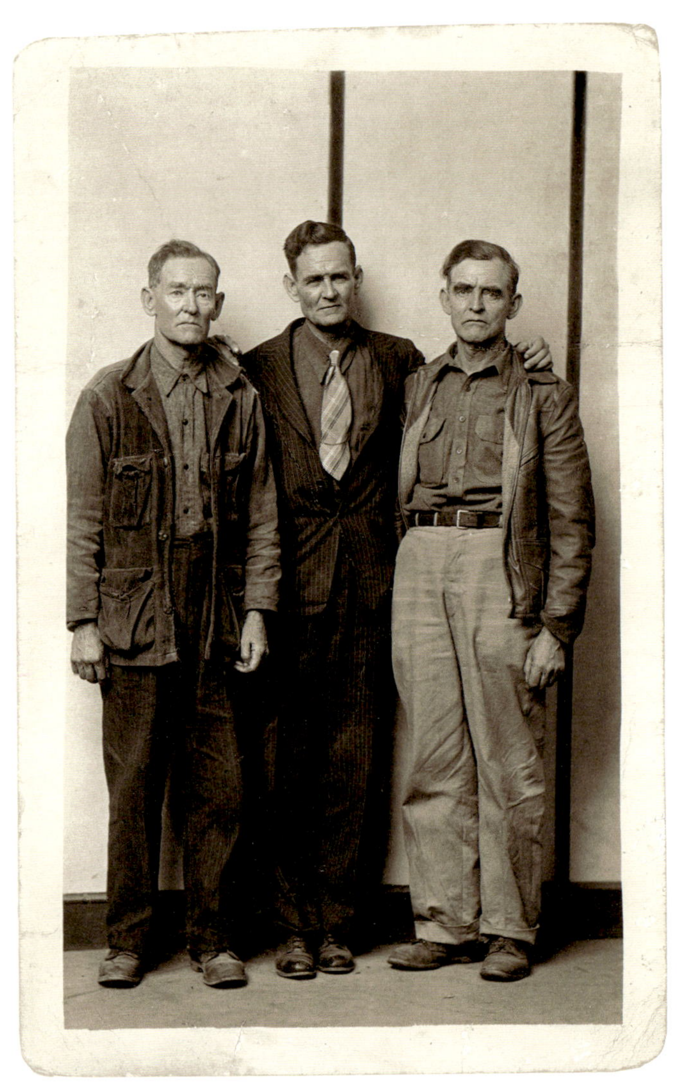

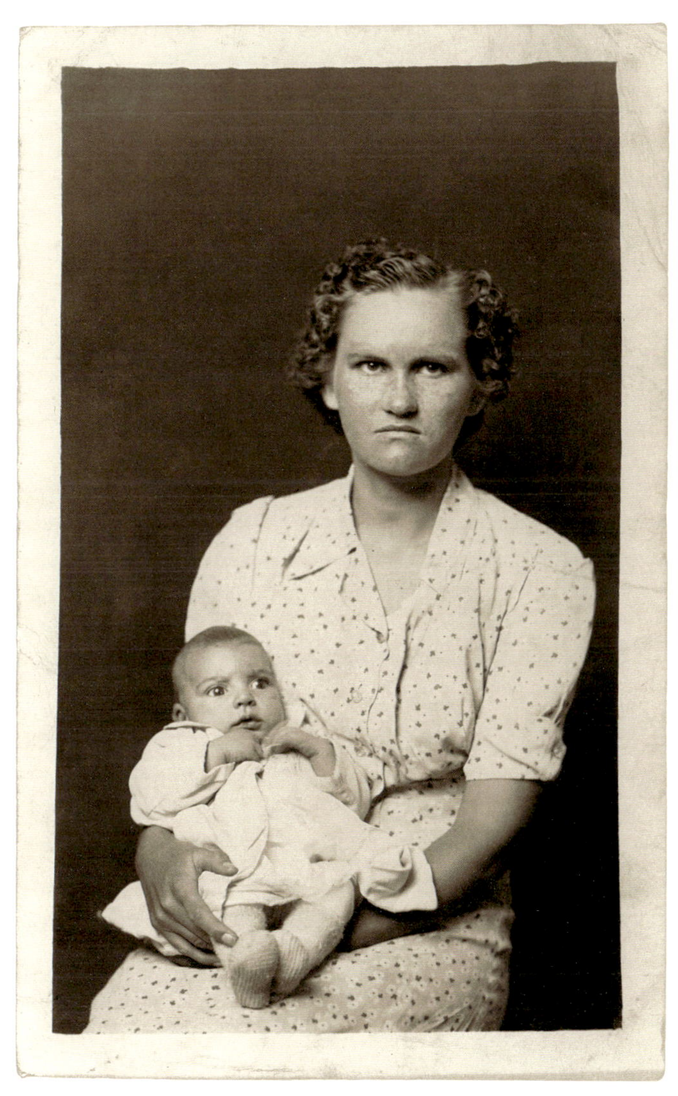

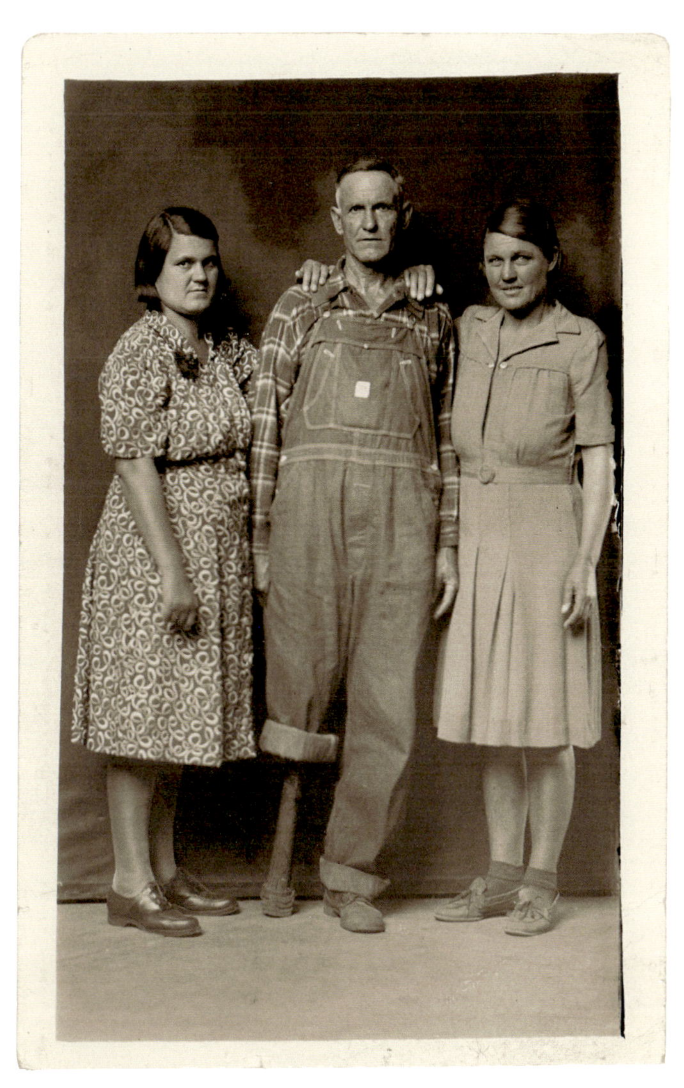

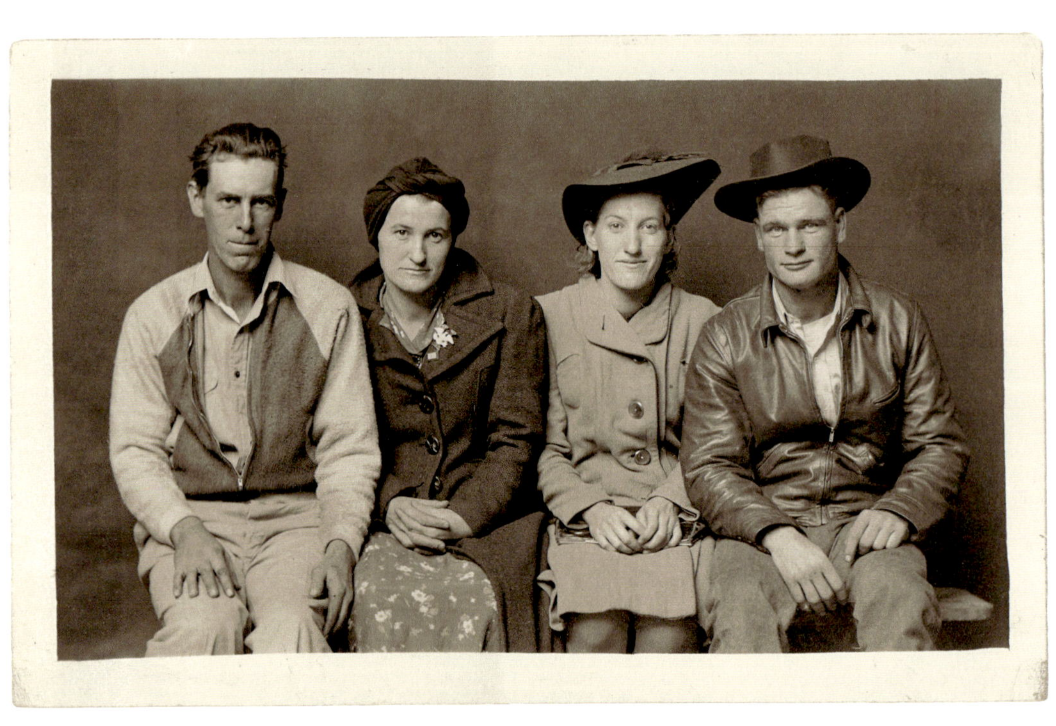

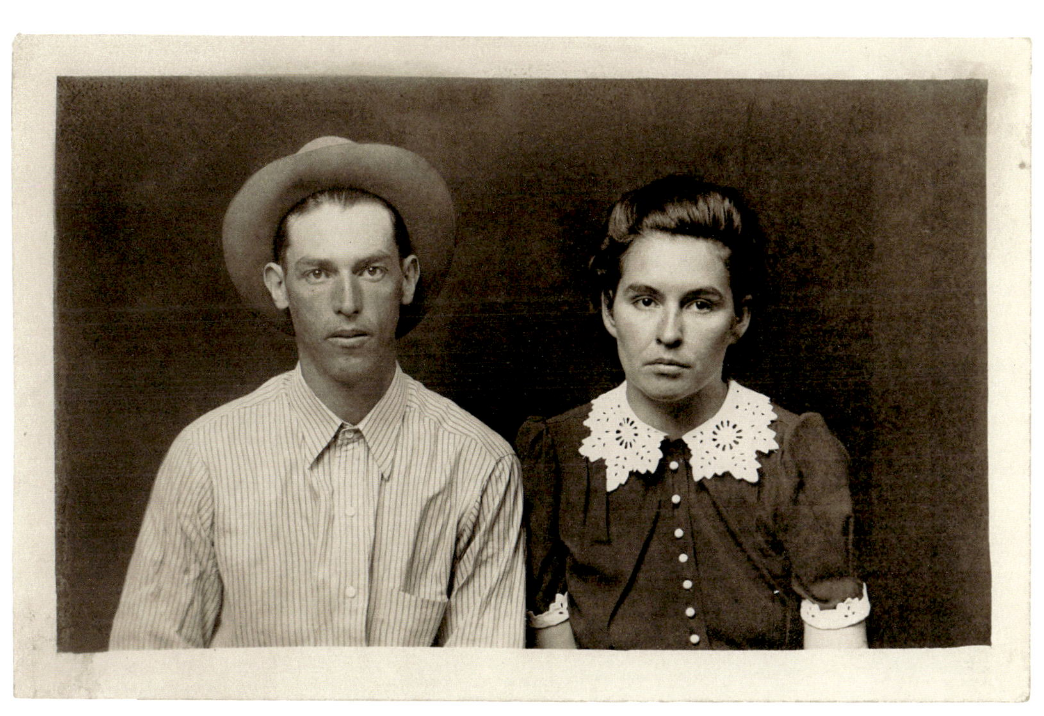

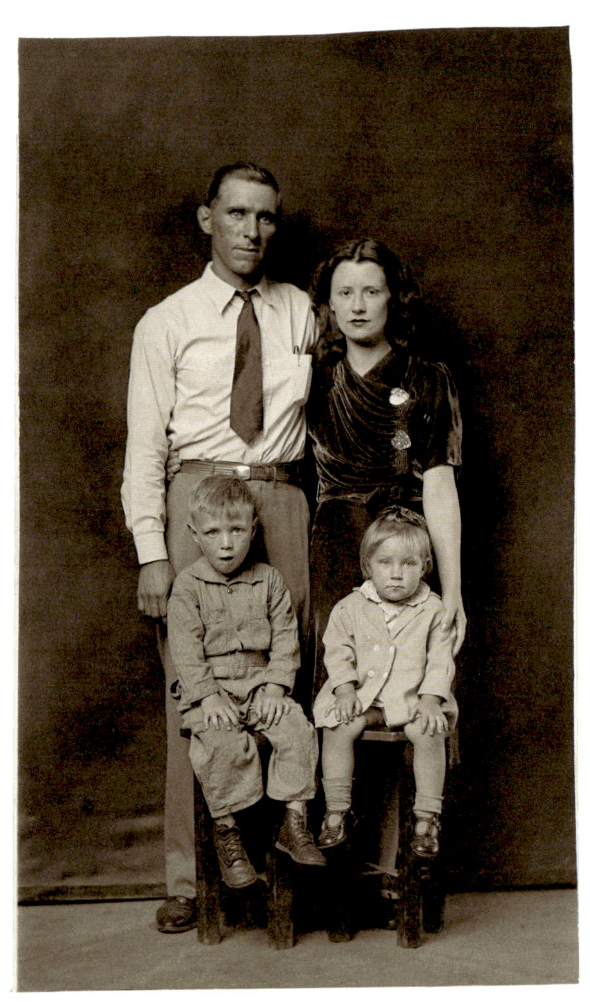

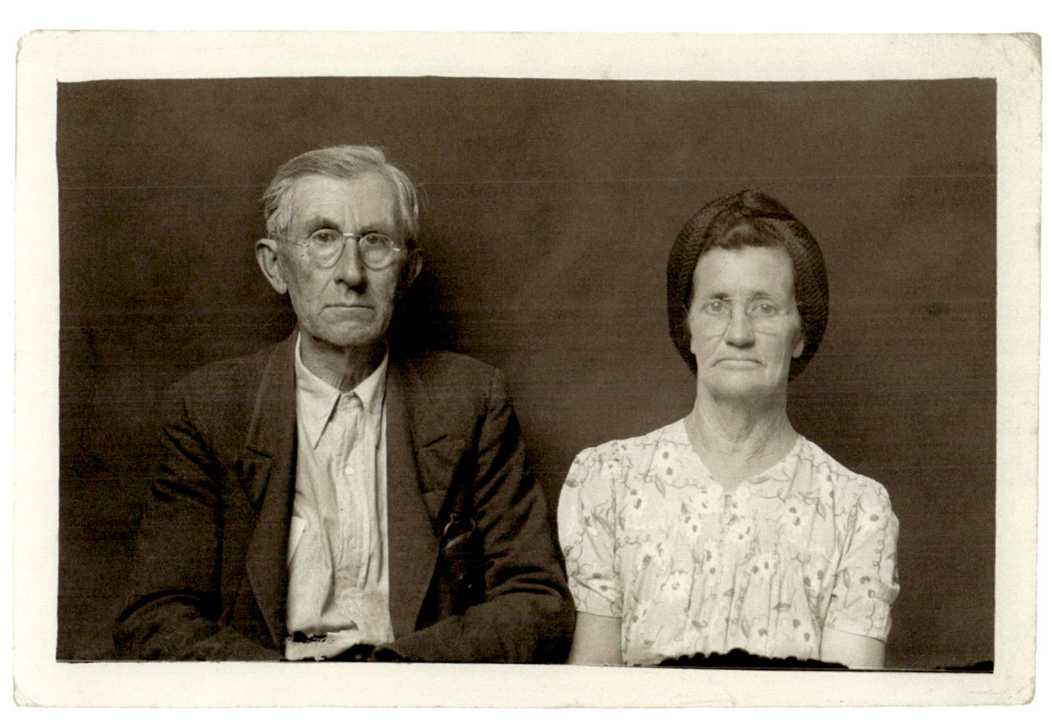

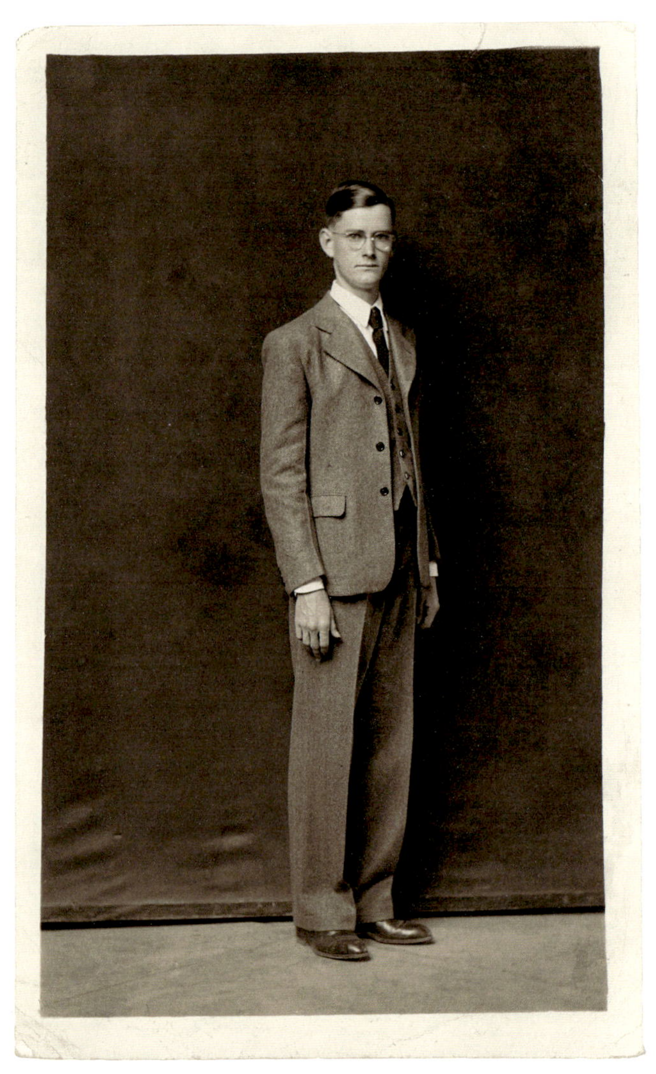

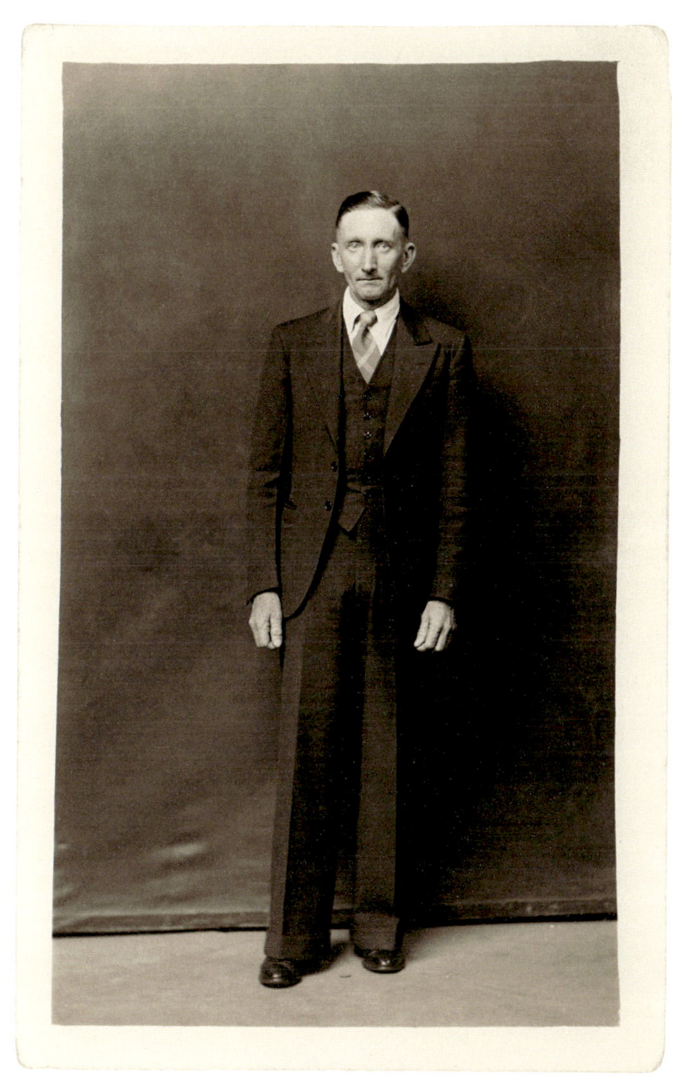

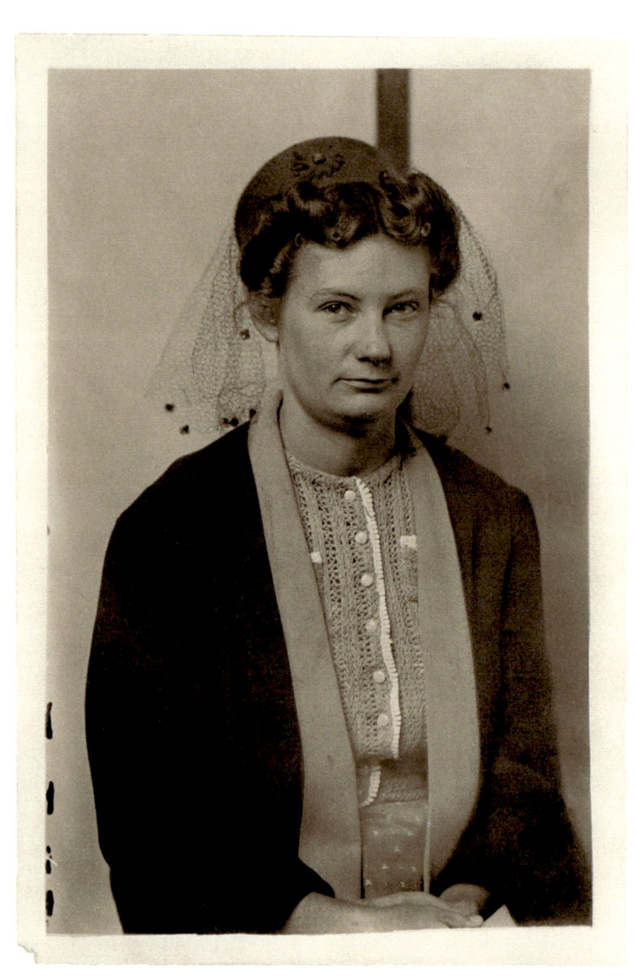

HELLO
BABY

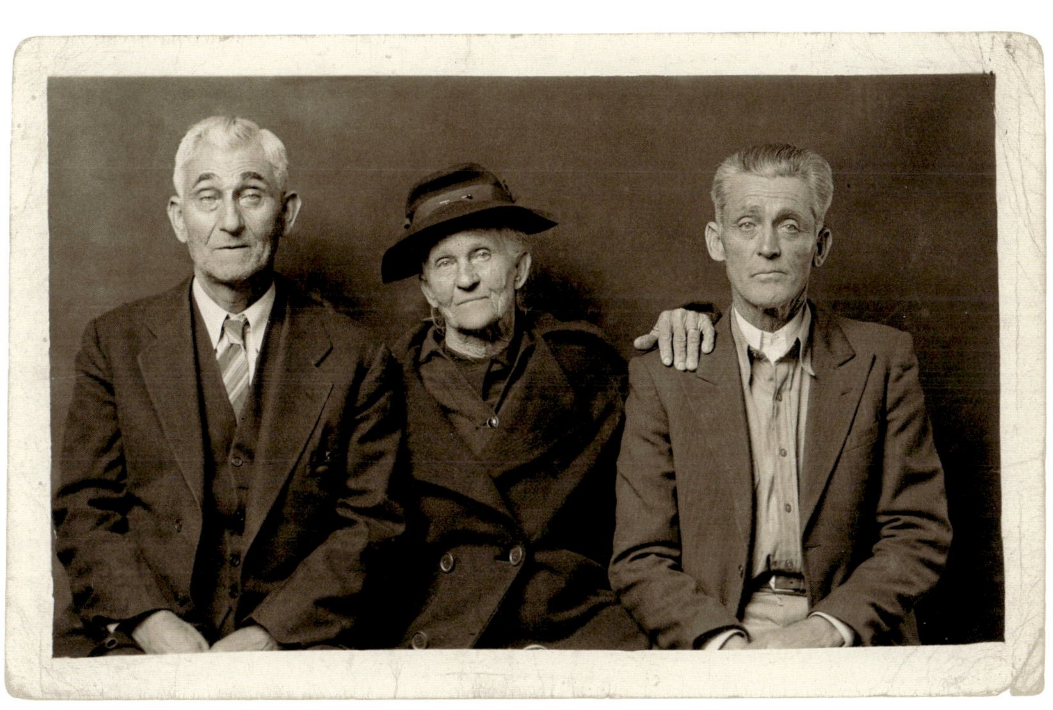

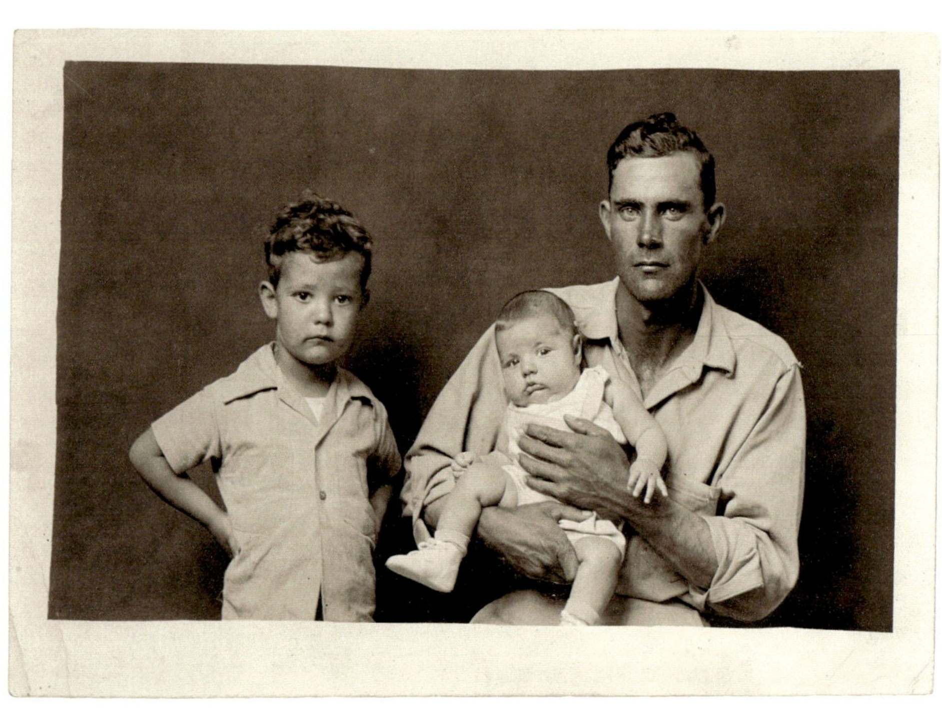

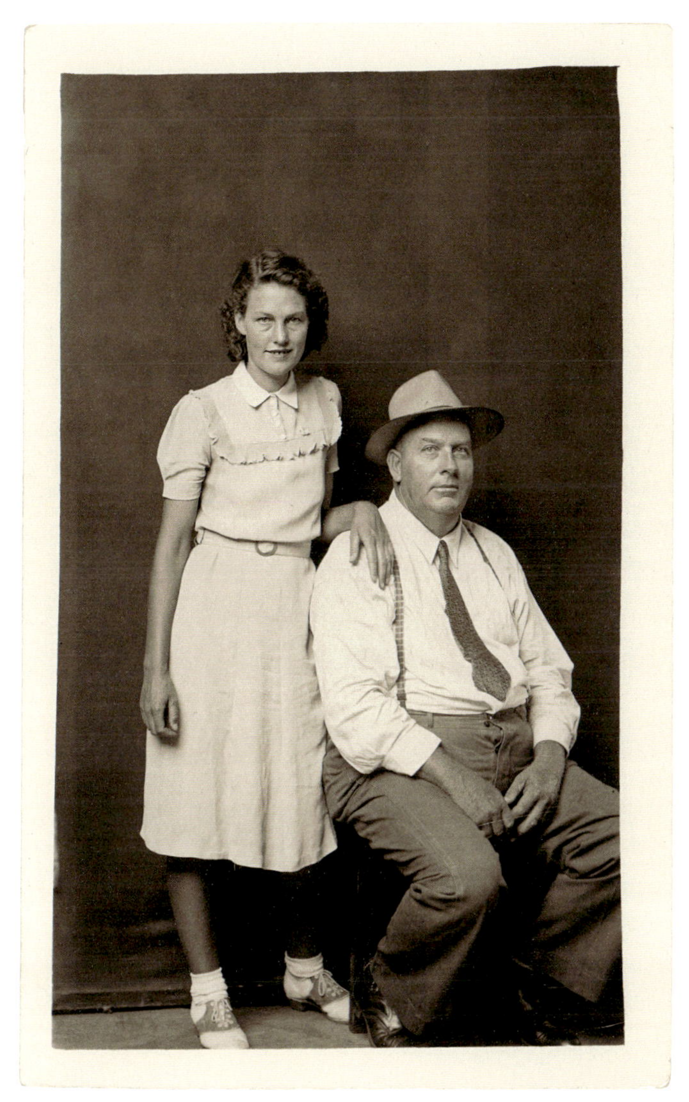

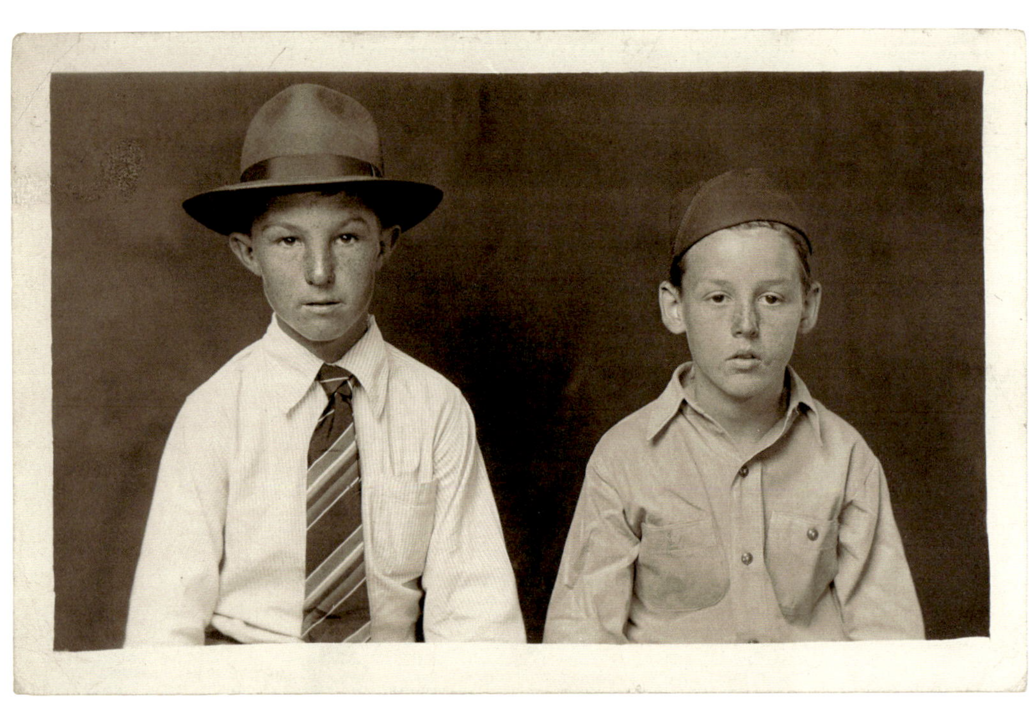

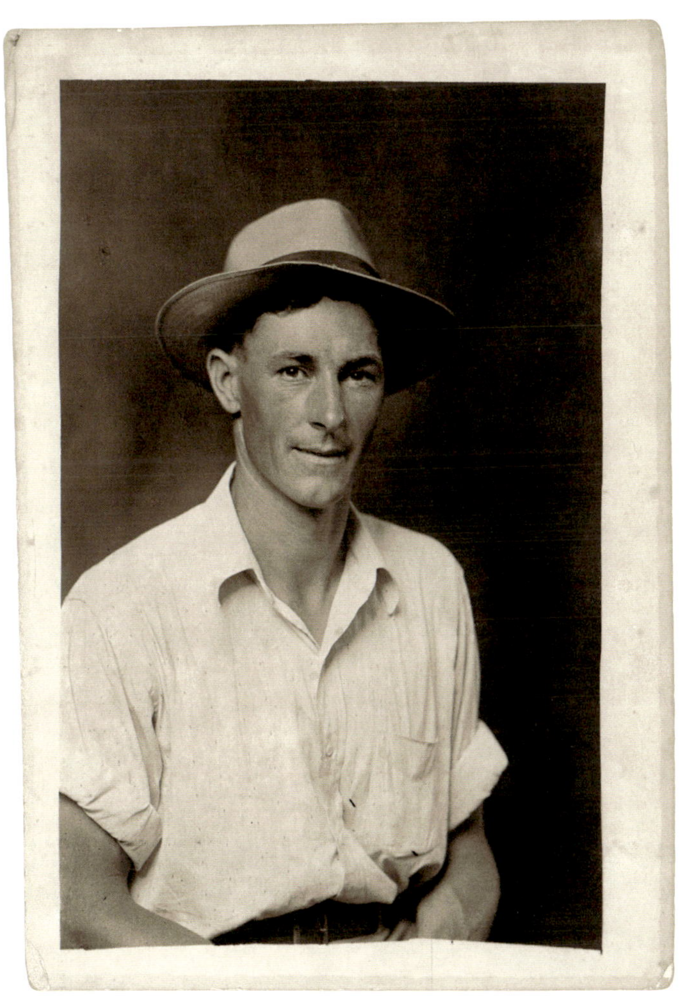

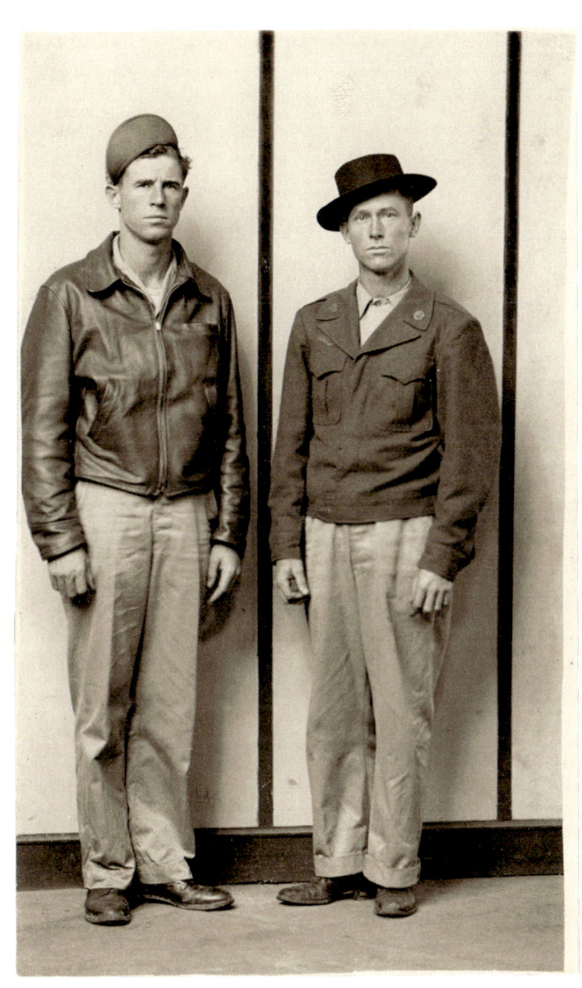

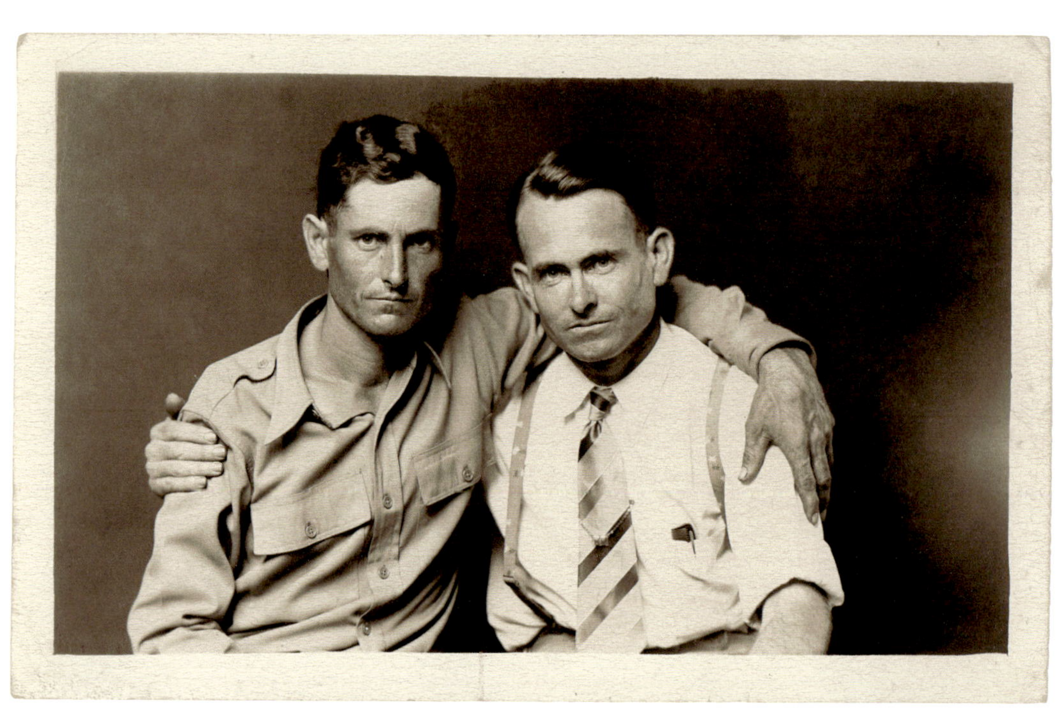

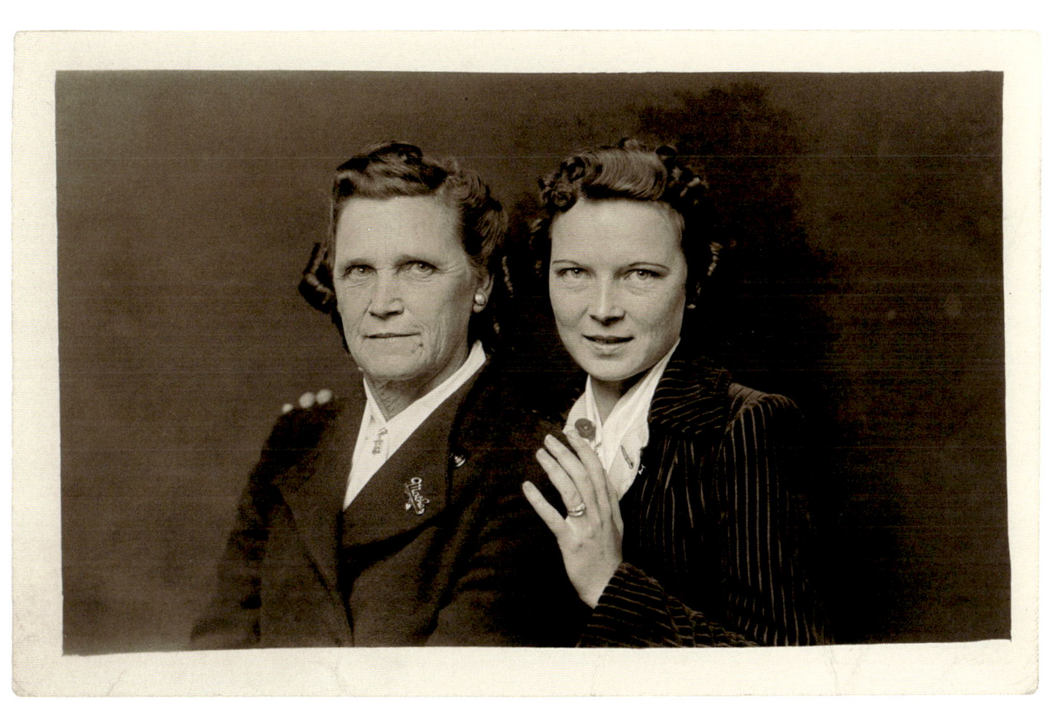

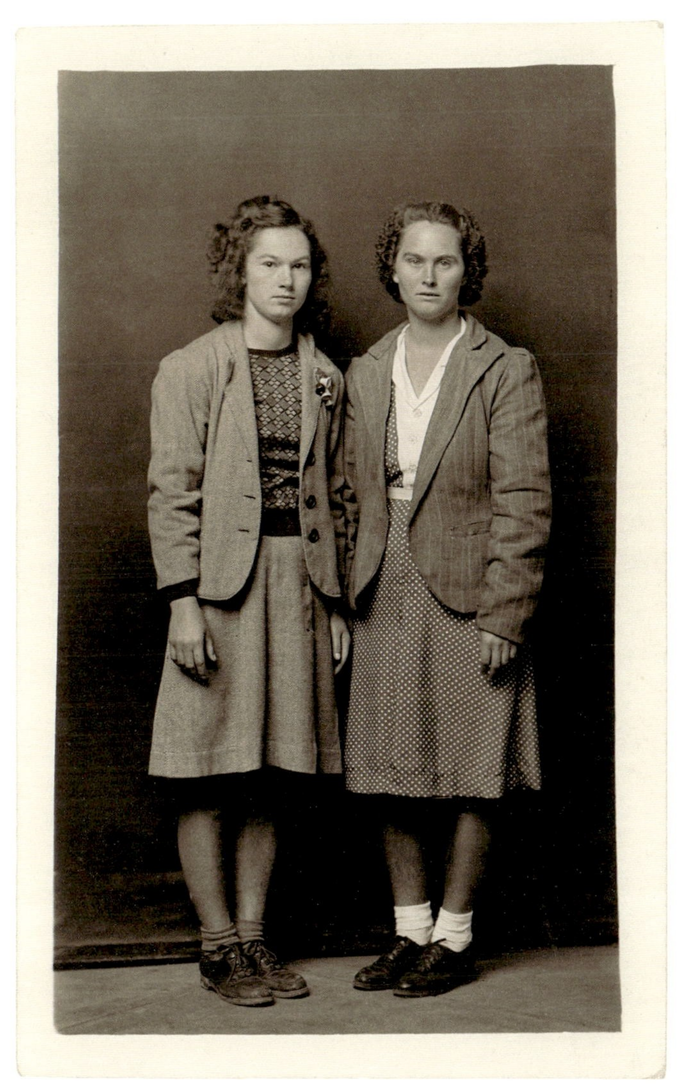

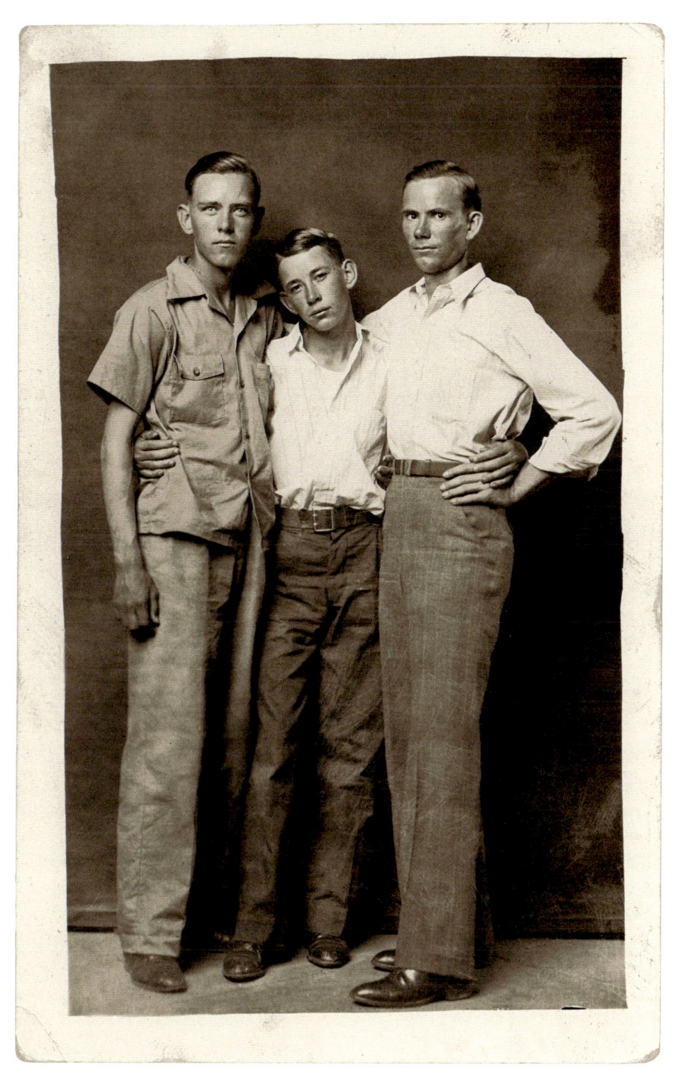

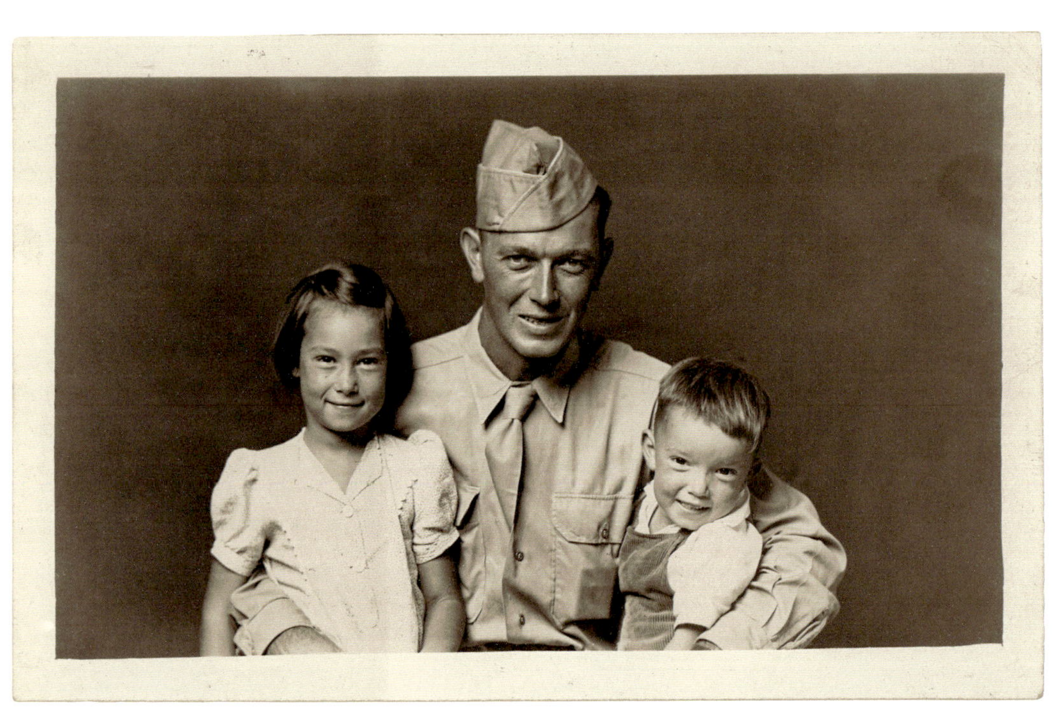

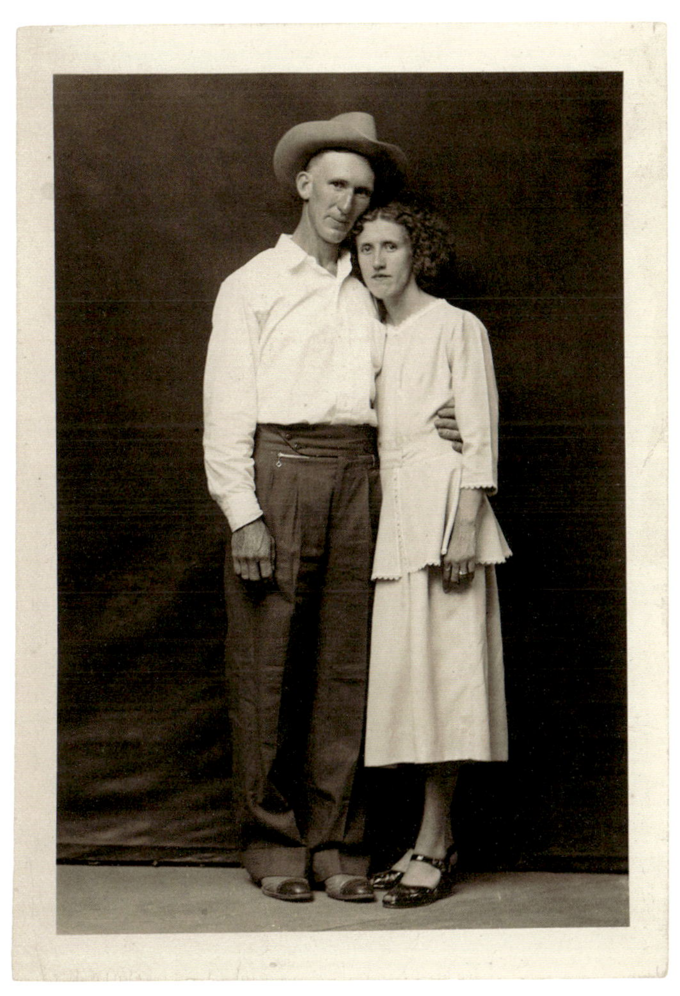

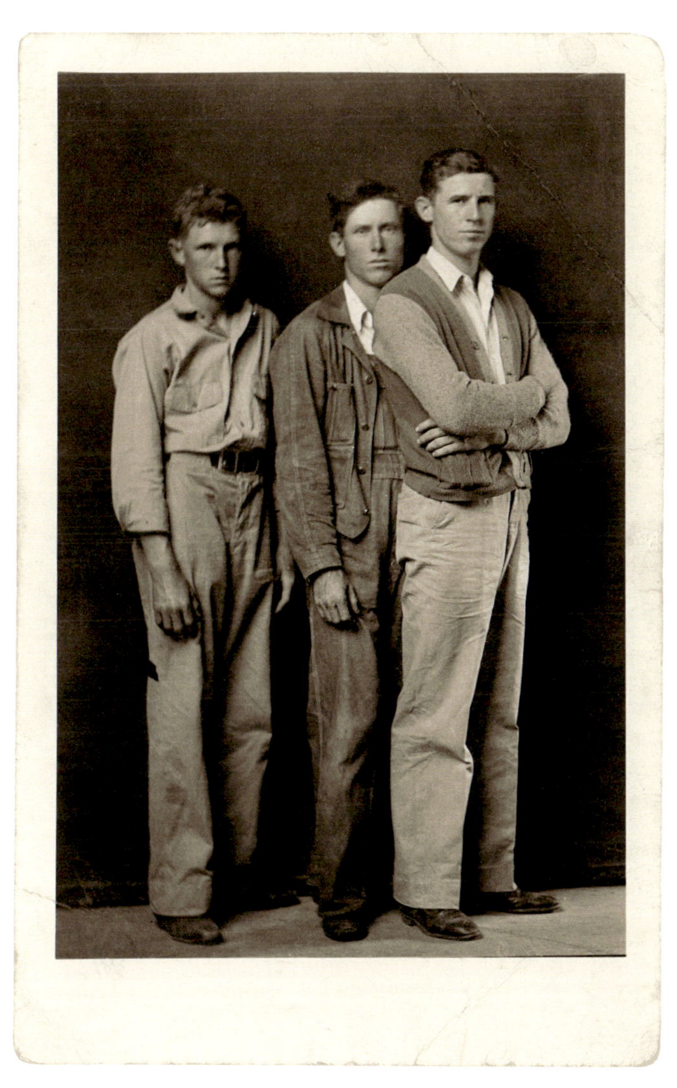

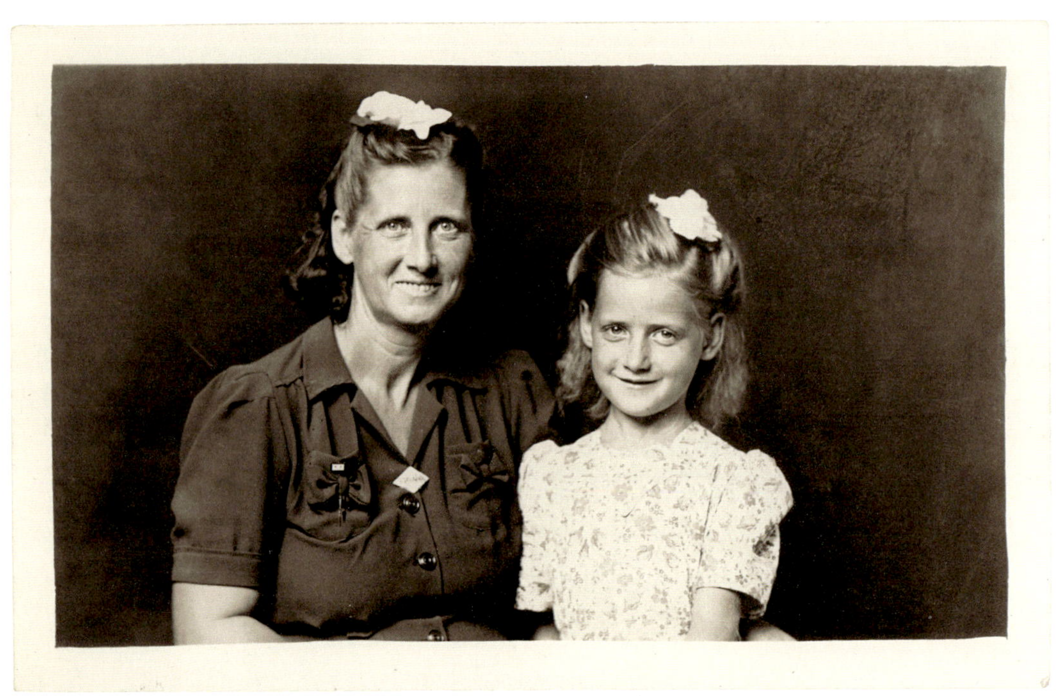

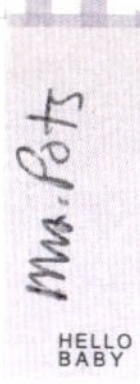
Mrs. Pots
HELLO
BABY

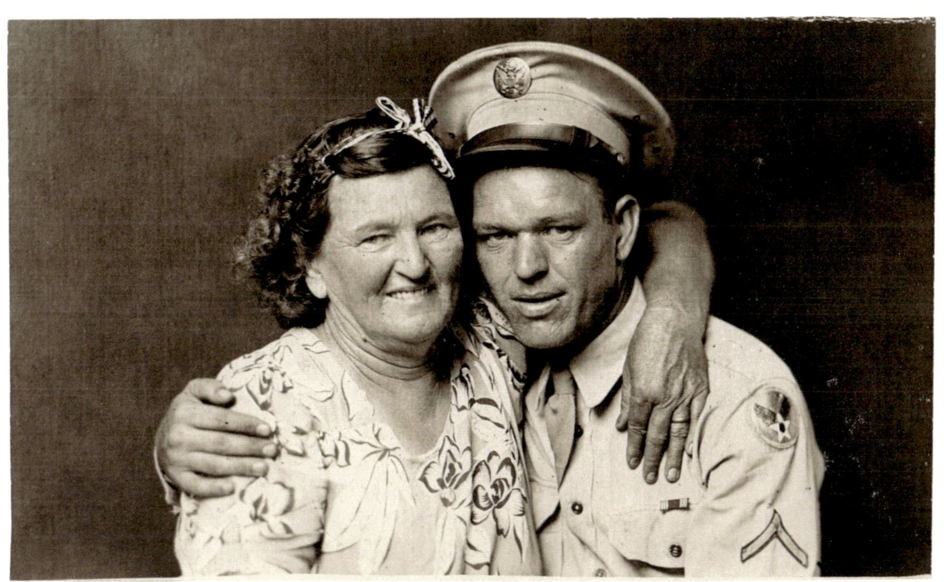

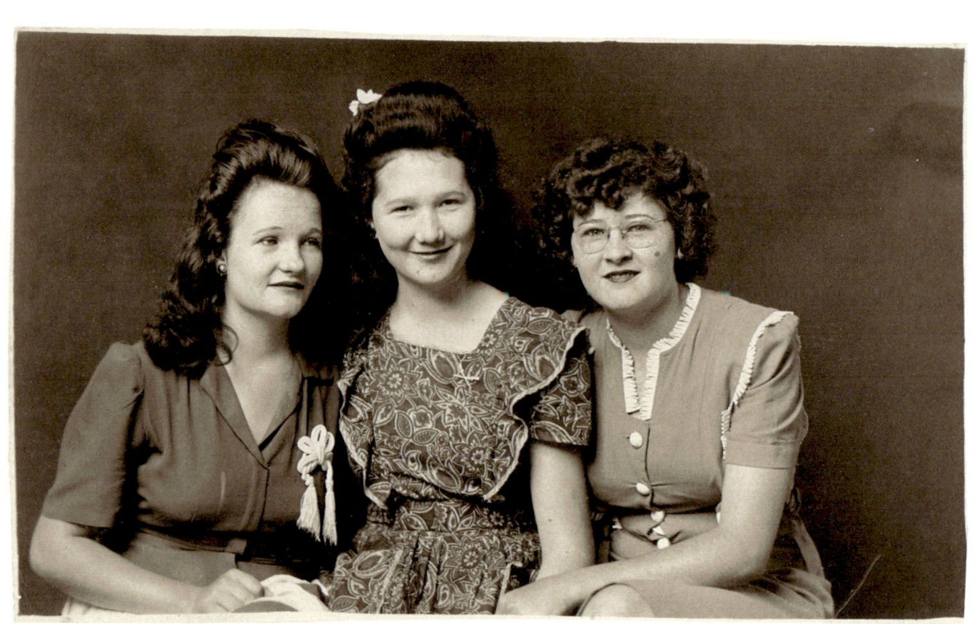

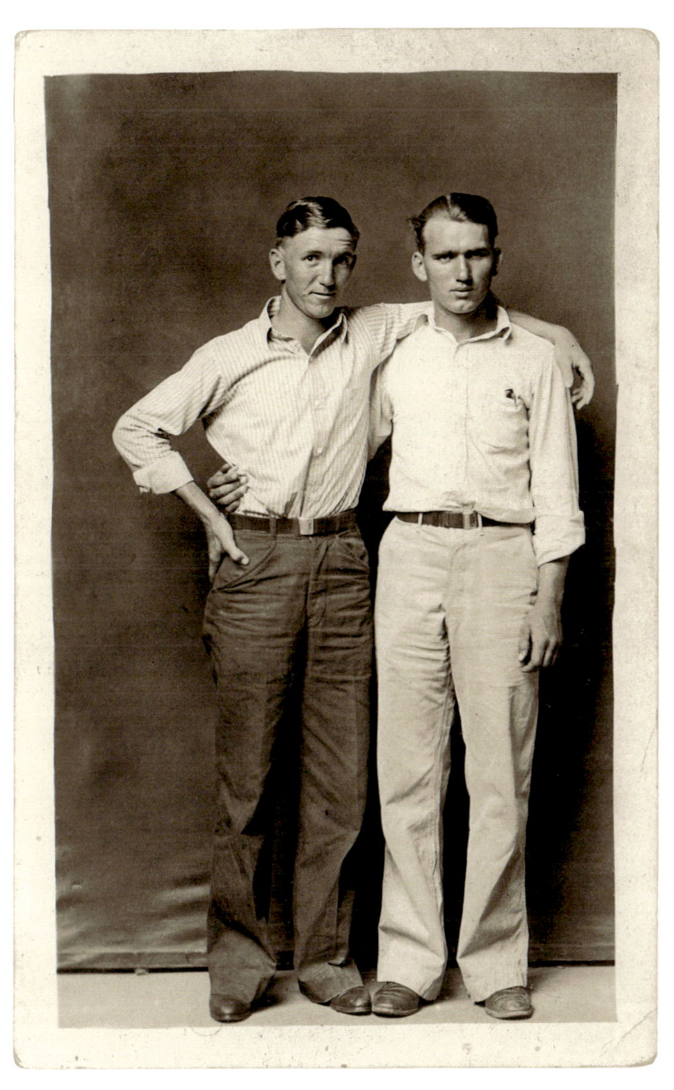

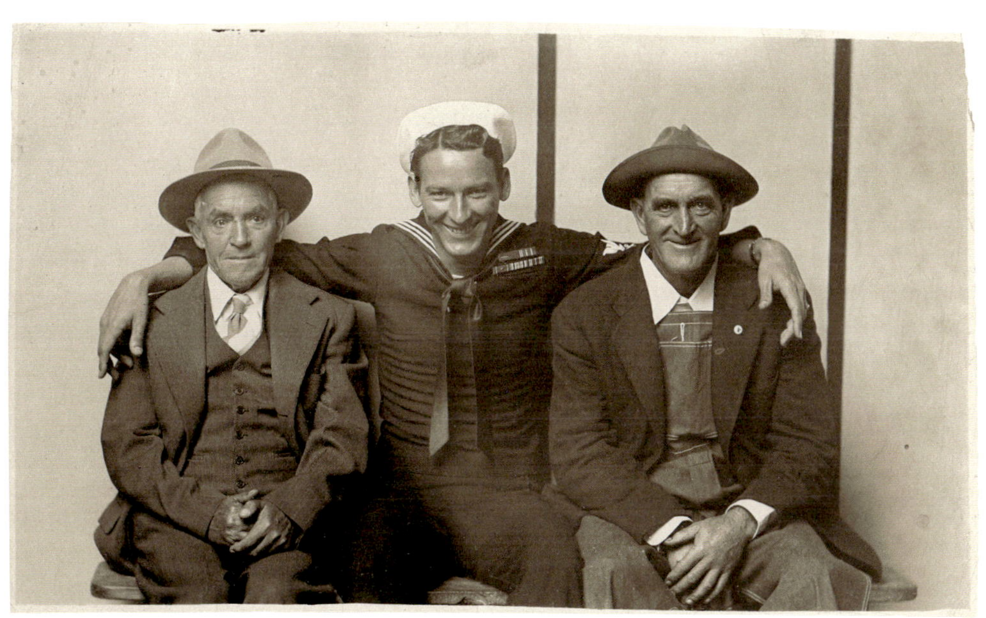

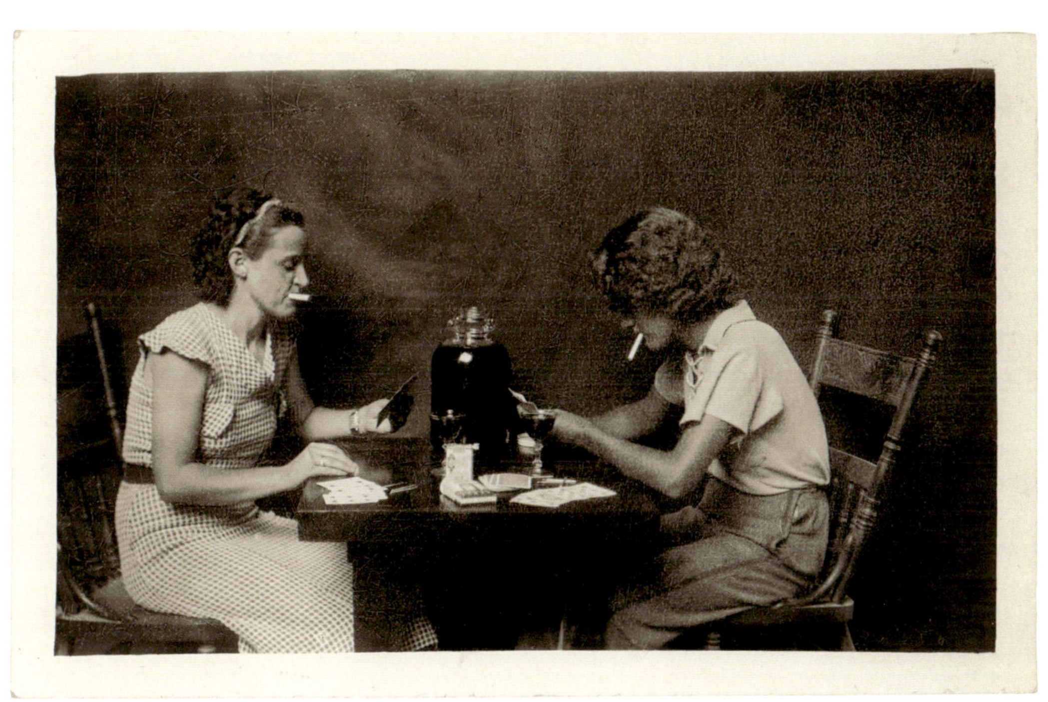

American Metamorphosis
Disfarmer and the Art of Studio Photography
by Richard B. Woodward

Small-town photographers in the first half of the twentieth century were once as plentiful as they were taken for granted. Their records of daily life over the last hundred and fifty years or so form the backbone of most local historical societies today, and are valued, along with newspapers, diaries, and letters, as personal testimony and verifiable evidence about the past. Reproductions of their work—images of a landmark event or of some now-forgotten men and women on horseback along streets long ago altered beyond recognition—can be found in the hallways of courthouses and the offices of county clerks, and as nostalgic decor in hotels and restaurants.

Most of these photographs are hung without attribution, as if anyone in the vicinity could have pressed the shutter. As unofficial historians for a community, keepers of its collective visual memory, photographers are still largely interchangeable in the public mind. They were merely there. They saw what everyone else saw, only they were holding a camera.

For anyone with an iota of artistic ambition, therefore, the frustrations of running a commercial studio in a small town were hard to overcome. Not only were you performing what was seen as a push-button service that any idiot could do, the job was also inherently passive. It was like being a girl at a high school dance. You had to sit and wait to be picked—for a partner to stand in front of you—before whatever gifts you were bursting to display could be recognized. No matter how intelligent or talented you imagined you might be, there was a good chance you would be overlooked, not chosen, forced to do nothing, for ten minutes, an hour, perhaps all day or all night. To be a portrait photographer in a small town was to be at the mercy of one's neighbors' whimsical and often ill-informed tastes.

Newspaper and magazine photographers—an overwhelmingly male breed throughout the years—have always enjoyed the freedom to venture into the world and train their cameras on any subject that caught their eye; even fashion and advertising photographers, cooped up in high-rent urban lofts, have editors or agencies to supply them with material. Southworth & Hawes and Matthew Brady could depend on their prime locations, in the thick of Boston and New York during the 1840s and '50s, as well as their well-earned reputation for high-quality work as a lure to bring illustrious and high-paying visitors through the door.

But without glamorous people as customers, the commercial portrait business is not glamorous. Its appeal, like dentistry, used to be the mundane steadiness of the job. Mainly it required patience and tact, not to mention a soothing manner or a cheerful line of patter, and a love of—or at least a tolerance for—children. Shmoozers and hustlers and pragmatists could feed their families while lonely dreamers were courting disaster. Young photographers entering the field, and planning for a reliable income, were well advised to join business organizations, such as the Rotary or Lions Club, or to ingratiate themselves with the superintendent of schools.

The emotional demands of the job could be formidable, even if the artistic challenges traditionally were not. When people lived in one place for many years, the relationships between photographers and subjects were often stable and long-term as well. The same person you had posed as a baby on her mother's lap might, if you became a trusted friend, ask for an Easter Sunday or a baptism or a graduation picture and maybe, eventually, for portraits of the wedding party. It's a puzzle that Mike Meyer, better known as Mike Disfarmer, fell into this gregarious profession and a miracle that he succeeded at it, for most reports indicate that he lacked even basic social skills. The people in the small town of Heber Springs, Arkansas, where he made photographic portraits for more than forty years, remember neither the places he worked nor the man himself as attractive. For a good part of his life (1884–1959) he seems to have been more feared than liked.

"He wasn't friendly," remembers Charlotte Lacey. "He was not talkative." There was not so much as a how do you do from the proprietor when you walked into the Disfarmer Studio, "this big open empty room" with "damp walls." (Doubling as his living quarters, the place no doubt over the years also acquired the moldy smells of seldom-cleaned bachelor quarters.) Photographed in her school band uniform as a girl, during the early 1940s, Lacey recalls the sight of the dour man vanishing under the camera cloth for minutes at a time as "very spooky and scary."[1]

"There wasn't much of a greeting when you walked in, I'll tell you that," says Tom Olmstead. He had his portrait taken, both as a boy and as a young man, and describes a studio that lacked any accoutrements to calm a restive child or impress a passerby. Only the large slanting glass-paneled roof in the back of the room, oriented at a sixty-degree angle to bathe the room in northern light, gave visitors any sign that the occupant might be out of the ordinary.

According to Olmstead, "it was a concrete building with a concrete floor, very plain. The furnishings were almost nil, a few sticks of furniture. Nothing on the walls." Nor are there records that the host ever thanked his customers for stopping by or helped them to get comfortable in front of the camera. "Instead of telling you to smile, he just took the picture," says Olmstead. "No 'cheese' or anything. You didn't even know when the picture was taken."[2]

Bessie Utley[3], who worked as Disfarmer's assistant in the '40s the only one he ever had, so far as we know—has not painted a picture of a businessman who wanted to ingratiate himself with his clients. "He could be real mean sometimes with 'em," she recalled. In particular he could be a martinet in posing his subjects, barking out instructions: "'You stand over here, you look this way or you look that,' and he wouldn't be nice."[4]

Then again, the oddity of a misanthrope like Disfarmer choosing to spend every day of every week (the studio was open seven days) in the company of strangers is no more puzzling than many other aspects of his life, most notably how this small-town photographer could have produced dozens of portraits that in their simplicity, restraint, elegance, and penetrating social gaze rank with the finest produced in the twentieth century.

What we don't know about Disfarmer far outweighs the collection of facts—and myths—that diligent researchers such as Peter Miller, Julia Scully, Toba Tucker, and Alan Trachtenberg have pieced together.[5] We still can't be sure, for example, why or exactly when he became a photographer; how many years of school he finished; what books or magazines he might have looked at, if any; whether he ever owned a car or might have traveled to New York or Chicago as a young man; which manufacturer supplied him with glass-plate negatives and why he continued with this antiquated process for so long; or his thoughts about photography in general and his own achievements in particular.

Prior to the body of research presented herein, the chief evidence about Disfarmer's career has consisted of the negatives saved by the late Joe Allbright. A recent resident in Heber Springs, having moved there only in the late 1950s, he had the foresight to recognize that the contents of a dead man's run-down photography studio might be valuable. (No one else thought so: in 1961 he bought the works—negatives, camera equipment, and plenty of junk—from a local bank for five dollars.) In 1973 he resold the ten to fifteen boxes of glass plates for one dollar to the newspaper editor (now attorney) Peter Miller who saw the pictures as special and spent a year cleaning the emulsion of mold and dirt, following a formula provided to him by Eastman Kodak.

Miller managed to rescue about three thousand of the four thousand negatives, make modern prints, and send a selection to Julia Scully, then an editor of *Modern Photography* magazine. Her sponsorship of the work, resulting in a 1976 book that coincided with an exhibition at the International Center of Photography in New York, is largely responsible for Disfarmer's posthumous fame. The biographical information unearthed by Toba Tucker during several trips to Heber Springs, beginning in 1989, when she interviewed and rephotographed many of Disfarmer's subjects, has also proven invaluable. Now, thanks to the efforts of collector Michael Mattis, who in the last two years has funded a massive search for Disfarmer vintage prints and ephemera in the Heber Springs and Cleburne County area, we have an even wider view of how the photographer functioned in his studio and the community. Or at least we can make a few more educated guesses.

***

So who was Mike Meyer/Mike Disfarmer?

In fairness to the photographer, the gruff aspects of his personality noted by his sitters and standers may reflect dodgy memories of him that date from the end of his life (and their childhoods), when he had become an increasingly hermit-like codger who drank too much and was basically a town joke. There is evidence that when he entered the portrait business, in the 1910s and '20s, he was much less abrasive and curt.[6] What little we know about his private life suggests that during his seventy-five years he may have undergone several transformations.

The most famous of these—his legal petition in 1939 to change his surname from Meyer to Disfarmer—is the source of his popular reputation as a kind of outsider artist, a naïve and slightly demented genius. If the tendency to mythologize any artist's suffering should be resisted, that impulse is harder to prevent in the case of Disfarmer who seems to have been a genuinely displaced person. The name change was the culmination of what should probably be seen as a slow mental breakdown.

He had apparently considered renaming himself for some time before taking legal action. The death of his mother, in 1935, seems to have been the emotional trigger for it, leading him to cut ties to all his relatives. In a bizarre letter that he wrote to his nephew on January 29, 1936, now in the possession of Toba Tucker, he related what in more recent decades might be labeled an "alien abduction" story—a jumbled creation myth about his origins, having nothing to do with his actual birth in Indiana in 1884.

For starters, he claimed that an "old man" told Mike he was not kin to the people who had known him all his life. Instead, his real name was "either Charles Cave or Charles August Cudahy" and he had been carried across the Indiana farmlands by a tornado and deposited in the Meyers' yard. There was a "Real Uncle Mike Meyer," he confided. (The letter is addressed "Dear Foster

Nephew.") That fellow, however, "blew away in the same storm I came in," then died, only to be found nine years later.

The story gets stranger. The remains of this other Mike Meyer were found—"a little piece of his dress, little pieces of bones"—and given to his real mother "who called it her little Mike and huged [*sic*] it and wept." She then put this bundle into a big doll, "played with it and huged [*sic*] and loved it and called it her little Mike." The bundle was supposed to be buried with Meyer's grandmother (a woman named Margretha Weidenhammer). The photographer Mike Meyer was never told about this secret, however, and so burned the bundle and the doll and "threw the ashes into the ditch in front of my studio." Thus was one Mike Meyer buried and another reborn.

His formal petition to become Disfarmer three years later is no less queer and was reported as such in the local newspaper under the headline: "Truth is Stranger Than Fiction." He was changing his name, the reporter said, because "'meyer' means 'farmer' in German, and since the petitioner was not a farmer, he chanced upon the name 'disfarmer.' 'Dis' is said to mean 'not' in German."[7] In another tale that Disfarmer liked to tell, he was the Lindbergh baby. Like many disturbed people, he picked up on a story that made headlines everywhere during the Depression—from the 1932 kidnapping until the suspect Bruno Hauptmann's electrocution in 1936—and adapted "the crime of the century" to his own needs.[8]

Emotional distress may well have plagued Meyer from an early age. In 1892, when he was 8, his father moved the family—a wife, three boys and four girls—from Indiana to Stuttgart, Arkansas in order to be part of a Lutheran religious community. Both parents were of German-American stock and Mr. Meyer had fought for the Union during the Civil War with the Indiana volunteers. But six years after the migration to the South, where he had taken up rice farming, he died. His second-to-youngest son, Mike, was only fourteen.

The next sixteen years of Disfarmer's life are a tantalizing blank. Perhaps he traveled to Elmira, New York, as he told one Arkansas acquaintance.[9] What we do know is that by 1914, when he was thirty, he and his mother had settled in Heber Springs. A photograph of the house suggests that they enjoyed a fair level of prosperity. A pair of dormers show two large bedrooms or more upstairs. There was a long front porch, and kitchen facilities off the back.[10] It was here that he set up his first known photography studio. He is remembered by a niece as a sweet and happy man.[11]

What stability these years may have represented did not last long. In 1926 a tornado touched down in Heber Springs and reduced the Meyer home to kindling. Both he and his mother escaped harm. Although he was by this time already in business for himself as a photographer, he was once again uprooted. He was forty-two.

Did this cataclysm so agitate Meyer's imagination that in coming years he saw himself swept up in storms and deposited in the backyard of a stranger? Or are the origins of the Disfarmer persona—of his alienation from the rural populace of Heber Springs—traceable to his father's fate as a Yankee who died young on his rice farm? Were superior airs to be found elsewhere in the Meyer family or just in this talented portrait photographer? Did his neighbors regard his fantastic story of personal transformation as entertainment, a hoax, what Huck Finn called "a stretcher"? Or did they view it as proof that he had completely lost his mind?

In searching for answers, Trachtenberg has written what may be the best explanation we are likely to find: "Motives for such a yarn, such a grand fiction of self-remaking, lie beyond all surmise. They belong to the realm of folklore and magic and to the shadier psychic recesses of the Ozark hills during the travail of the Great Depression."[12]

It is also possible that the Disfarmer persona has foundations in his ambitions to be a serious (if locally unappreciated) artist. The social status of a portrait photographer was ambiguous in a place like Heber Springs. Neither blue collar nor white collar, the job ranked below minister, banker, doctor, or lawyer in prestige. On the one hand, it was a trade that involved manual labor and the stinky mixing of chemicals; on the other hand, it required a level of scientific knowledge and technological sleight-of-hand, situating it above grocery or hardware store owner; and, at the end of the day, squeezing a bulb on a shutter release hardly qualifies as heavy lifting. You don't come home with dirty overalls, as would a mechanic or farmer.

Bessie Utley, who paid her daughter's college education with the money that Disfarmer gave her to assist him in processing other people's film, sounded grateful for studio employment when she stated with a laugh: "It was better than picking cotton, I'll tell you that."[13]

Heber Springs was the center of a farming area during Meyer's lifetime. From 1862 until 1934 anyone who came to Cleburne County was guaranteed 160 acres if he built a home and cleared five acres of trees and bramble. Most of the residents outside the town center worked in the fields or maintained the animals and machinery for such labor. Everyone raised corn and took it to the grist mills, and most grew sorghum to make molasses. Cotton was the cash crop that paid for everything else.[14]

During the early '20s, the area was also a dangerous place to live. A railroad strike in 1922 dragged on for years. Violence begat violence. The railroad lines, which had opened up Cleburne County's hot springs to tourism in 1908, were sabotaged, and some of Heber Springs' leading citizens meted out vigilante justice against the strikers.[15]

There were whippings and lynchings, and marches by the Ku Klux Klan down Main Street. (Without a population of African-Americans to terrorize, the KKK seems to have settled for dissident railroad workers.) The National Guard was called up. People were afraid to leave their homes at night. According to Charles Stuart, president of the Cleburne County Historical Society, "strong feelings about those years linger to this day."[16]

It is sometimes forgotten that Meyer was not a native, having first set foot in Heber Springs, so far we know, at the age of thirty when his mother moved there in 1914. He was therefore neither lifelong nor even high school pals with any of the people he photographed. What's more, in a place where many had family roots going back several generations, his went back to Indiana. (Or, if you believe the international version of his wind-blown conception, to Germany.) He was not technically a Southerner.

Unusual personal habits further distanced him from his neighbors. He never married. Utley is the only woman with whom he has been linked, and her testimony is contradictory. She claimed that he "never made any passes or anything—he was a perfect gentleman", but also that "he couldn't keep his hands off of me, and I told him that's what he'd better do is keep his hands off of me. And he said he would."[17]

There was no shame in being a bachelor, a type long accepted and gently joked about across rural America. (Lutheran bachelor farmers are recurrent characters in Garrison Keillor's comic monologues about the fictional town of Lake Woebegone on "Prairie Home Companion.") Much more outside the local moral code and harder for the people of Heber Springs to tolerate was Disfarmer's religious life: he did not attend church. In an area dense with Baptist and Methodist places of worship, he stayed home on Sundays. What's more, he made a point of telling people he didn't believe in the Bible.[18]

Nor did he have friends, male or female. Heber Springs was a town of about 3,800 people when he moved there, and he seemed eager to get to know none of them. He attended a few meetings at the Mason Lodge; and he liked to play the fiddle with a barber/guitarist named Albert Hendrix. Country music was Disfarmer's only known interest other than photography and Hendrix his only known companion. But as Scully notes, these regular musical get-togethers "hardly amounted to friendship."[19] He paid far more attention to people as artistic problems to solve, sometimes taking as long as an hour to make a portrait, than as individuals with lives outside his studio. His adopting the name

Disfarmer put on a legal document what was already a fait accompli. Neither by birth nor temperament was Mike Meyer a member of this community.

Thirty is a late age to be taking up photography, so it is more than likely that Meyer had educated himself in the basics of exposing film and making prints much earlier than 1914, when his mother moved to Heber Springs. The town of Stuttgart, a hundred miles away, where he lived from ages eight to sixteen (and maybe until he was thirty?), had a series of photography studios—E.K. Blush, Buerkle, H.E. Downing, Kettering, and Snodgrass—from the 1890s to the 1940s[20] Meyer may have apprenticed at one of them. Or perhaps, like photographers before and since, he taught himself. However it happened, he was proficient enough by 1915 to have his name affixed to a business sign on the south side of Main Street in Heber Springs.

The Penrose & Meyer Studio, located in the lobby of the Jackson Theatre, seems to have reached a swankier customer base than the one Disfarmer later relied on. In the dozen or so surviving prints located by Mattis and his team, dating from approximately 1915-20, the portrait subjects are for the most part well-dressed and middle-class.[21] They don't wear overalls or bear other traces of the working poor. Heber Springs in the early decades of the century was a tourist destination, with many summer hotels, cinemas and a bowling alley. Before Prohibition it was wide open, with numerous bars and much rowdiness. Penrose & Meyer may well have solicited visitors to the Jackson Theatre who were in town to catch a play or vaudeville act and who wanted to top off the excursion with a photograph.

The burning of the Jackson Theatre in 1921[22] ended the partnership, with Penrose leaving town soon thereafter. Meyer set up business on his own, buying up plots of land in 1923-24 on First Street, just off of Main, and building his studio there in either 1925 or 1926. After the tornado wiped out his mother's house, he made the place his new residence.[23]

The Meyer Studio (at the same address that became, after the name change in 1939, the Disfarmer Studio) was modern for its time and place. Such a design, with its slanting skylight and northern exposure, had long been familiar in urban areas. But in the rural South in the mid-'20s it must have been a striking sight, especially with its stripped-down concrete interior and stucco façade.

Like most portrait businesses in small towns, the Meyer studio made money both by taking your picture and by processing your dropped-off film. Cameras were familiar items in middle-class homes after George Eastman revolutionized photography in 1888 with the cheap and easy Kodak. Independent studios had to compete by offering a special portrait experience or attractive rates for handling film from your own camera.

A price list from the Meyer Studio—dated February 6, 1928 and now in Mattis's collection—shows that his was a high-volume but not a high-grossing business. This unknown customer ordered fifteen prints (three each from five negatives) and paid four cents a piece. To develop pack film cost twenty-five cents, while roll film cost ten cents. It is shocking to learn, from another receipt in Mattis's hands, that twenty-seven years later—in 1955, four years before his death—Disfarmer was still only charging four cents for extra prints.[24] This may reflect either his low-key attitude toward money or a commercial need to keep prices at rock bottom in order to survive against mail-order processors like Eastman.

The core of his business was portraiture, however; a session seems to have cost fifty cents, for which you received three prints. (Records indicate that for decades Disfarmer failed to raise prices for this service either.[25]) Contrary to previous research, Mattis has uncovered a few enlargements.[26] These are rare, though. In the majority of cases Meyer/Disfarmer made contact prints, a few from 5x7 negatives but predominantly in the 3 1/2 x 5 1/2 format. This latter size enabled him to do a swift turnover in photographic postcards, his bread-and-butter.

The negatives were glass-plate.[27] Such technology would have been considered eccentrically old-fashioned in 1920 and, in the opinion of John Szarkowski, downright "Luddite"[28] by 1952 when Disfarmer at last switched to celluloid film.[29] But it may be that he learned to photograph with this antiquated method, liked the results, and never saw a compelling reason to update his equipment.[30]

By the early '30s, both the railroad strike and the onset of the Great Depression must have hurt Meyer's trade as they hurt most businesses in Heber Springs. The dress of the clients in his portraits at the end of the decade has become increasingly workaday. Laborers begin to crowd out the middle-class. But perhaps by keeping his rates low, and with no competitors in town—or any overhead other than himself and Utley's wages—he did fairly well.

The ritual of having your portrait made by Disfarmer, the crazy man who claimed he grew up in a potato hole, did not lose its charm for many years. Utley remembered "it was terrible busy on Saturdays because that's when all the farmers come to town. I don't care if they had their picture made last week, they wanted it made again this week.... It just went on and on like that. That was a good paying business."[31]

He did even better during World War II, when photographs became precious keepsakes for wives and mothers who wanted images of their men before they were shipped overseas, perhaps to die. These men, too, wanted portraits of the people back home so they could remember why they were fighting a war.

The style of portraiture changed with the times. The props seen in the Penrose & Meyer prints—a mirror and flower vase—gradually disappear; and the operatic fantasy scenes of clouds and castles that flanked his clients in the '20s are later reduced to two plain, almost severe, backdrops: one, a dark monochrome; the other, lighter-colored and more reflective, with a few incongruous dark tape-stripes, like a Mondrian painting.

These backdrops were freestanding. (Note the exposed wooden feet in Figures 3 and 4 in the Afterword in the present volume.) Disfarmer could have moved them according to changing light conditions during the day. But most of his subjects don't remember that being the case. The traditional view of Disfarmer is that he used only natural light from the dramatic skylight above. This may have been true in daylight hours. But it is hard to see how he could do business late in the afternoon, especially in winter months or on cloudy days, without artificial illumination, much less on Saturday nights when farmhands and their girlfriends rode into town.

One of the most intriguing finds from Mattis's team is a series of prints (e.g., page 201) that seem to show Disfarmer experimenting with a lighting set-up. What's more, during interviews about their portrait sessions, some of his subjects don't recall the skylight. Instead, they speak of Disfarmer's having a "flash" gun in the studio.

Kenneth Foust, who was born in 1928 and had his portrait taken by Disfarmer from eight to ten times between 1944 and 1950, remembers that the photographer "had a flash bulb that he used. I don't remember there being any glass wall, if there was it was covered by a curtain. We'd walk in and it was a dark room. I can't remember if it was a 'blast' of light or a big reflector that he held in his hand, not sure. I think it flashed, it caught you off guard...."[32]

The startled look noticeable on the faces of many Disfarmer subjects may be explained by his use of this technique, so familiar from the work of Weegee and Diane Arbus, photographers with whom Disfarmer is often compared. How often it was used, and whether alone or in combination with natural light, deserves further investigation.

Two lenses were found in his studio after his death: a twelve inch Tessar made by Bausch and Lomb; and a shorter Wollensak Double Anistigmat.[33] A few subjects have reported that his camera was mounted in a partition through which he could also view entering customers.[34] But Kenneth Foust remembers Disfarmer standing behind a camera mounted on a tripod in the middle of a bare room. Others, including his wife Sue Foust, concur.[35] It would be surprising if the photographer, who occupied the same studio for thirty-three to thirty-four years, did not tinker at least once with his approach to portraiture. Exposures were relatively long (Peter Miller estimates a 1/2 second; Alan Trachtenberg 1/25 of a second) and the sessions varied from ten minutes to an hour, depending on the number of people in the picture and the line-up of customers at the door and how much time Disfarmer had to kill.

At a time when many photographers were on the front lines with soldiers in Europe and Asia, making a splash with dramatic wartime shots published in glossy magazines such as *Fortune* and *Life*, Disfarmer was grounded in an Arkansas portrait studio. It is hard to believe that a man in his mid-fifties, even in a small town like Heber Springs, would never have seen the photographs of Margaret Bourke-White or Robert Capa or W. Eugene Smith. But if he did, nothing about his own pictures indicates that he wanted to emulate their more flamboyant style.

***

There is no evidence that Disfarmer ever thought of himself as an artist. The same could be said of Timothy O'Sullivan or Eugene Atget, however, or any number of figures now in the pantheon of photography who worked before museums and other institutions legitimized their trade as an art. There *is* testimony that Disfarmer knew how good a photographer he was. An anecdote from a prominent citizen of Heber Springs reveals that he had a prickly streak of pride: "Wasn't anyone any better 'n he was, in his opinion," remembered Judge Reed. Utley also reports that he showed a degree of hauteur from his surroundings. "He was just like he was so much superior...it was like he had a brain and we never had."[36]

Without a statement from the man himself, the question of self-consciousness will remain unresolved. But emphasis on Disfarmer the naïf and the nut has over the years distorted the scope of an achievement that depended on control and a scrutinizing eye. Most of all, the issue of whether or not he arranged the people or let them stand "naturally" has deflected attention from his evident shaping hand.

When his subjects have claimed that he did not pose them, what they may mean is that he did not always tell them when the shutter would be tripped. "No 'cheese' or anything," as Olmstead has said. This could well have been a strategy of Disfarmer's to increase the chances of an uncanned expression or posture. Utley's description of her boss brusquely ordering his sitters "to look this way and look that" suggests that at times he exercised stern mastery. The pictures themselves offer overwhelming proof that he spent considerable effort placing figures and limbs. He was smart enough to recognize happy accidents, such as the almost identical clothes worn by the two women and two boys as seen in page 163. But he is the one who likely put the tiny child in the center and then waited for the faces of all five to evince their separate discomfort.

It is not believable that the five family members on page 85 composed themselves in such perfect rhythm—hand on shoulder, right arms crooked at ninety degrees—without guidance from the photographer. The tall young man on the left anchors the picture with his oak-like fortitude, a strength that seems to diminish down the line until we reach the slouching grandmother on the end. The man second from the right has the left side of his vest open. How could Disfarmer, focusing the quintet for minutes in his ground glass, not see this "mistake"? More likely, he decided to weave the slice of white lining into the checkered pattern made by the collars, shirts, pants, dresses, and the darker outer side of the vest.

The photographer Lee Friedlander has observed that people no longer pose with the awkward ease that they showed when he began making portraits fifty years ago.[37] A blasé attitude about picture-taking coupled with a resentment toward the ubiquity of cameras in our midst has infected photographic portraits with a stilted self-awareness and an air of ironic performance.

Almost any page of this book reveals how lucky Disfarmer was to stand his camera in front of so many Americans in the years before they caught this disease. Touching people of the same sex was not a taboo when these pictures were taken. Not everyone had a camera, at least not on a tripod in a studio, and so anyone who had such an ornate set-up qualified as an unusual character.

The young man with a hat on page 24 or the tall brothers leaning against one another on page 31 want to make the right impression for the photographer. But they seem unsure exactly how this should be done. Disfarmer zeroes in on their gawkiness and commends their effort without turning them into a Norman Rockwell cartoon of American goodness.

In other cases, Disfarmer seems to oblige the myth-making wishes of his customers. The handsome young tough framed in a half-portrait close-up (page 27) wears a hat, a leather jacket, and a scowl as though determined to come off like a movie outlaw or Hank Williams. A portrait suitable for a magazine cover or a wanted poster, it was likely done to impress a sweetheart or for the fellow himself.

Disfarmer was a master at portraying family groups, one of the major challenges for any photographer. The degree of difficulty seems to increase exponentially not arithmetically with the number of children and grand-parents. So much more can go wrong. His compositions were never elaborate; he kept everyone within a frieze-like plane. But his symmetries invariably look smart, alive, and witty (pages 74, 115, 170) rather than coldly manipulative.

The luminosity of so many Disfarmer portraits is no accident either. His negatives were coated with an orthochromatic emulsion, a film sensitive to the green, blue, and violet parts of the spectrum, and not to red. This lends the flesh of his people a burnished, ruddy tone. Eyes and faces stand out, as though sculpted, perhaps also in alarm at the flash going off a few feet away or the sound of a cow bell he was known to bang.[38]

Many pictures are heartbreaking studies of poverty. The battle to keep a household together in the rural South during these decades must have been lost by more than a few of the people here. Even those young couples who hung on and stayed married seem to have paid a price. The blank background in Disfarmer's photographs encourages us to fill it in with stories about people who were standing before a camera that was in some sense judgmental.

Disfarmer is not cruel, patronizing, or sentimental about their plight. But neither is he a friend or pastor. Like Weegee, he is there to do a job. He is like a crime scene photographer, determined to record the details because the details are what ultimately will exonerate a person. The reality of their condition—the hats, creases in their jeans and dresses, lines in faces and hands, bad posture, dangling cigarettes and arms, staring eyes—can be preserved in a photograph and serve as existential evidence.

In his ruthless clarity and in his zest for viewing the material world through a glass lens, Disfarmer belongs in the company of August Sander, Brassaï, Walker Evans, Irving Penn, Atget, Weegee, and Arbus, although comparisons of this sort are perhaps ultimately a disservice to all.

Disfarmer's achievement was at once smaller and greater than theirs. Lacking the education of well-traveled urban aesthetes like Evans and Arbus, he was anything but a sophisticate. His mind was probably damaged. His range of subject matter was narrow—studio portraits of citizens in an American small town—and his vintage prints, on many kinds of papers, were often done in a hurry and lack the consistently high finish of a classic Penn, Sander, or Brassaï. Disfarmer's audience could not have afforded the work of an "artist," and he often had to make do with materials dictated by wartime or backcountry shortages. But even though it was the taking of the picture and not the final product that seems to have kept the photographer behind a camera for four decades, a high proportion of the prints that have been gleaned from the family albums in the present project (most of which were made on relatively expensive Velox or Azo papers) clearly exceed the norms of a typical commercial enterprise from that era.

Moreover, Disfarmer did not have the opportunities of these other photographers. Atget was a commercial photographer who roamed the streets and country-side of France, setting up his camera whenever he saw something that he thought might please his Parisian customers or just himself. Sander spent twenty years and traveled thousands of miles to collect the portraits for his monumental project. Penn had Alexander Liberman.

Disfarmer didn't leave Heber Springs for forty years, so far as we know. Perhaps he couldn't. He relied on daily walk-in traffic to survive. Waiting for someone to enter his studio before he could begin work, he was the girl at the high school dance. He had no wealthy patrons, state or national government sponsors, magazine editors, art galleries or museums curious to see his latest images. He was completely alone.

The two photographers to whom he seems most comparable are Martin Chambi of Peru and Seydou Keita of Mali. Each ran a portrait studio in his native country during the same years as Disfarmer—the '30s, '40s, and '50s—and each produced many pictures of the same impressive artistic and social pungency as his.

And yet neither was regarded as crazy by his neighbors. Each led successful, moderately happy lives as respected men of their community. The local honor that they knew late in life has only swelled since their death. In none of these respects was Mike Disfarmer so lucky.

***

Eventually the customers stopped coming. The steep drop-off in Disfarmer's productivity during the early '50s may be the result of several factors. He was approaching seventy and starting to drink more heavily. He kept up appearances by wearing his uniform of a clean white shirt and dark pants. But his diet was poor, consisting of nothing but chocolate ice cream, according to one witness. His eccentricities made him a target for children who would knock on his door and run away. He became a kind of male witch, the Boo Radley of Heber Springs.

He had been photographing there since 1915. There could not have been more than a few townspeople whose portraits he had not made once, twice, or thirty times. Disfarmer was known to spend an inordinate amount of time adjusting light for a portrait, perhaps previously because he was serious about his trade, perhaps now because he had nothing else to do. Working was a way to put off having to go home, which was a shabby room twenty paces or so away from his camera.

He was dead for a couple of days before anyone missed him. Breaking into the studio, they found him lying on some newspapers. Two years later when Allbright, his wife, and children gained permission to search the place in hopes of finding something worth salvaging, they discovered more than $8,000 in saving bonds and hundreds of dollars in cash.[39]

But according to Olmstead, whose family runs a local funeral business, there was no money forthcoming from relatives for the burial in 1959. "We had to bury him for free," he says. "We do those sorts of things for people down here." Even so, the simple headstone in Old Cemetery, Heber Springs, notes only the deceased's birth and death year. The day and month are blank. And the name chiseled on the grave reads Mike Meyer.

Many older citizens of Cleburne County have been amazed that critics, curators, collectors and eminent photographers from around the world should treat "Old Mike Meyer" as worthy of respect. In the wake of Scully's 1976 book, a local historian named Evalina Berry voiced her skepticism about all the fuss being made over him.

"It was a big surprise that Disfarmer—or Mike Meyer—was being acclaimed as a master photographer and that his work was cited by the author of the book as nothing short of genius," she wrote in her 1982 history of Cleburne County.[40]

To Berry the only explanation for the to-do lay in the social reality embedded in the pictures: Disfarmer had captured the mood of the county during and after World War II, a time of privation, worry, struggle and validated hope. "Therein lies their significance," she wrote rather dismissively.[41] That Disfarmer might be an artist of a high order who had extracted qualities from the people of Cleburne County that they didn't know they had—indeed that they may not have shown until photographed by him—seems to her a little preposterous, an invention of artistic types from outside Arkansas.

In a sense she is right. Only within a tradition of modernist photography, with its aesthetic of spareness, brutal honesty and uncontrived narrative, do Disfarmer's pictures look extraordinary. If the sorry grotesqueries of his life belong in a Sherwood Anderson or Flannery O'Conner story, the integrity of his work puts him in the company of other tough-minded American realists, with Grant Wood and Edward Hopper.

To the citizens of Heber Springs, the photographs of his that they can pick out in family albums represent first of all—and most of all—individuals that they or their parents or grandparents knew. They are names before they are faces.

For the rest of us, though, it is the reverse. It is the expressions and gestures, clothes and hairstyles—the anonymous humanity—that holds our attention. To many of the people here we can feel inexplicably attached even though we never knew them or their families. Disfarmer's photographs—inadvertent elegies for a small town, a region, an era, a way of life—have to been seen outside their origins to be fully appreciated.

They are also a tribute to the passing of a profession. It is tempting to think that many other towns had photographers as gifted as Disfarmer, and that their work was either destroyed by locals who didn't recognize its worth or still lies buried in an archive. But what Disfarmer accomplished was not easily duplicated. The small-town photographer is figuratively and literally a thing of the past, and Disfarmer sui generis.

Julia Scully from time to time receives old photographs from people who know of her connection to Disfarmer and who want her to validate their finds. "It's been more than thirty years since I first saw the work of Disfarmer," she says, "and I haven't seen anything comparable in quality or emotional impact. Nothing even close."

[1] "Disfarmer" documentary film, produced circa 1995 by Dale Carpenter for the Arkansas Educational Television Network and their weekly television program "The Arkansas Traveler."
[2] Phone interview with the author, 6/12/05
[3] Bessie Utley is the figure on the right in pages 83 and 147, and the figure on the left in page 201; her sister Josie Stokes appears in pages 54 and 147.
[4] "Disfarmer" documentary film, op cit.
[5] Julia Scully's writing on Disfarmer can be found in *Aperture*, Number 78 (New York, 1977), pages 6-12; and in *Disfarmer* (Twin Palms Publishers, Santa Fe, NM, 1996). Alan Trachtenberg's essay, "Imagining Heber Springs," was published on pages 3-20 in *Heber Springs Portraits: Continuity and Change in the World Disfarmer Photographed* by Toba Pato Tucker (University of New Mexico Press, Albuquerque, NM, 1996). Tucker's two essays "Continuity and Change" and "The Town of Heber Springs," describing her years spent interviewing and photographing residents there, can be found in the same volume on pages 21-43 and 45-48 respectively.
[6] Page 181, *Disfarmer*, op. cit.
[7] Pages 11-12, *Heber Springs Portraits*, op. cit.
[8] Phone interview with Charles Stuart, president of Cleburne County Historical Society, 6/11/05
[9] See the Afterword in the present volume by Michael Mattis.
[10] Photographs on page 11 of *Heber Springs Portraits*, op. cit.
[11] Page 181, *Disfarmer*, op. cit.
[12] Page 13, *Heber Springs Portraits*, op. cit.
[13] "Disfarmer" documentary film, op. cit.
[14] *Time and the River: A History of Cleburne County* by Evalina Berry (Rose Publishing Co. Little Rock, Arkansas, 1982), pp. 274-76.
[15] Ibid., pp. 256-57.
[16] Phone interview with the author, 6/14/05.
[17] Page 183, *Disfarmer*, op. cit.
[18] Ibid., page 182.
[19] Ibid.
[20] Information provided by the Museum of the Arkansas Grand Prairie.
[21] See the Afterword in the present volume by Michael Mattis.
[22] Information provided by the Cleburne County Historical Society.
[23] Ibid.
[24] See Figure 6 of the Afterword in the present volume by Michael Mattis.
[25] Mattis collection.
[26] Mattis collection. Disfarmer probably sent negatives to larger cities, perhaps Little Rock, for clients who requested larger prints. No enlarger was found in his studio.

[27] Peter Miller no longer has the crates that held the negatives Allbright retrieved from the Disfarmer Studio. But the manufacturer was, he believes, located in St. Louis.

[28] Szarkowski comments from email correspondence with the author.

[29] Mattis collection, envelope with celluloid negative, dated 1952.

[30] A number of photographers were still working with glass plates in the 1920s, including the Frenchman Louis Clergeau (1877-1936), who for more than thirty years documented life in his village of Pontlevoy, France; William E. "Ed" Irwin, active in the Oklahoma Territory, West Texas, and Arizona from about 1894 to 1920; and Eugene Buechel (1874-1954), born in Germany but best known for his portraits of American Indians on the Rosebud Reservation, South Dakota.

[31] "Disfarmer" documentary, op. cit.

[32] Interview with Hava Gurevich, 11/6/04.

[33] Page 17, *Heber Springs Portraits*, op.cit.

[34] Ibid., page 14.

[35] Phone interview with Kenneth and Sue Foust and with Tom Olmstead, 6/15/05

[36] Page 12, *Aperture*, op. cit.

[37] Conversation with the author.

[38] Interview with Charlotte Lacey by Hava Gurevich 11/04.

[39] "Disfarmer" documentary.

[40] Page 272, *Time and the River*, op. cit.

[41] Ibid.

Afterword
Disfarmer Rediscovered
by Michael P. Mattis

The legend of Mike Disfarmer has intrigued the photographic community for nearly thirty years. The bizarre story of a hermit-like Arkansas studio photographer named Mike Meyer legally changing his name to Disfarmer in order to disassociate himself not only from his family, but from the very farming community of Heber Springs in which he plied his trade, is irresistible. But even more compelling are the pictures themselves. The beautifully sequenced book by Julia Scully and Peter Miller that introduced his work to the art world revealed searing portraits from the American heartland, captured at a defining moment in history in which the Great Depression yielded to World War II, and the sons of the farm donned their country's uniform and headed off to foreign shores.[1] The camera's unsentimental gaze suggests a photographer who was simultaneously an insider and an outsider in his own community.

Scully and Miller's book caused a sensation at the time. "Nobody famous ever posed for Mike Disfarmer," Gene Thornton wrote in *ARTnews*, "but his portraits are among the best ever taken by any photographer."[2] Richard Avedon termed the book "indispensable"; his own series of rural portraits, *In the American West*, published a decade later, reveals a kinship with—and likely the influence of—Disfarmer's unblinking eye. To Sean Callahan writing in the *Village Voice*, Disfarmer's portraits constituted "a compelling and comprehensive record of the home front from 1939 to 1946...a microcosm of the nation during hard times."[3] And in its end-of-year review, *The New York Times* hailed the book and the accompanying exhibition of posthumous enlargements at the International Center for Photography as one of the ten outstanding photographic events of 1976—stating flatly that Disfarmer's portraits "can stand comparison with August Sander, Diane Arbus and Irving Penn."[4]

So it was somewhat deflating for collectors to learn that no original vintage Disfarmers could be had.[5] Rather, the discovery of this photographer stemmed

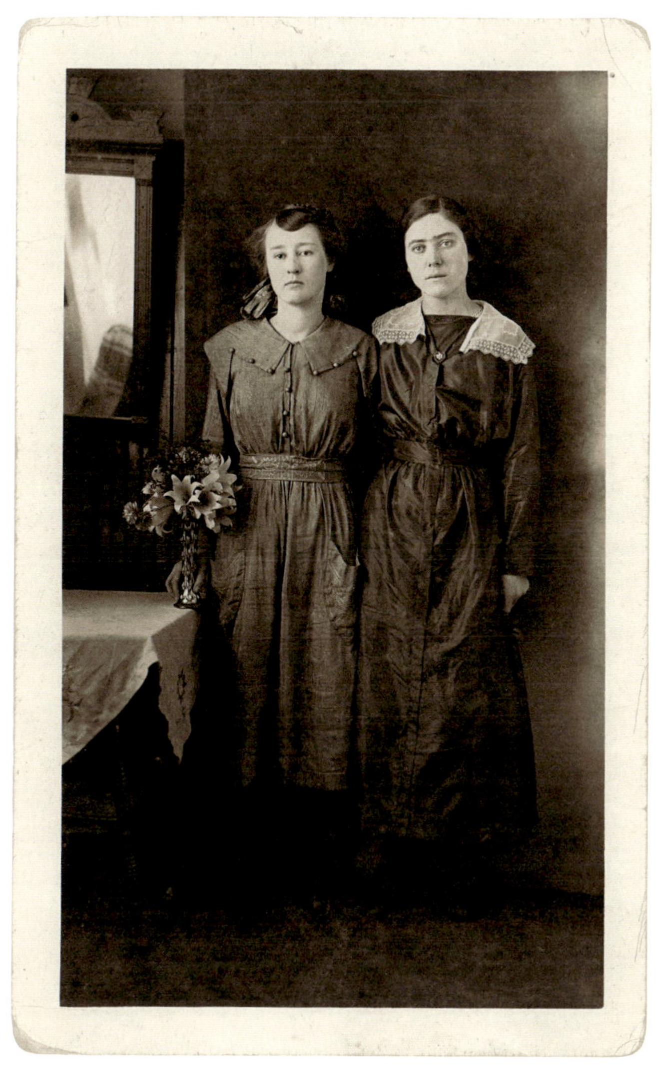

Figure 1

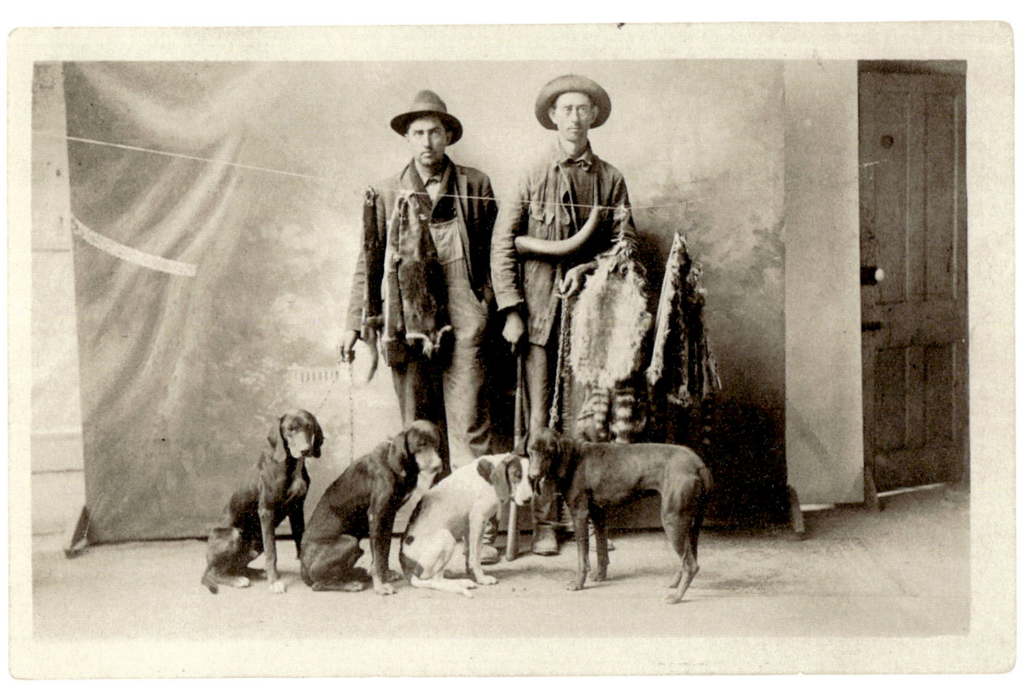

Figure 2

entirely from a trove of four thousand glass-plate negatives that had been rescued from destruction by Joe Allbright, a retired army engineer who had purchased the contents of Disfarmer's studio after his death; the negatives were later given to the local newspaper publisher Peter Miller. Scully's essay contained the tantalizing comment, "Many of these originals are still to be found in the photo albums of Heber Springs families," but rumor had it that some enterprising art dealers had already flown down to Arkansas in search of such "originals," only to have doors slammed in their faces by the untrusting locals.

The present historical reclamation project began in February 2004, when I was serendipitously offered the family collection of vintage Disfarmers assembled by Ashleigha and David Pratt, a young couple who had grown up in Heber Springs and recently relocated to Chicago. The intimacy and sheer beauty of the vintage contact prints was undeniable—and a spur to action.[6] With Scully's tantalizing comment as a touchstone, a dedicated team of historically-minded locals was quickly trained and mobilized; ultimately they combed every dirt road in Cleburne County in search of Disfarmer originals. From the outset, an integral part of the project was educating an initially skeptical rural community that their albums of old family photos were likely to contain objects of significant artistic and cultural value that could—and indeed should—be brought to the attention of a wider audience. To this end, art researcher Hava Gurevich joined the project to gather oral history and perform geneological research. In addition, members of the team worked closely with the Cleburne County Historical Society, providing materials for exhibitions that celebrated Disfarmer's achievement. Today, after nearly two years, it can categorically be stated that the bulk of Disfarmer's extant oeuvre has been recovered.

What have we learned along the way? To begin with, note that prior to the present book, all published Disfarmer portraits[7] dated from the short period 1939-46 corresponding to the dates of Allbright's cache of glass negatives. So it is especially eye-opening to have uncovered vintage prints spanning Disfarmer's full forty year career in Heber Springs. Dated examples in the collection range from 1917 to 1956.[8] Thus anxious young soldiers are portrayed prior to shipping off, not only

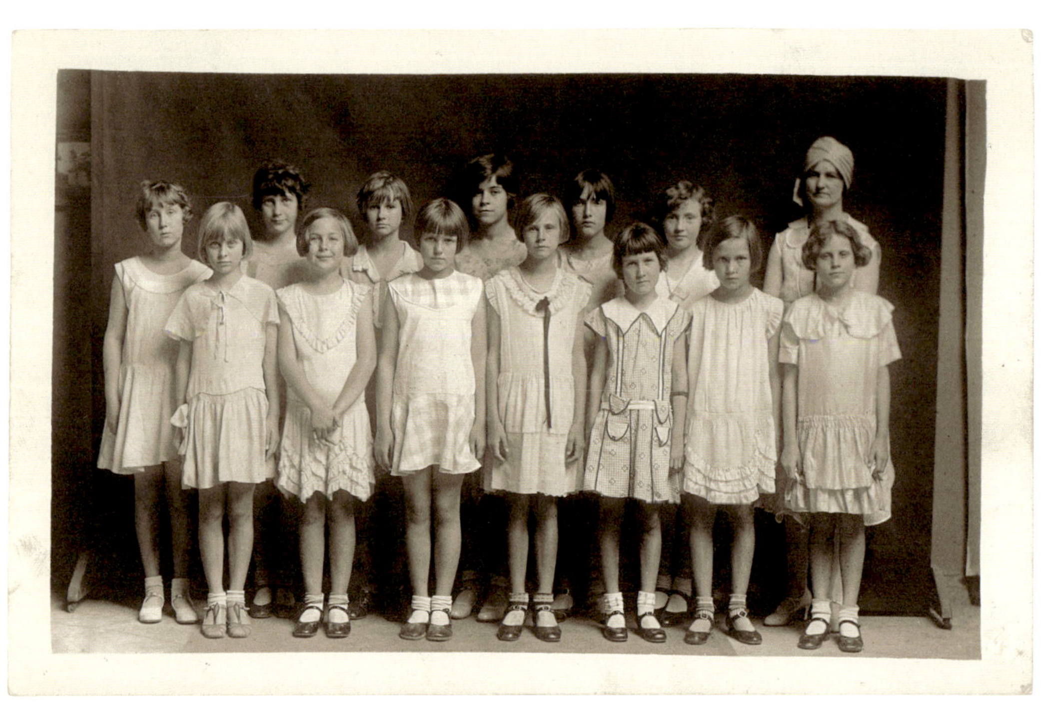

Figure 3

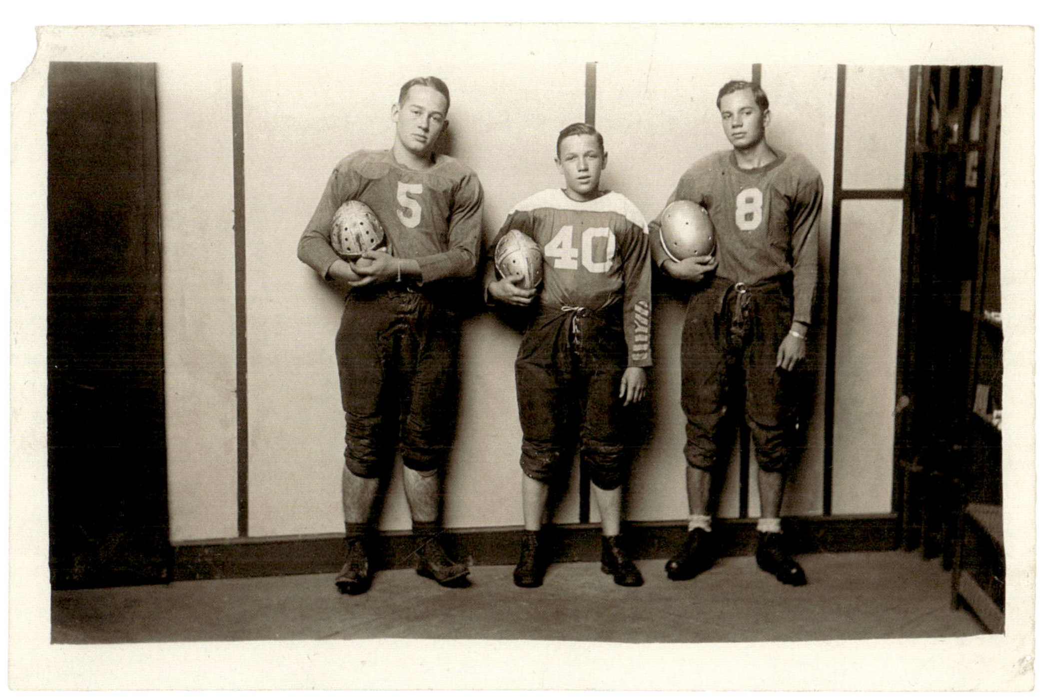

Figure 4

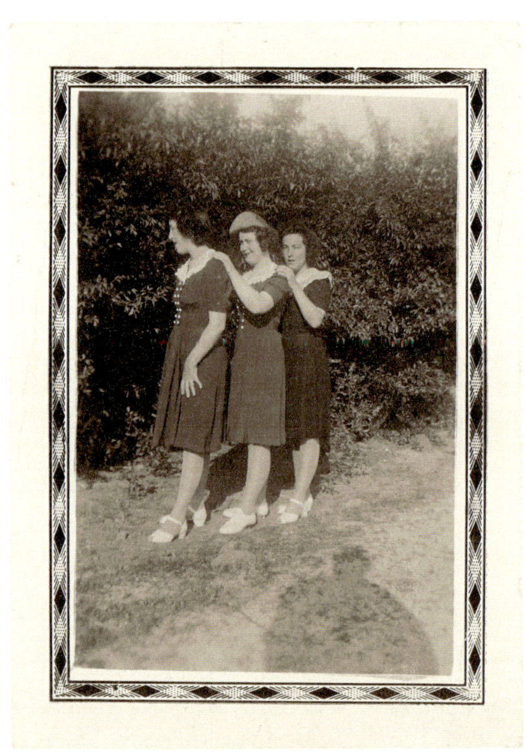

Figure 5

to World War II, but also to World War I (page 43), whereas towards the end of his career (when his anachronistic glass plates do inevitably give way to film negatives) Disfarmer's previously somber camera joyfully captures the pairings of bobby-soxed young women with their James Dean wannabe boyfriends.

Much that is new can now be said about Disfarmer's life work.[9] Mike Meyer/Disfarmer is known to have settled in Heber Springs some time after 1910[10]—by 1915 the Penrose & Meyer Studio was open for business in the lobby of the Jackson Theatre, an elegant Victorian building on the south side of Main Street.[11] During this time Heber Springs was undergoing a revival as a spa town. Figure 1 illustrates a photograph that bears the rare Penrose & Meyer Studio stamp on the verso and is dated 1917. Whereas hints of the later Disfarmer "look" are certainly present, the psychological power of the double portrait is attenuated by the typical props of a turn-of-the-century studio, in this case a mirror, a tablecloth, and a floral bouquet.

Figure 2 shows the freestanding moveable backdrop that appears in most of Disfarmer's portraits between 1918 and 1928 (pages 41-45).[12] The painted trompe l'oeil features include a pulled-back curtain to the left, a Roman "temple," and an overall pattern of clouds and/or foliage. Often the subjects from this time period pose on an oriental carpet.

Figure 3 depicts the freestanding moveable solid black backdrop that characterizes the majority of Disfarmer's work beginning around 1930. The spare and somber background seems appropriate for a time in which prosperity in Heber Springs had come to a halt and the Great Depression had settled in for the decade. Starting in 1940, this black backdrop alternates in usage (possibly depending on the available natural light) with the distinctive Mondrian-like white background with black stripes shown in Figure 4. It is these two backgrounds that are already familiar from the earlier publications, and that, to modern eyes, harmonize most successfully with Disfarmer's psychologically direct approach to portraiture. The two backgrounds continue past 1950, although in that decade Disfarmer's overall productivity seems to have dropped precipitously.

Disfarmer's output was not wholly confined to the studio. Long-time residents of Heber Springs recall a gangly, Zorro-like figure in a black cloak riding about town on his horse, view camera and tripod at the ready, offering to photograph families relaxing on their porches; a particularly fine early example bears the Penrose & Meyer stamp. And on weekends he frequently set up his camera in Spring Park, a central gathering place for the young and young-at-heart.[13] Figure 5 shows one such photograph; the light-hearted spirit is disturbed by the ominous shadow of the photographer hunched under the black cloth. The diamond border of this small-format print dates it to 1935-1938 which is when Disfarmer favored this particular stock.[14]

Despite the dramatic changes in his studio interiors, physical addresses, and of his very name over the span of his career, Disfarmer did manage to hold the line on prices. Figure 6 reproduces his price-list from 1928. A single-picture sitting cost fifty cents and included three free prints; additional prints ranged from three to five cents each depending on size. An Edward Weston nautilus shell, which at that time would have cost twenty-five dollars, seems pricey by comparison.

How to summarize Disfarmer's (dare I say) artistic achievement? By virtue of his trade as a small-town studio photographer, Disfarmer was the ultimate insider, privy to each family's rites of passage—from first birthdays to high school graduations, engagements and army furloughs, anniversaries and reunions—as well as to the private joys of close friends celebrating a night on the town. But in fundamental ways (described in detail in Woodward's essay in the present volume) he remained a lifelong outsider: an agnostic from Lutheran stock among church-going Baptists and Methodists, the son of a German-born Union soldier in the heart of the South, a man of perception among men of action, a confirmed bachelor in a community of large families. In my view, it is this unique insider/outsider mix, so evident in the pictures themselves, that is the essence of his genius, and the reason why—despite three decades of intense searching—no other studio photographer from that era has been uncovered whose accomplishment remotely matches Disfarmer's.

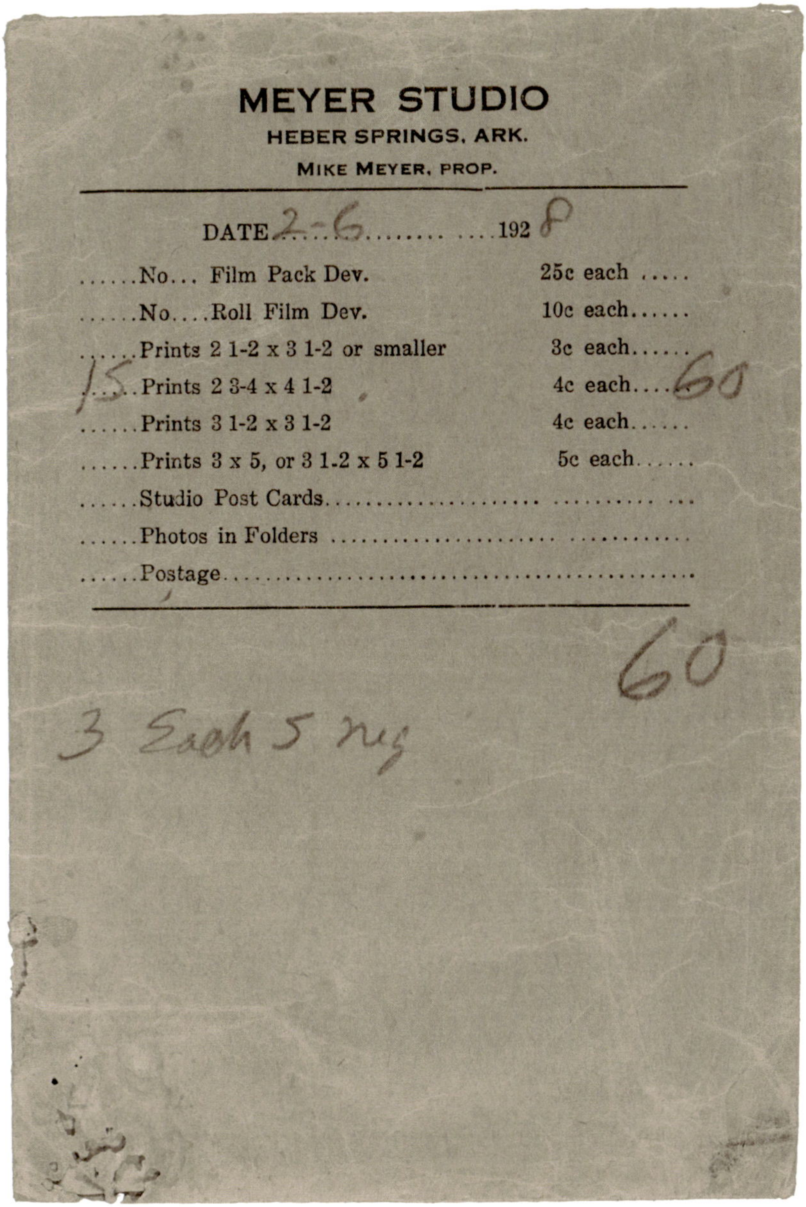

MEYER STUDIO
HEBER SPRINGS, ARK.
MIKE MEYER, PROP.

DATE 2-6 1928

......No... Film Pack Dev.	25c each	
......No....Roll Film Dev.	10c each......	
......Prints 2 1-2 x 3 1-2 or smaller	3c each......	
15 ...Prints 2 3-4 x 4 1-2	4c each....	60
......Prints 3 1-2 x 3 1-2	4c each......	
......Prints 3 x 5, or 3 1-2 x 5 1-2	5c each......	
......Studio Post Cards..............................		
......Photos in Folders		
......Postage..		

60

3 Each 5 neg

Figure 6

[1] J. Scully and P. Miller, *Disfarmer: The Heber Springs Portraits 1939-1946*, Addison House, Danbury, N.H., 1976.

[2] *ARTnews*, November 1976.

[3] *Village Voice*, January 1977.

[4] *New York Times*, 26 December 1976.

[5] At the time, the only other major photographer for whom no original vintage prints were available was the chronicler of the French *belle époque*, Jacques-Henri Lartigue, who was born ten years after Disfarmer; but unlike Disfarmer, since Lartigue lived into his nineties, modern signed prints could be ordered. In the last decade vintage Lartigues have finally surfaced, as several unique family albums have been disassembled; as with Disfarmer, these are contact prints (see *Imprints of Joy*, Edwynn Houk Gallery catalog, 2000).

[6] Most vintage Disfarmers are printed on Azo or Velox papers which were high-quality papers that were particularly well suited to contact printing (with the exception of the dustjacket, the prints in the present volume are reproduced actual size). Over his long career Disfarmer experimented with many different types of such papers, both single- and double-weight, warmer and cooler toned, and in finishes ranging from dead matte to high gloss.

[7] The prior literature consists of J. Scully and P. Miller, op. cit., and the revised and expanded edition, Twin Palms, Santa Fe, 1996; Toba Tucker and Alan Trachtenberg, *Heber Springs Portraits: Continuity and Change in the World Disfarmer Photographed*, UNM Press, Albuquerque, 1996; *Aperture* magazine no. 78, 1977; *Photography Year 1977 Edition*, Time-Life Books, New York, 1977.

[8] Fewer than 20% of the photographs are dated, some by hand by the sitters, others with Disfarmer's 6-digit ink stamp in which the first four digits give month and year, and the last two digits indicate the negative number.

[9] For further details, see R. Woodward's essay in the present volume.

[10] His estranged family members reported to Scully that Disfarmer and his mother moved from Indiana, but Disfarmer told at least one close acquaintance that he had actually lived in Elmira, NY, prior to Heber Springs (Col. Carl F. Baswell, interview with Daniel Hipp, 18 June 2005). The 1920 Cleburne County census lists his occupation as photographer and his birthplace as Indiana.

[11] Unfortunately, very little is known about George A. Penrose.

[12] Other, less common, backdrops are also occasionally used prior to 1930.

[13] Evalina Berry, *Time and the River: A History of Cleburne County*, Rose Publishing Co. Little Rock, Arkansas, 1982, p. 270. The cautionary note should be sounded that the large majority of the outdoor shots from Heber Springs, even those bearing one of Disfarmer's studio stamps, were not made by Disfarmer but merely printed by him, as his studio performed such standard photo-finishing services for the community.

[14] See also pages 48-49, 82-83, 92, and 116-117.

DISFARMER

The Vintage Prints

Published in the United States by

Edwynn Houk Gallery, New York
750 Fifth Avenue, New York, NY 10151
telephone 212 750 7070, fax 212 688 4848
email: info@houkgallery.com
website: www.houkgallery.com

and powerHouse Books,
a division of powerHouse Cultural Entertainment, Inc.
68 Charlton Street, New York, NY 10014-4601
telephone 212 604 9074, fax 212 366 5247
e-mail: info@powerHouseBooks.com
website: www.powerHouseBooks.com

First edition, 2005

Library of Congress Control Number: 2005929961

Hardcover ISBN 1-57687-304-8

A Limited Edition of this book is available with a modern print.
Please inquire with the Publisher.

The publication of this book accompanies an exhibition of vintage photographs
at the Edwynn Houk Gallery, New York
8 September—15 October, 2005

Duotone separations by Robert Hennessey
Printing and binding by EBS, Verona

Endpaper design by Arlene Levine

A complete catalog of powerHouse Books and Limited Editions is available upon request;
please call, write, or visit our website.

10 9 8 7 6 5 4 3 2 1

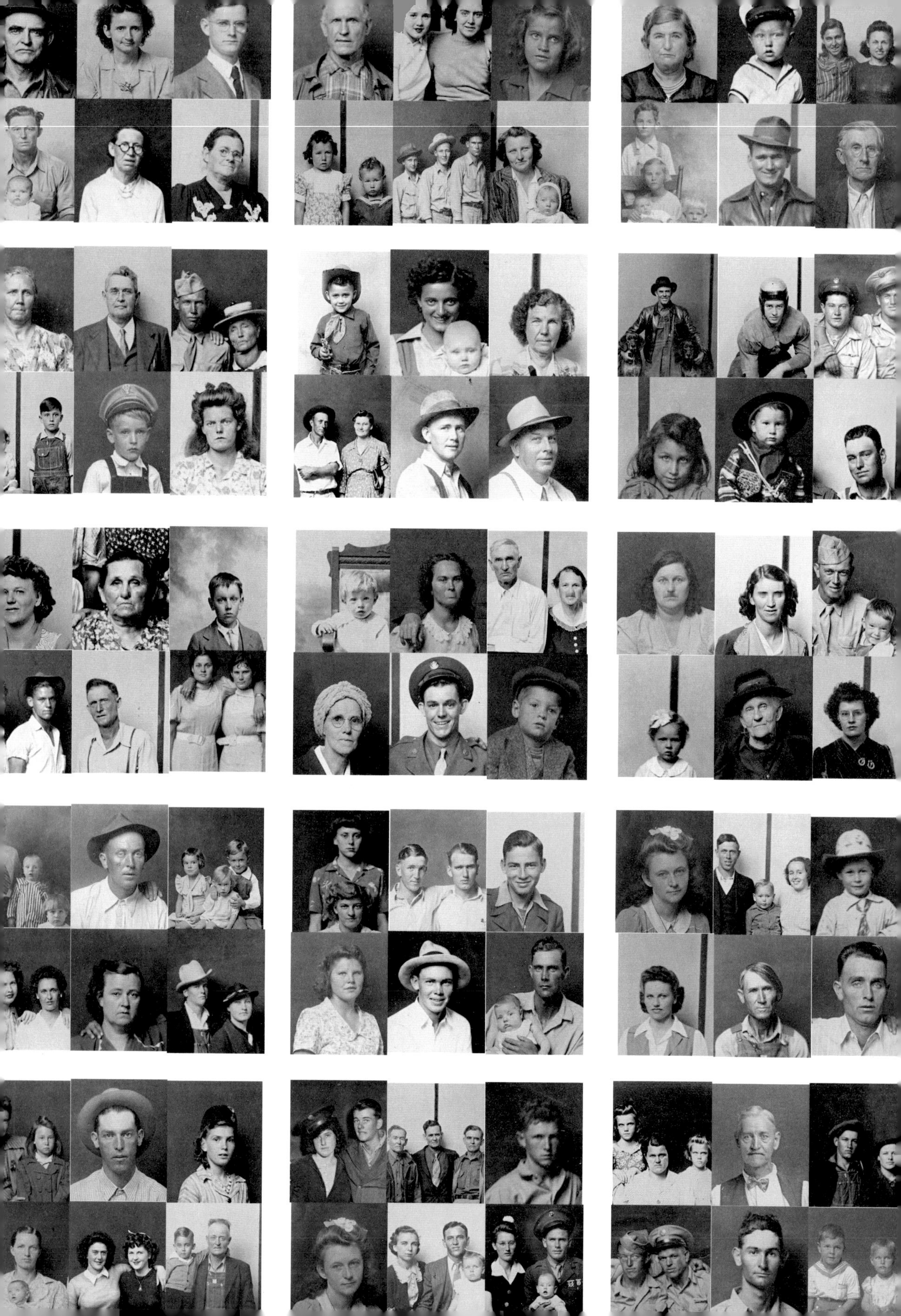